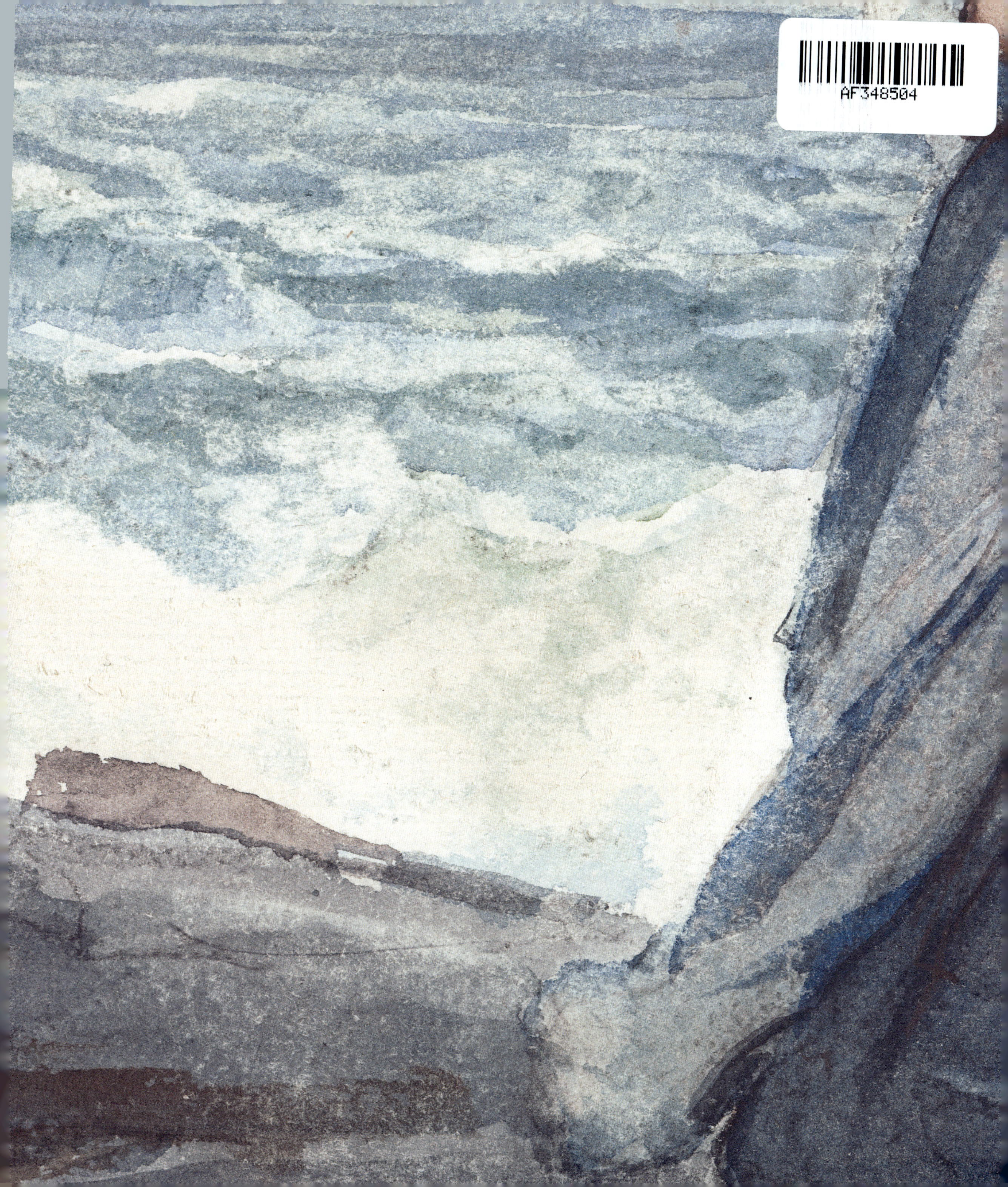

Winslow Homer | *in Watercolor*

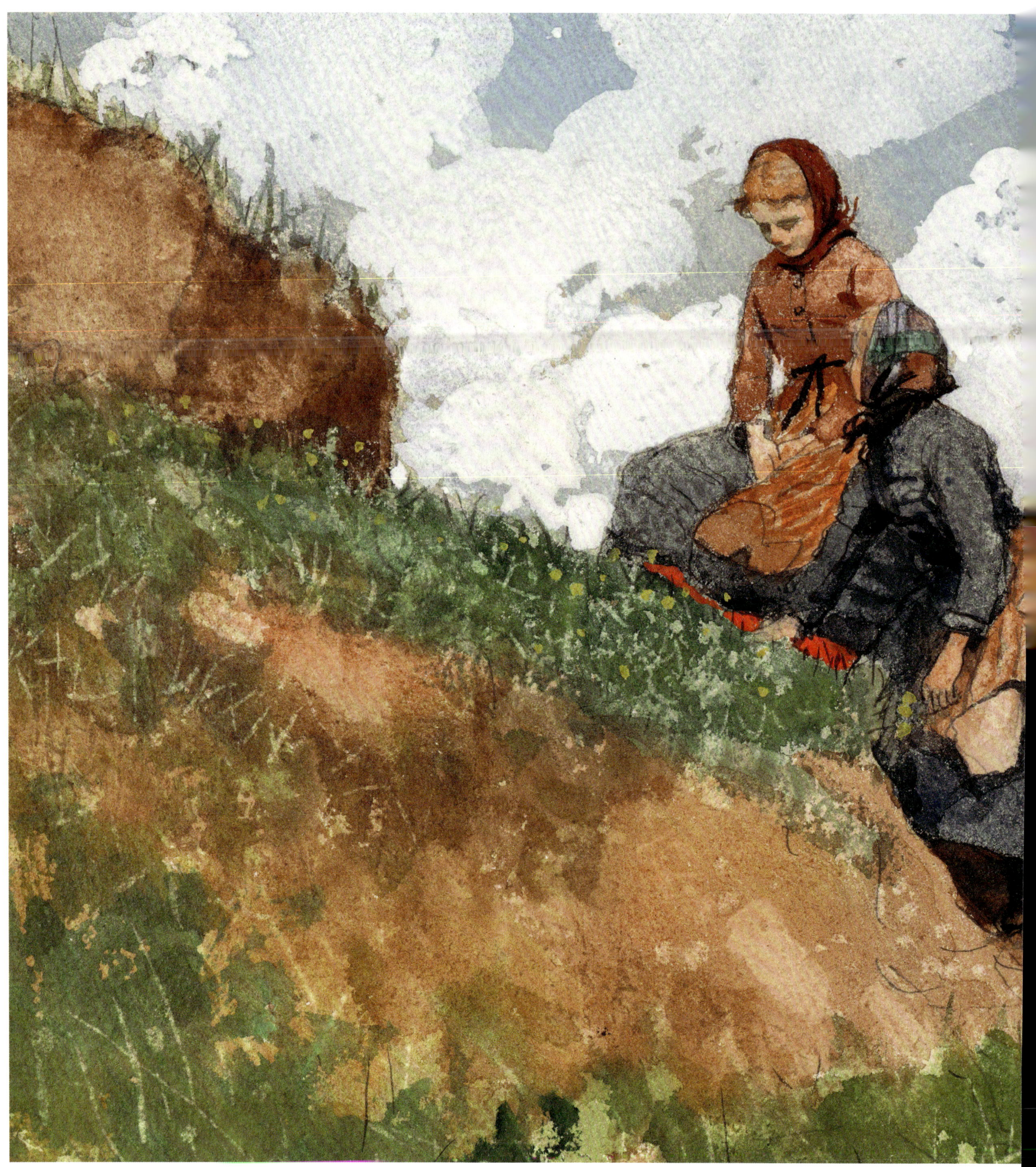

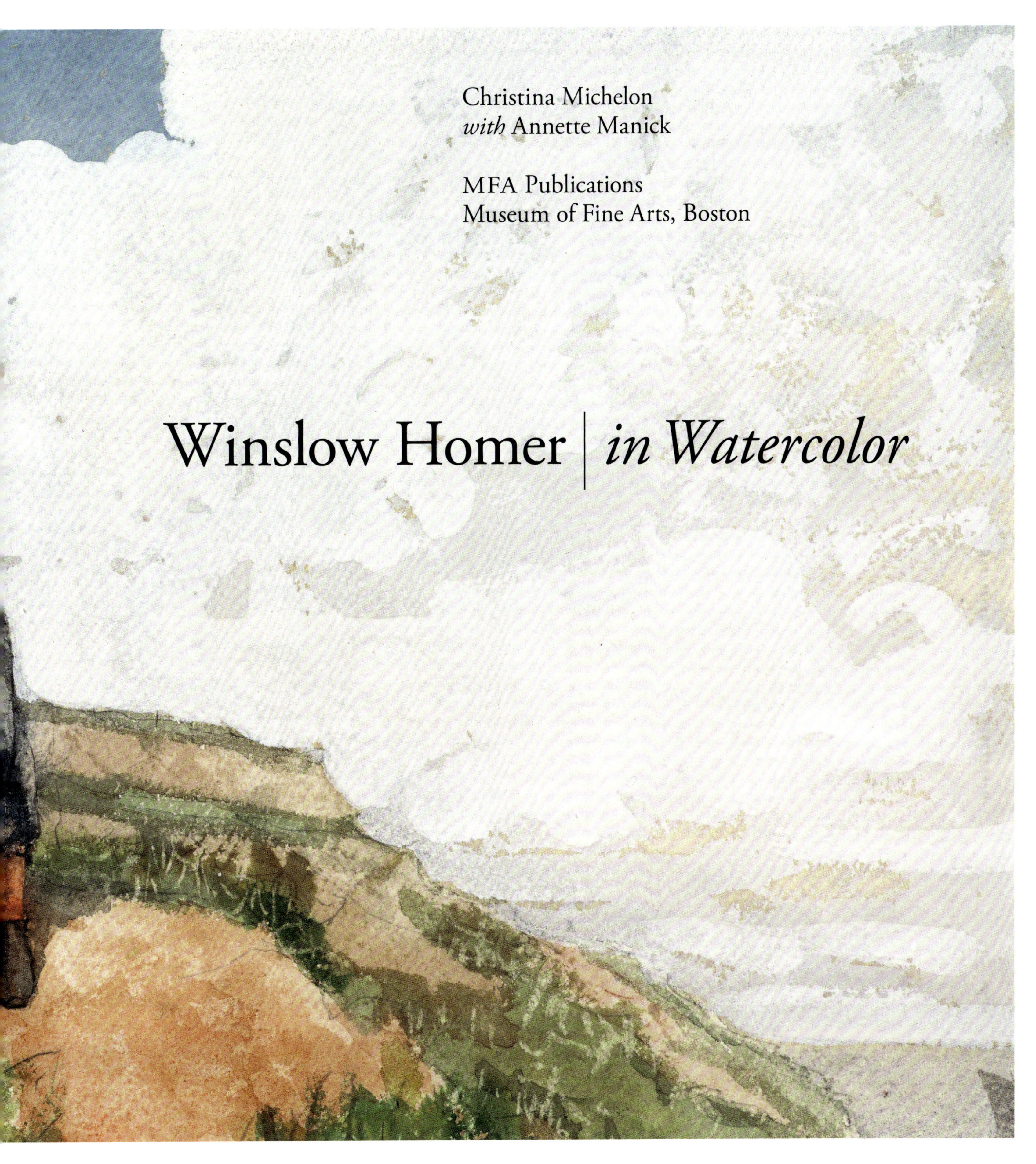

Christina Michelon
with Annette Manick

MFA Publications
Museum of Fine Arts, Boston

Winslow Homer | *in Watercolor*

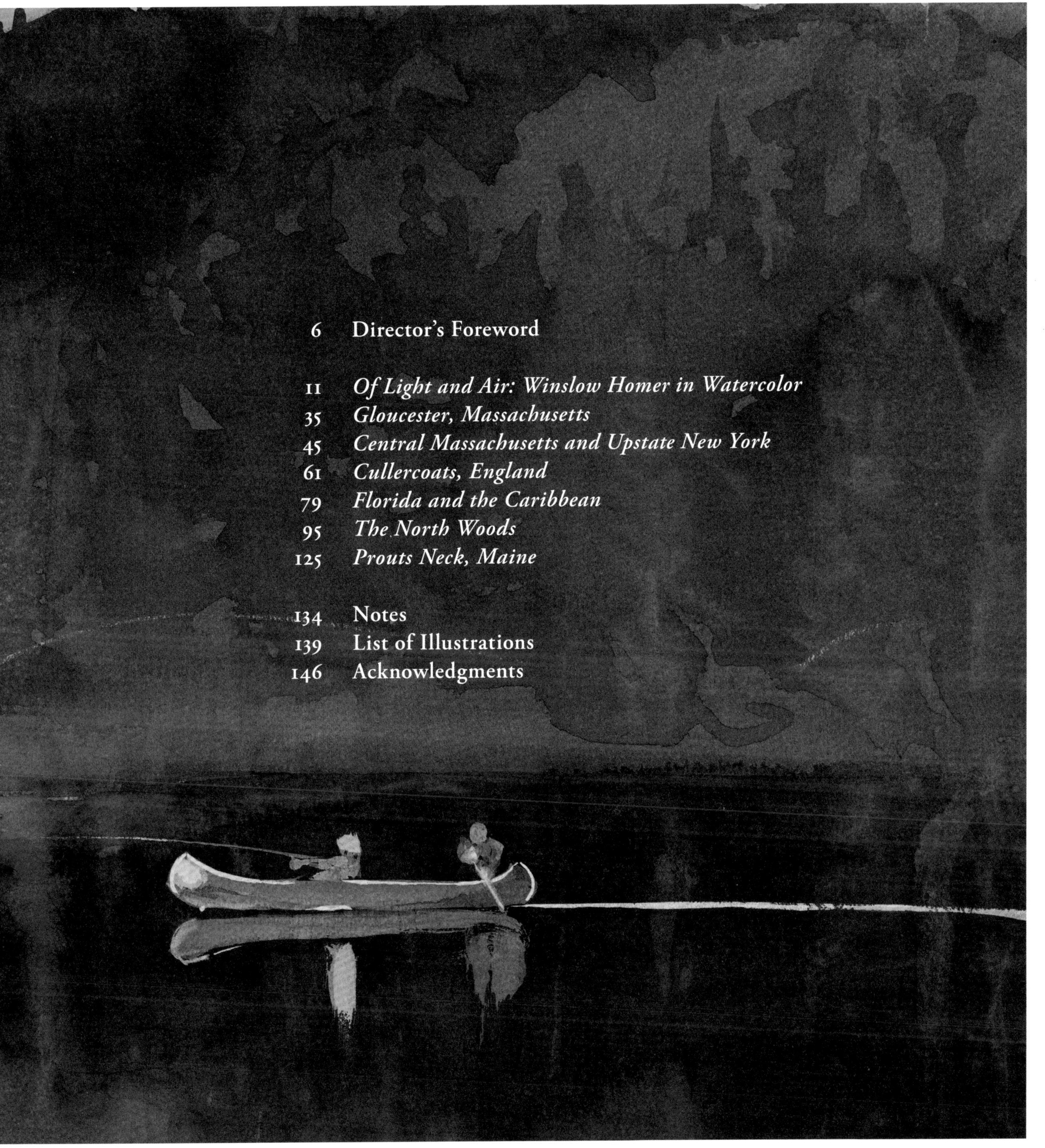

Director's Foreword

Winslow Homer transformed the medium of watercolor through his relentless spirit of experimentation. With fluid brushstrokes, dynamic compositions, and a vibrant palette, Homer created immersive scenes that transport us to the rugged Maine coast, the mountains of the Adirondacks, the shores of seaside England, and the bright suns of the Caribbean. The Museum of Fine Arts, Boston, is proud to steward the largest collection of Homer's watercolors in the world, all of which are reproduced in this volume.

Born in Boston, Homer had a long relationship with New England and the MFA. One of the artist's most ambitious compositions, *The Fog Warning*, became the first Homer painting to be gifted to an institution. Donated to the MFA in 1894, the painting—an icon of the Museum's collection—laid the foundation for what was to come. Five years later, the Museum purchased its first watercolor by Homer, and over the course of the twentieth century we were able to acquire nearly fifty watercolors, mostly through the generosity of local benefactors. Along with eleven oil paintings, a dozen drawings, and over three hundred prints by or after the artist, the Museum holds one of the most significant collections of Homer's work across media.

Since its establishment over a century and a half ago, the Museum has cared for and preserved fragile works of art for future generations. Homer's iconic watercolor *The Blue Boat*, a favorite among art lovers around the world, remains nearly as vibrant as the day Homer painted it. Watercolor is extremely sensitive to light, which limits how often these precious pictures can be displayed in our galleries. This publication, and the exhibition it accompanies, offer a rare opportunity to revel in these luminous works on paper. Moreover, they situate the watercolors in relation to Homer's larger body of work, including drawings, prints, and paintings, while illuminating the enduring significance of Boston and New England to the artist's career.

We are pleased to celebrate not only the majesty of Homer's watercolors, but the generations of collectors and benefactors that have enabled the Museum to become a critical repository for the artist's oeuvre. We also gratefully acknowledge the Bowdoin College Museum of Art, Currier Museum of Art, and Portland Museum of Art for lending key works to this exhibition and enabling us to tell a more complete story of Homer's work in watercolor.

Winslow Homer lore paints the artist as a loner; however, he did not work in isolation. Homer was buoyed by the support of his family and networks of fellow artists, dealers, and patrons, and in turn he was a devoted son, brother, and neighbor. Likewise, this project is the result of mutual support and fruitful collaboration, not just among curators and conservators, but our entire staff, as well as colleagues throughout New England, and beyond.

The exhibition *Of Light and Air: Winslow Homer in Watercolor* is sponsored by the Abrams Foundation. Generous support provided by the Governor Carlton Skinner and Dr. Solange Skinner Fund for the Exhibition of Art of the Americas and by Kate Enroth and Dana Schmaltz. Additional support provided by the Jean S. and Frederic A. Sharf Exhibition Fund, the Dr. Lawrence H. and Roberta Cohn Exhibition Fund, and the Eugenie Prendergast Memorial Fund.

Generous support for this publication provided by the Andrew W. Mellon Publications Fund.

PIERRE TERJANIAN
Ann and Graham Gund Director, Museum of Fine Arts, Boston

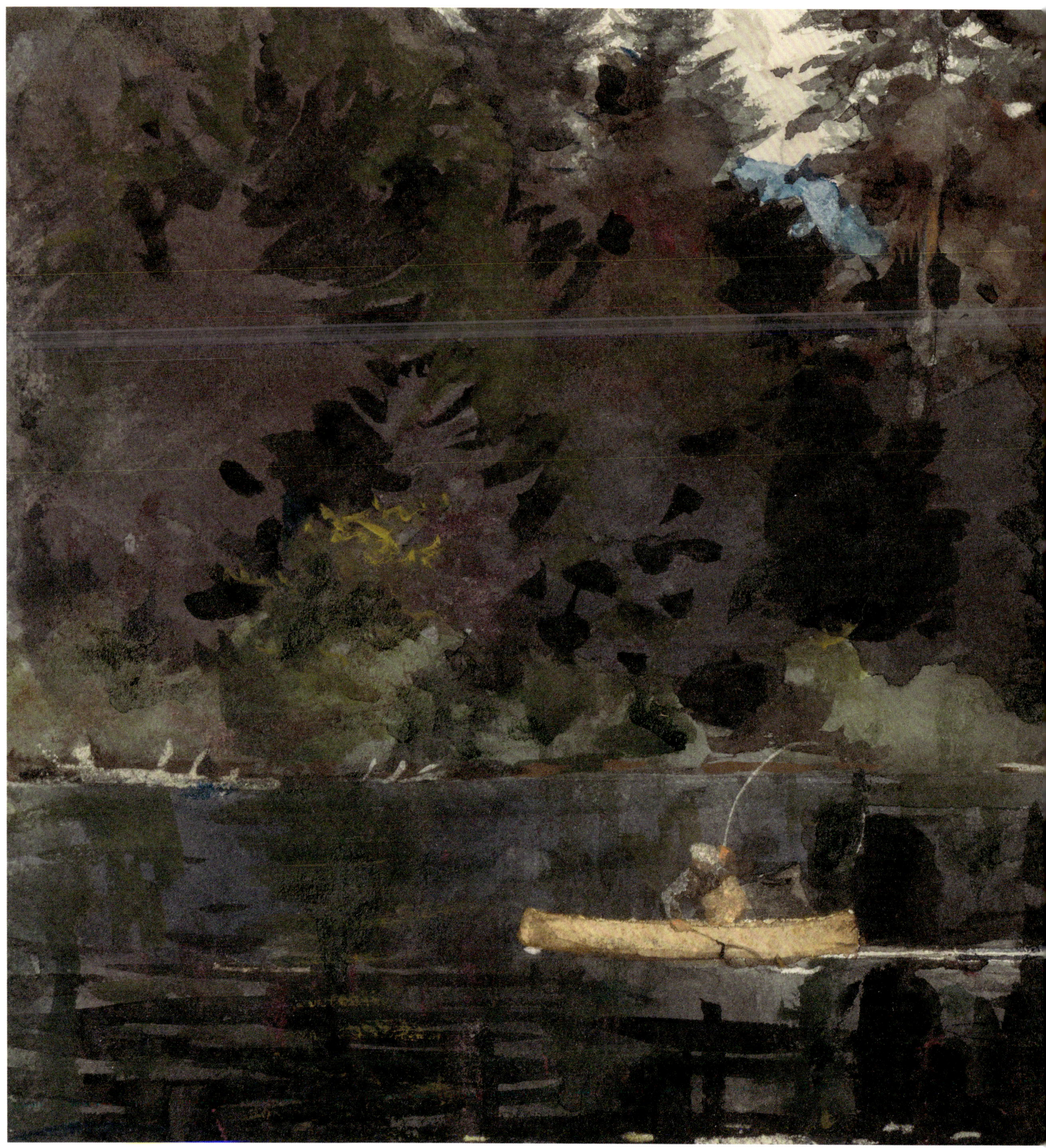

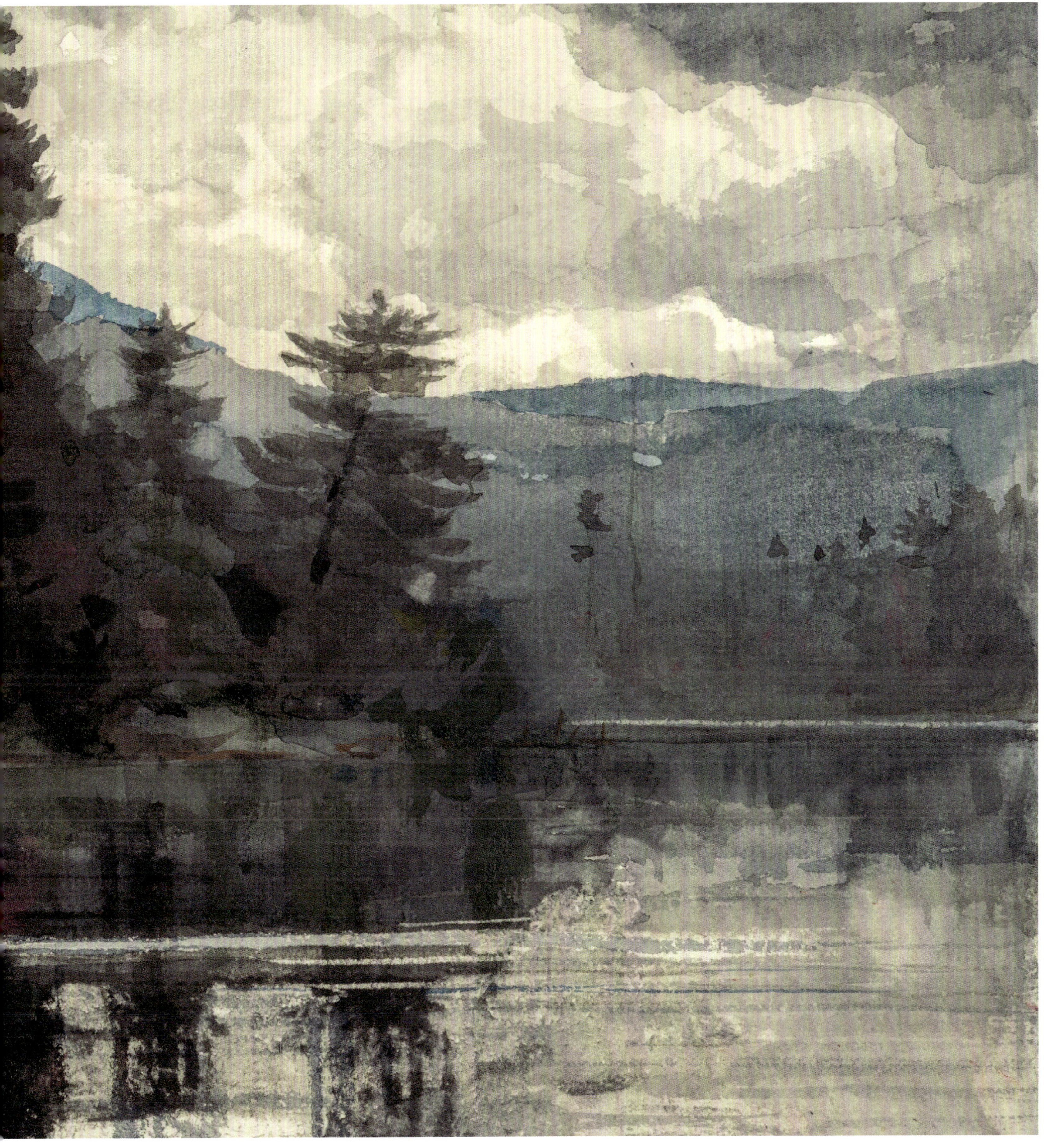

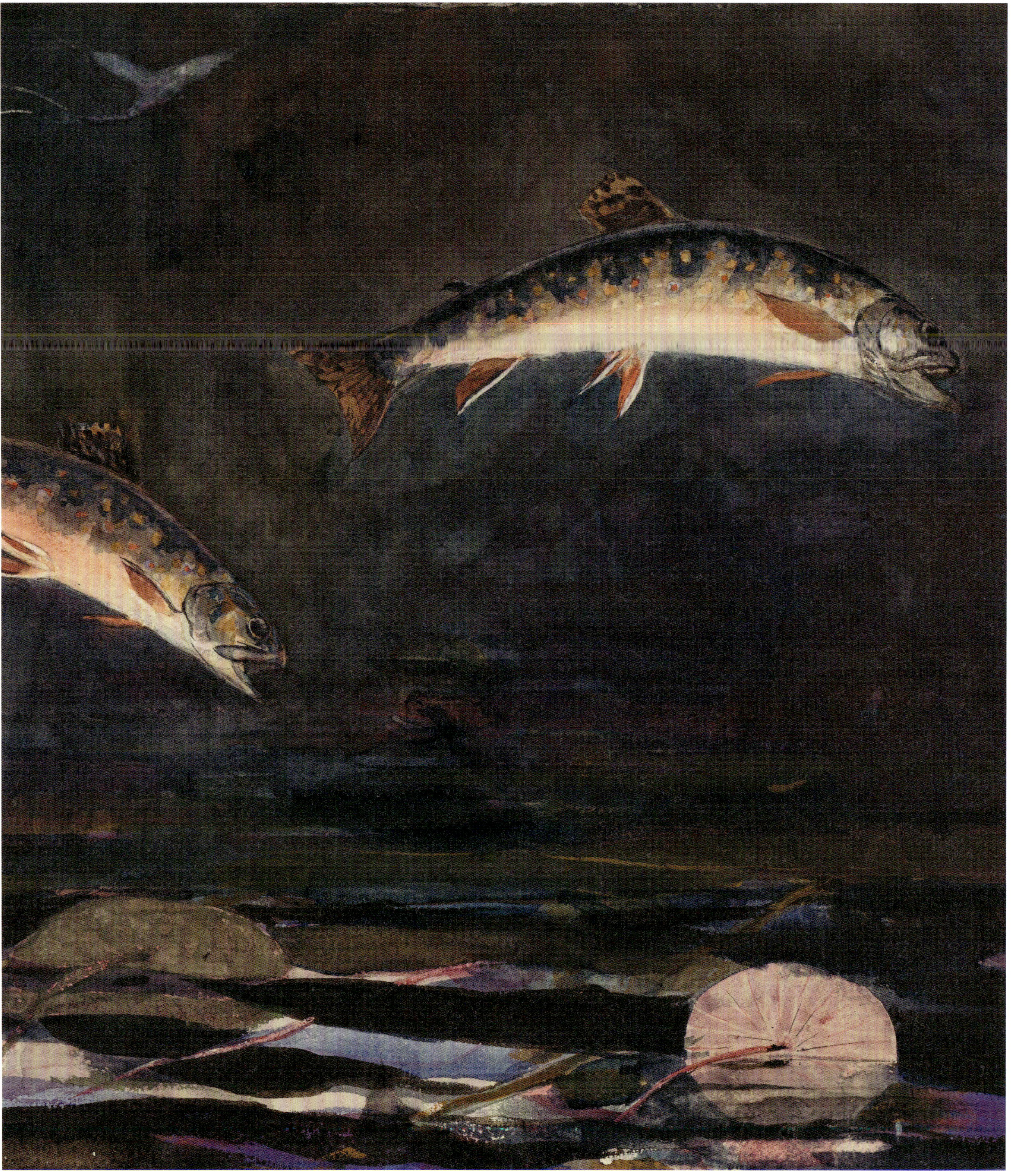

Of Light and Air: Winslow Homer in Watercolor

"I prefer every time a picture composed and painted outdoors." —*Winslow Homer*[1]

Few American artists are as closely associated with the outdoors as Winslow Homer, and few rival his ability to depict it in watercolor. An avid fisherman, Homer took inspiration from fishing trips in the Adirondack Mountains and other remote locales to create some of his best watercolors, recognizing the medium's unique ability to capture a fleeting moment.[2] In one such work, two iridescent brook trout leap from the surface of a lily-pad-laden pond in pursuit of a mayfly. Suspended in the air, the fish shimmer against an ethereal background before the inevitable splash. Homer created the mayfly's spectral silhouette through the subtractive process of blotting, one of the many advanced techniques he used here. He also layered numerous washes of various pigments to achieve the dark, atmospheric setting, and then used a sharp tool to scrape those pigments away in the lower left, creating a textured highlight with the exposed paper. Homer signed the work twice: he blotted his initials in the upper right, the same register as the mayfly, and scratched "HOMER" into the lower left corner, just beneath the scraped highlight in the water's surface. His mastery of watercolor as well as the innovative methods he employed to create breathtaking landscapes and iconic genre scenes cement his place as one of the greatest watercolorists of all time.

In contrast to the grand narratives in his later oil paintings, Homer's watercolors are rooted in the moment and the surface effects of light. Though often ambiguous, they are not without symbolism. In the numerous representations of leaping fish done throughout his career, Homer illustrated both real insects and artificial lures. In *Leaping Trout*, it is unclear if the mayfly is real or fake, underscoring the art of artifice inherent in both Homer's painting and in the act of fishing itself (see fig. 65).[3] Mayflies—the object of the trout's acrobatic efforts—only live for about twenty-four hours and have been deployed as a metaphor for ephemerality by artists for centuries. Thematically and compositionally, this watercolor also evinces Homer's fascination with life and death. The pairing of twin bodies mid-air is reminiscent of Homer's late oil painting *Right and Left* (fig. 1). Finished a year before the artist's death and depicting a

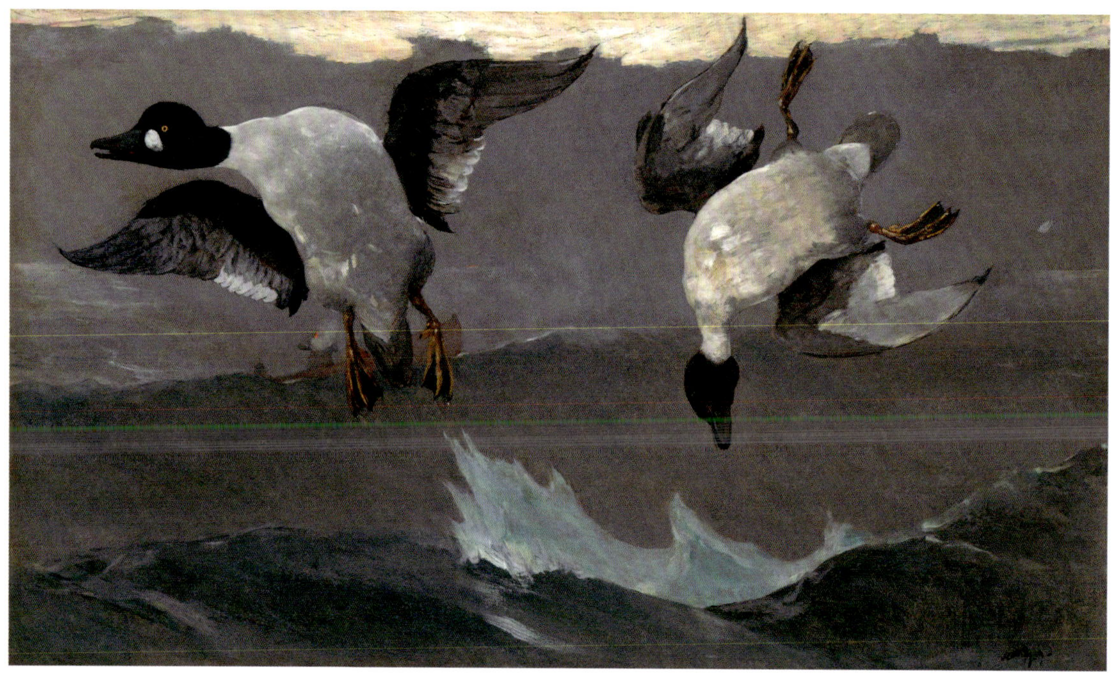

1. *Right and Left*, 1909, National Gallery of Art

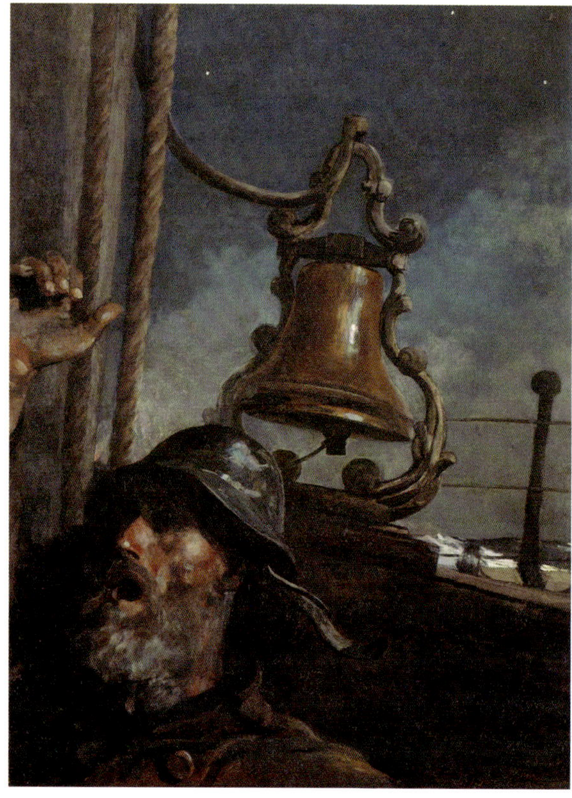

2. *The Lookout—"All's Well,"* 1896

hunter taking aim at the two birds in the foreground, the painting is rife with references to mortality. However, *Leaping Trout*'s narrative is more enigmatic: are the fish predators or prey?

Watercolor, pioneered by Homer as a medium for capturing the ephemeral, can be materially ephemeral itself. Extremely sensitive to light, watercolor's fugitive pigments can disappear under the wrong circumstances. Remarkably, *Leaping Trout* remains nearly as vibrant as Homer intended, likely because it was safely housed in museum storage the majority of its life. One of the finest examples of Homer's skill in the medium, *Leaping Trout* was the first Homer watercolor to be purchased by a museum, and it laid the foundation for what would become the largest collection of Homer watercolors in the world.[4] *Leaping Trout* was acquired in 1899, along with the iconic oil painting *The Lookout—"All's Well"*; later that year, the Museum purchased three more watercolors (fig. 2). These acquisitions joined Homer's masterwork in oil, *The Fog Warning*, a momentous gift to the Museum in 1894 (fig. 3). *The Fog Warning* was the first painting by the artist to join the Museum's collection and one of the first works by Homer to join any museum collection. The Museum owns another ten paintings—including *Driftwood*, his last completed canvas— and over a dozen drawings by Homer, as well as nearly three hundred prints made by or after the artist (fig. 4). Some of this work joined the collection during the artist's lifetime, but much of it came to the Museum during the

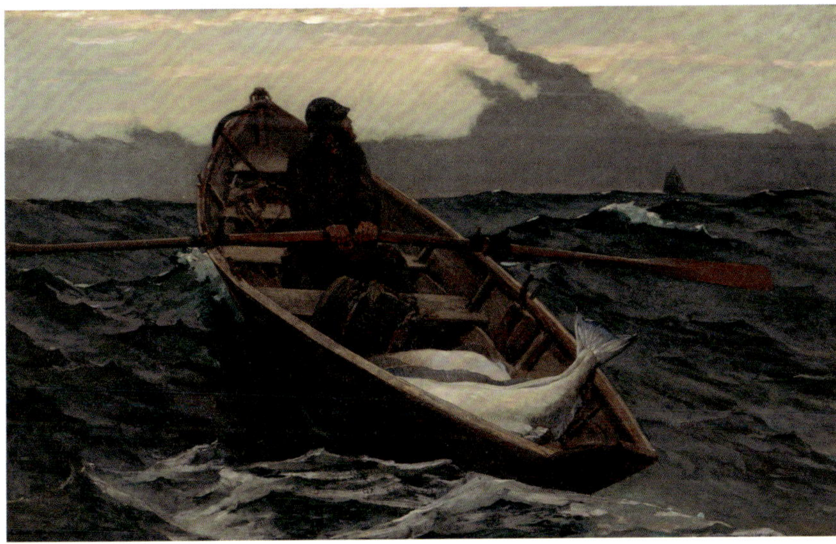

3. *The Fog Warning*, 1885

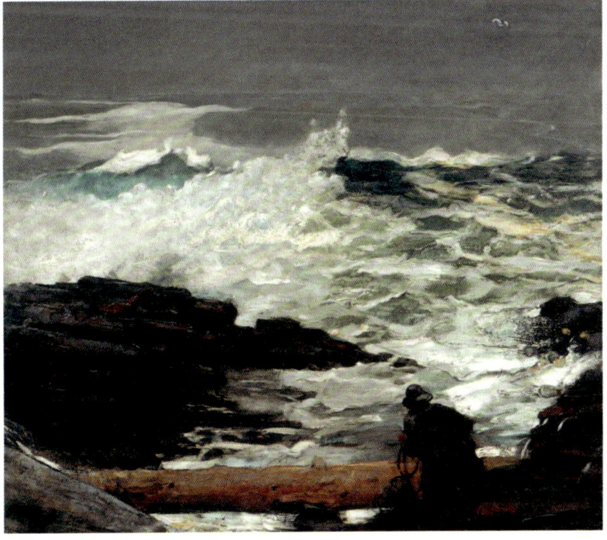

4. *Driftwood*, 1909

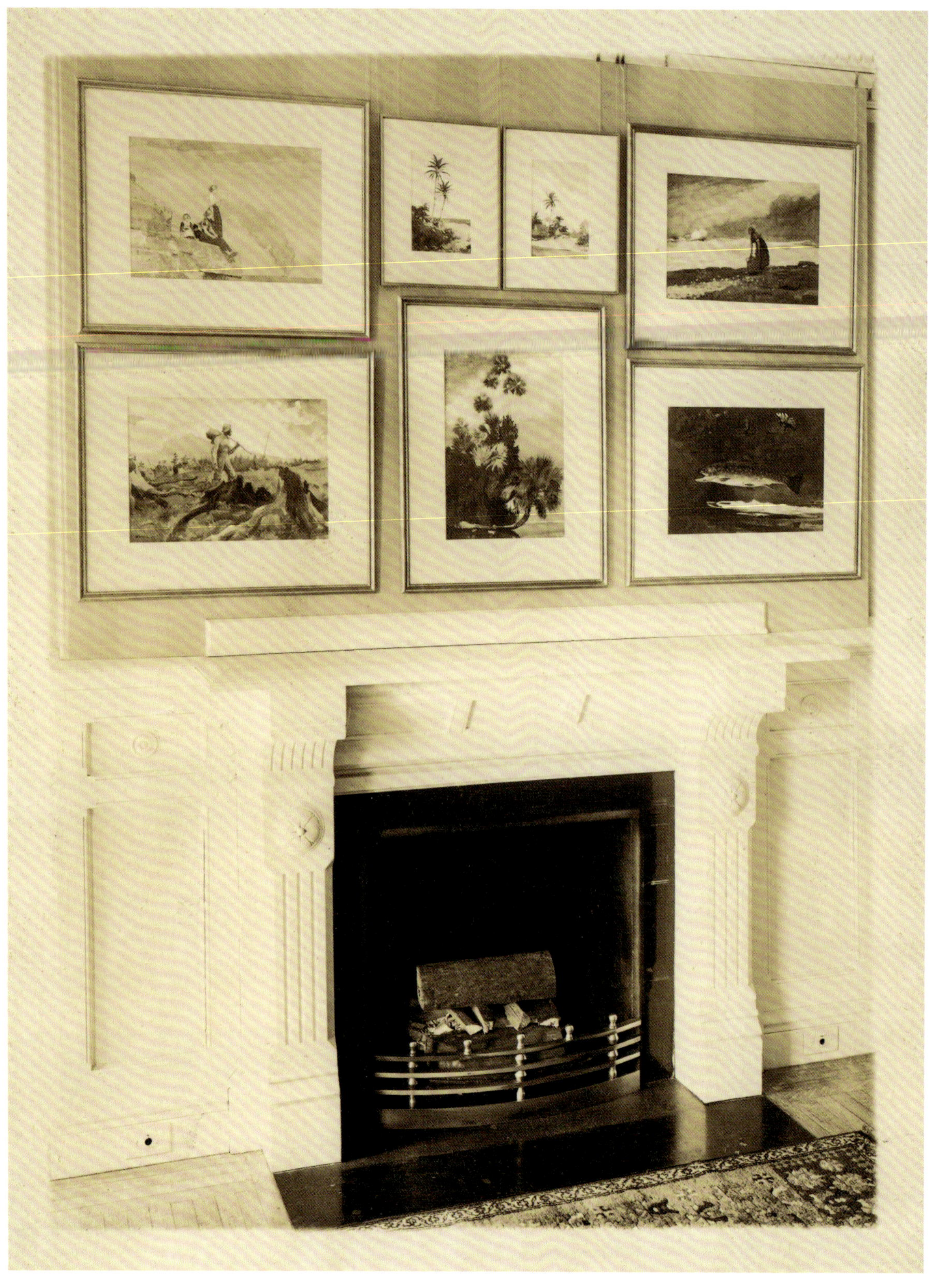

5. Homer watercolors, including *Fisherman's Family* (fig. 43), *Girl with Red Stockings* (fig. 50), *Trout Breaking* (fig. 65), *Palm Trees, Florida* (fig. 61), and *The Guide and Woodsman* (fig. 63), in the home of John Taylor Spaulding, between 1923 and 1948

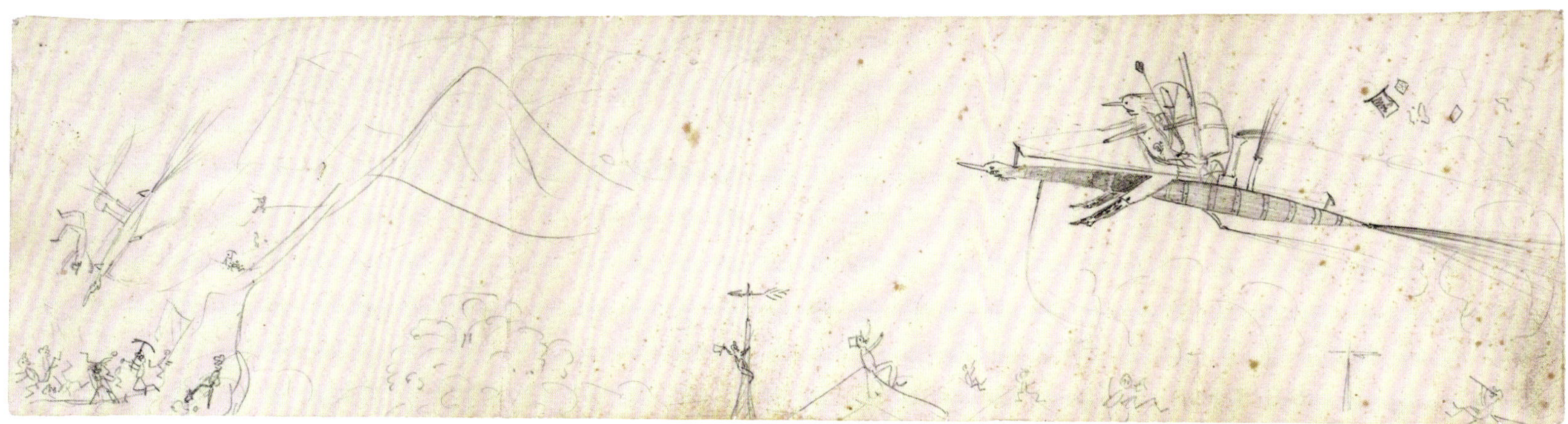

6. *Rocket Ship*, 1849–50

first half of the twentieth century, either by purchase or through the generosity of Homer's local patrons or connections in the region (fig. 5). The Museum's collection, one of the broadest and most significant holdings of Homer's art across media, serves as the framework for this brief overview of the artist's life and work.

Born in Boston and raised in rural Cambridge, Homer's parents were Charles S. Homer, an inventor whose ambitions often put the family in situations of financial precarity, and Henrietta Benson Homer, an accomplished watercolorist. Both of Homer's parents encouraged his artistic talent. At the age of thirteen or fourteen, Homer drew *Rocket Ship*, based on the Currier and Ives print *The Way They Go to California*, on the occasion of his father's departure for the gold fields of the West Coast (fig. 6). Henrietta introduced her son to watercolor in his youth, and an early work by Homer is anecdotally believed to be a copy of one of his mother's paintings (fig. 7). From butterflies to blueberry branches, Henrietta keenly observed the natural world around her and created a large number of nature studies, most likely from actual specimens, given the details she included (fig. 8). Homer held onto many of his mother's paintings after her death in 1884, and they were the only art he displayed in his Prouts Neck studio besides his own. In *Trout Breaking*, another of Homer's masterful Adirondack fishing studies, the swallowtail butterflies seem almost a quotation of Henrietta's study of monarchs from just a few years prior (fig. 9; see fig. 65). Though Homer left Boston for New York City in 1859, he frequently returned to New England. His parents moved from Cambridge to the nearby town of Belmont, and he

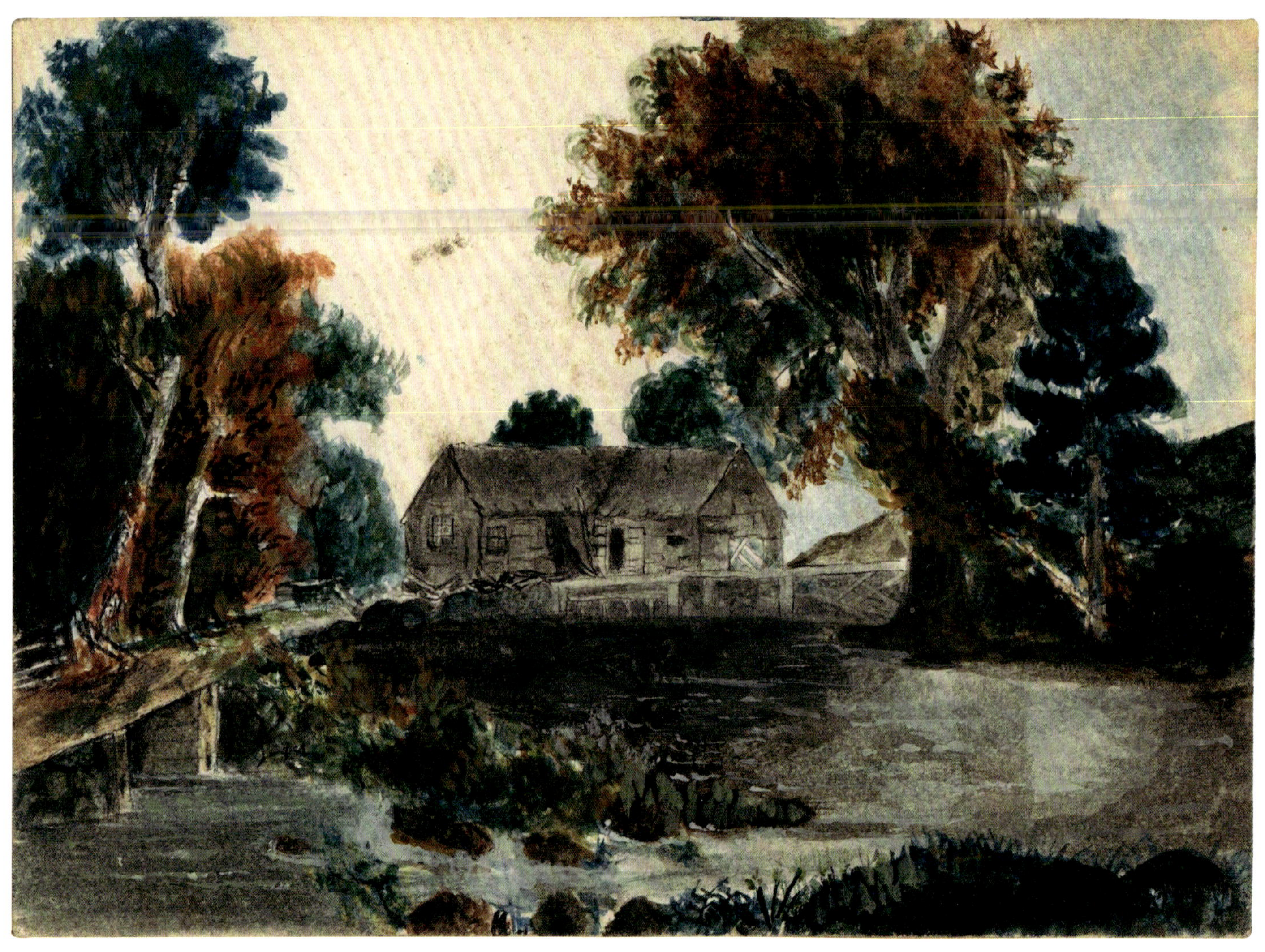

7. *Farm Scene*, 1847, Bowdoin College Museum of Art

often visited throughout the 1860s and early 1870s.[5] He occasionally integrated references to Belmont into his illustrations, sometimes featuring friends or family, such as his cousin Florence Tryon (fig. 10). In a review surveying Homer at mid-career, one art critic wrote, "We get the very essence of New England forms and faces and gestures, and of New England fields and hillsides, in this early work. … No man could mistake the home and people of this artist."[6]

Before his ascent as a leading American artist and his embrace of watercolor, Homer worked as an illustrator. Around 1853, when Homer was seventeen years old, his father arranged an apprenticeship at the lithography shop of John Henry Bufford in Boston's Beacon Hill neighborhood. Here, Homer contributed illustrations for sheet music, books, and other printed matter (fig. 11). At Bufford's, Homer learned not only about the processes and business of printing, but composition and draftsmanship. Though Homer loathed

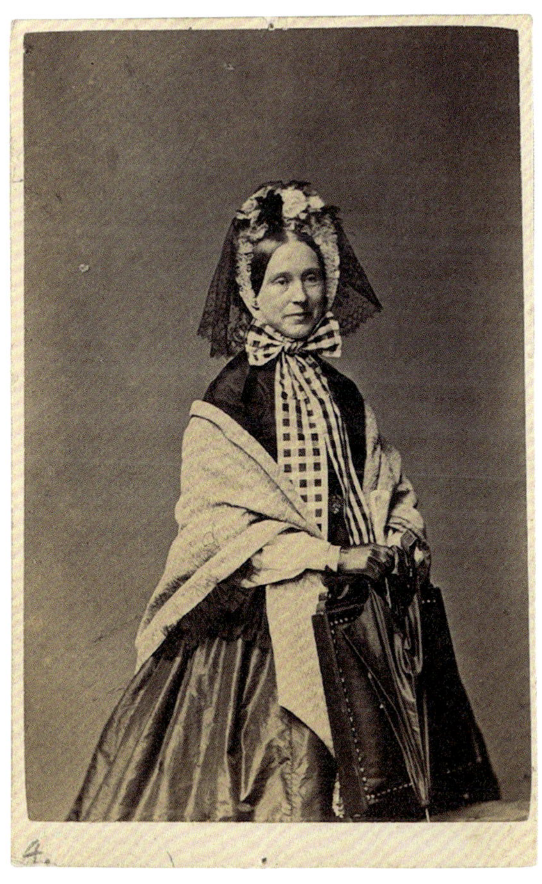

8. Henrietta Benson Homer, 19th century, Bowdoin College Museum of Art

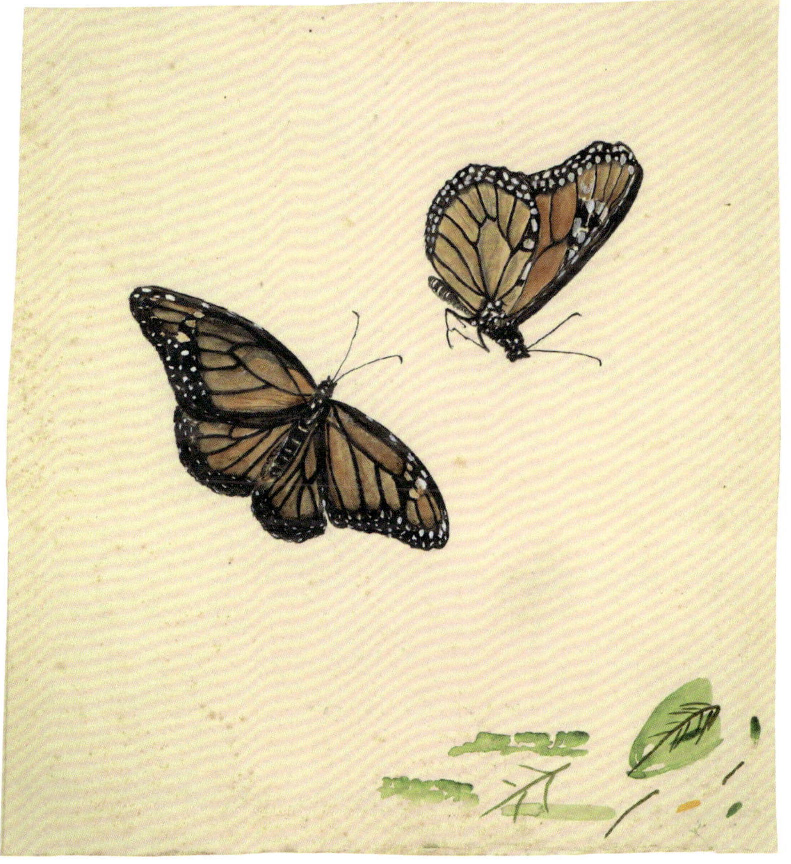

9. Henrietta Benson Homer, untitled (study of two butterflies), 19th century, Bowdoin College Museum of Art

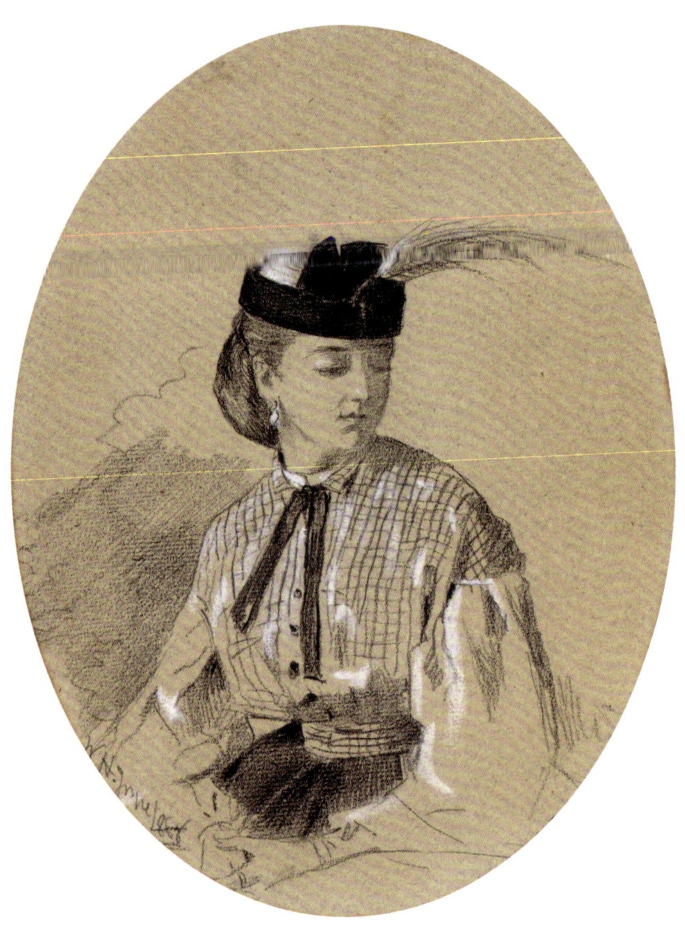

10. *Miss Florence Tryon*, 1868

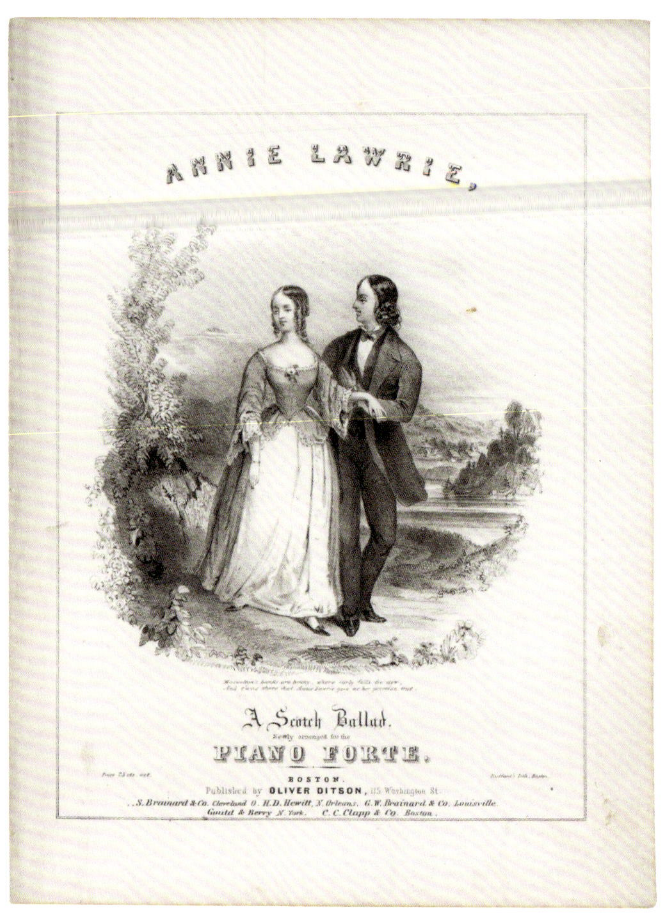

11. Winslow Homer and J. H. Bufford & Company,
Annie Lawrie, 1856

the formulaic and dirty work of the lithography shop, his early training as an illustrator would serve him well for the rest of his career. After ending his apprenticeship, Homer declared that he wished to be self-employed and from then on worked as a freelance illustrator while pursuing a career as a painter. Homer all but gave up lithography after his initial employment at Bufford's in the 1850s, but he continued to explore the potential of his work in that print medium and others throughout his career. Another Boston lithographer, Louis Prang, collaborated with Homer during the Civil War on the publication of *Campaign Sketches* and *Life in Camp*, portfolios featuring both serious and humorous representations of soldiers' day-to-day experiences. Prang and Homer collaborated again some decades later, when Prang purchased two of Homer's mature watercolors from Boston dealer Doll & Richards and reproduced them in the 1890s. Prang had perfected the medium of chromolithography, an advanced method of color printing, and could brilliantly reproduce the appearance of watercolor on a mass scale, effectively enabling consumers to possess a Homer watercolor for a fraction of the cost (figs. 12 and 13). In 1895, again in collaboration with Prang, Homer picked up a lithography crayon, likely for the first time in nearly forty years, to create *Sea and Rocks During a Storm*, a small seascape of which only a few impressions are known (fig. 14). Homer's interest and utilization of print were not limited to lithography and wood engraving, but also included etching, which he pursued with enthusiasm

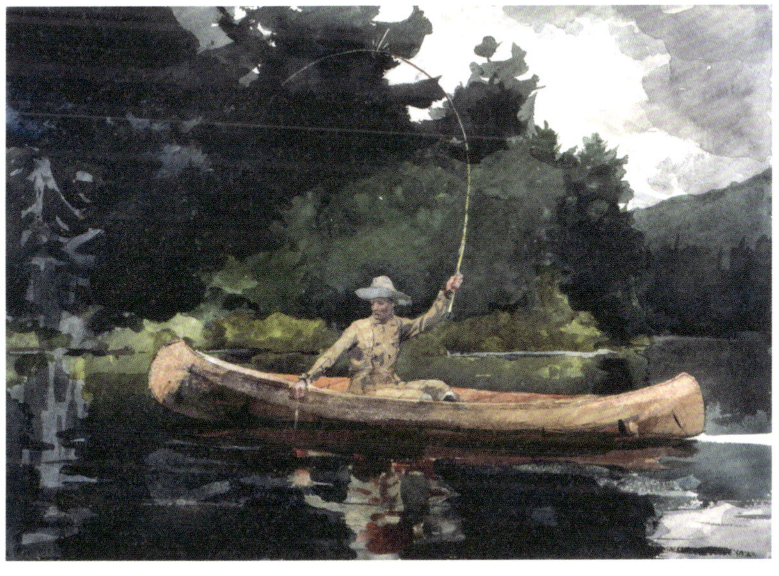

12. *The North Woods (Playing Him)*, 1894, Currier Museum of Art

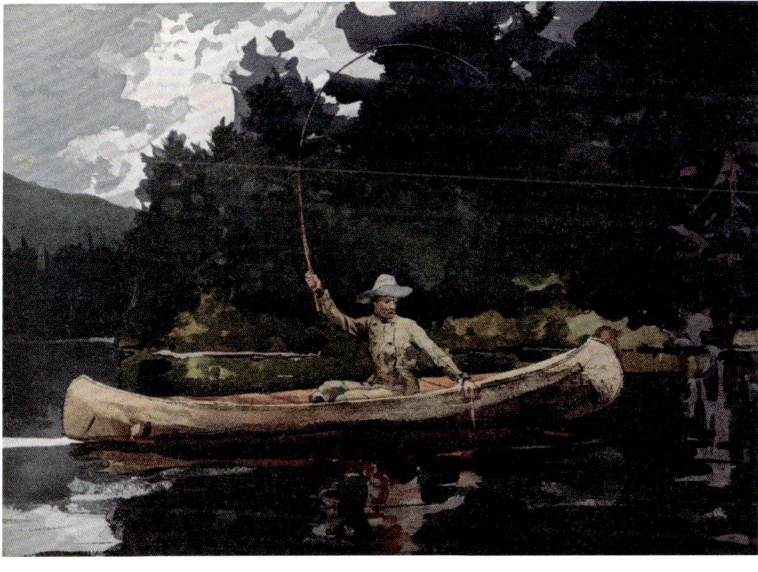

13. Winslow Homer and Louis Prang & Company, *Fly Fishing from a Canoe, North Woods*, 1895

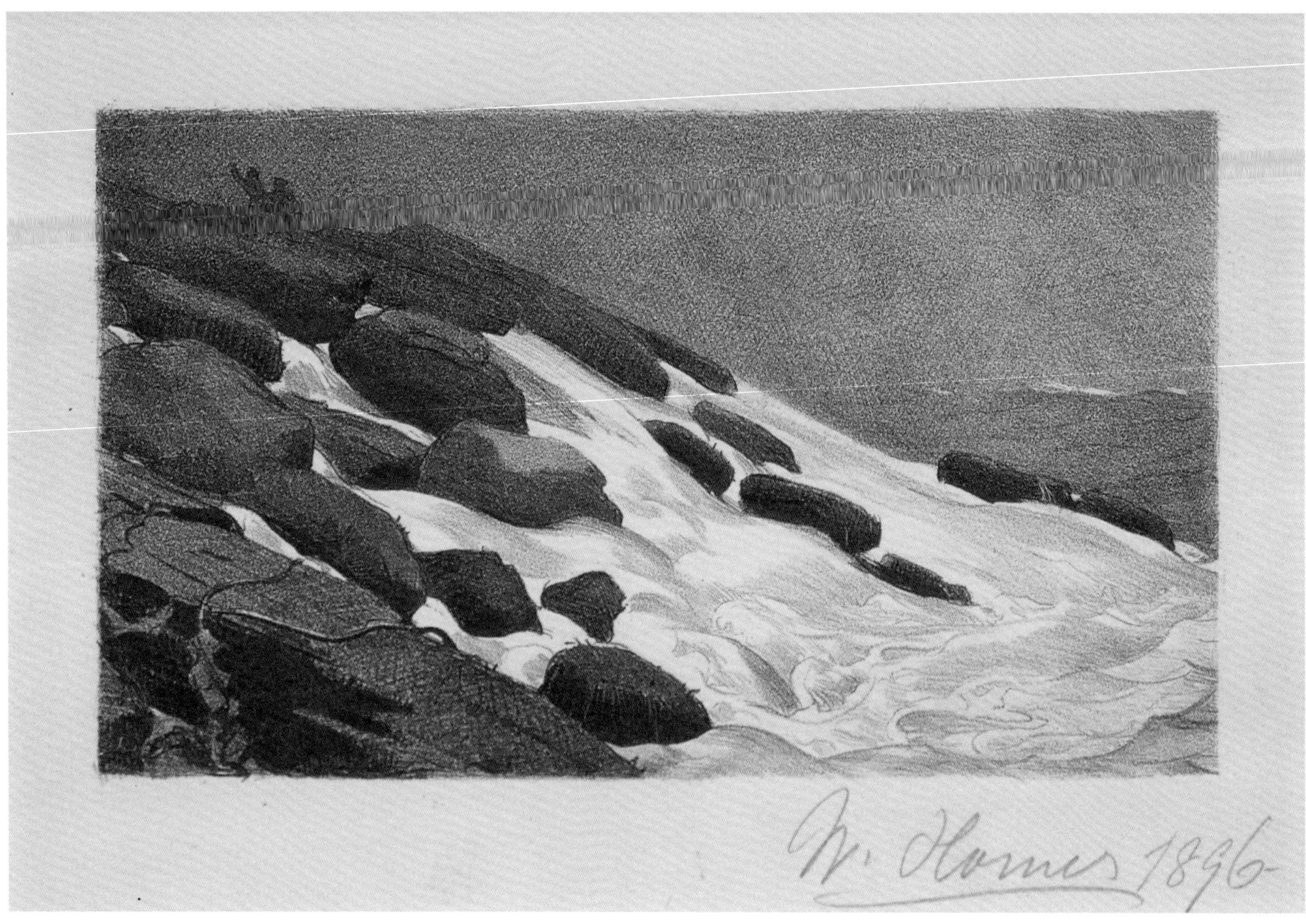

14. Winslow Homer and Louis Prang & Company, *Sea and Rocks During a Storm*, 1896, The Art Students League

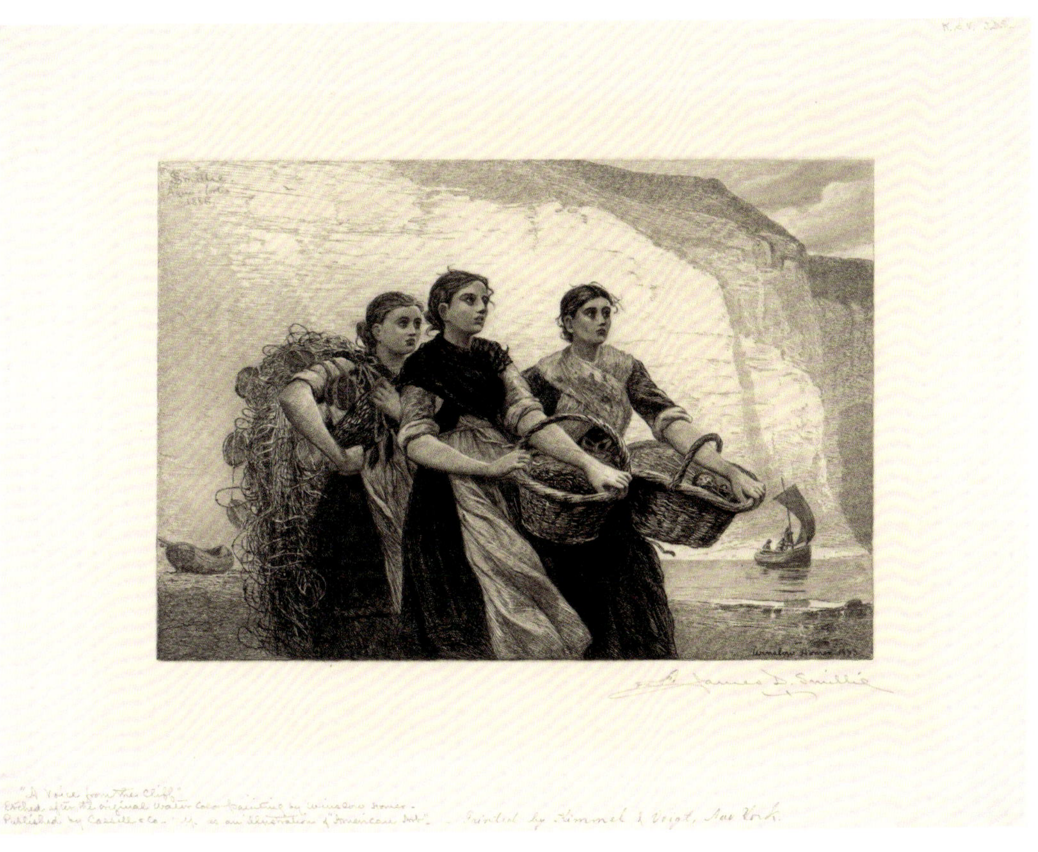

15. James David Smillie after Winslow Homer, *A Voice from the Cliffs*

during the 1880s.[7] In addition to making his own monumental etchings, he also worked closely with the Museum's first curator of prints and drawings, Sylvester Rosa Koehler, and printmaker James David Smillie on a Koehler-published and Smillie-printed etching of Homer's painting *A Voice from the Cliffs* (fig. 15).[8]

From the late 1850s through 1874, Homer provided designs for wood engravings that would appear in illustrated magazines such as the Boston-based *Ballou's Pictorial Drawing Room Companion*, New York's popular *Harper's Weekly*, and others. *Harper's* sent Homer to the front lines of the Civil War in October 1861 to serve as an artist-correspondent, where he focused especially on everyday life in camp. Original drawings for some of Homer's early illustrations show not only his skill in crafting dynamic compositions, but also his embrace of wash, a technique he would use more fully in his later watercolors. In *Rebel Works Seen from General Porter's Division, Yorktown*, he used a brush to paint a wash of gray tones to develop the sky above and trees in the foreground and to add greater dimension to the field at center and houses in the distance (fig. 16). He annotated the image with "Sketched from life," attesting to the veracity of what he depicted. In the printed version of the drawing, the pastoral scene—akin to views Homer would create on farms in rural Massachusetts and upstate New York a decade later—became militarized with the inclusion of Confederate soldiers marching on horseback (fig. 17). Homer continued producing illustrations for *Harper's Weekly* and others through the conclusion of the Civil War in 1865 and for the next ten years. Homer's work as an illustrator taught him how to create a dynamic and legible composition through an economy of line and a balance of tonal values, skills that would provide a strong foundation for a career painting in both oil and watercolor.

Following the Civil War, many American artists, including Homer, who began studying color theory and working seriously in oil in the 1860s, shifted to representations of the pastoral. Artists embraced poems such as John Greenleaf Whittier's "The Barefoot Boy" of 1855 that, although written during the ante-

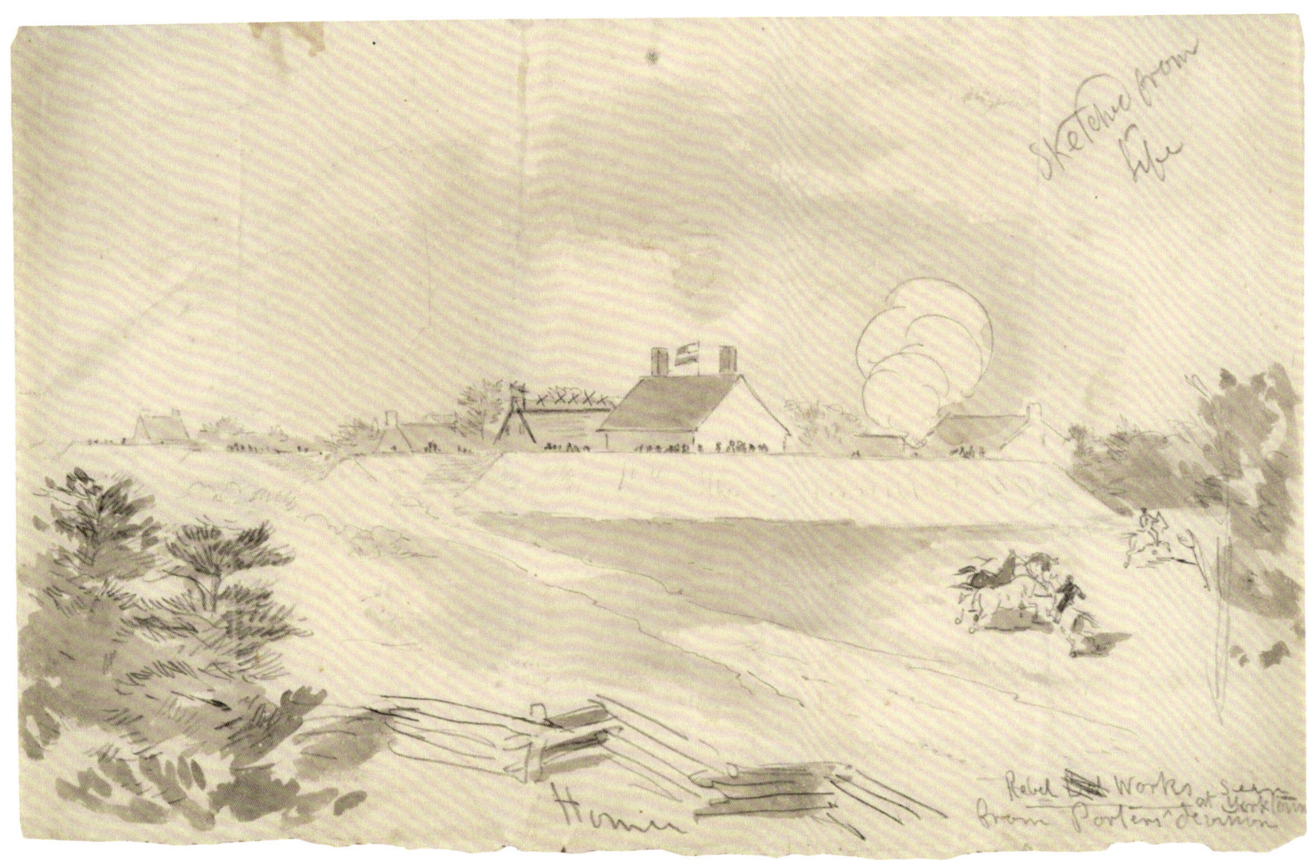

16. *Rebel Works Seen from General Porter's Division, Yorktown*, 1862

bellum period, articulated the innocence of youth and a deepened appreciation of nature.[9] Homer provided bucolic illustrations for Whittier's *The Ballads of New England* (1870) and the poetic works of other leading authors of the day, subject matter that also influenced his work in oil and watercolor. Sentimental literature and imagery took on new significance after the war, as some audiences yearned for the idea of simpler times while others saw hope for a brighter future in depictions of childhood. The preparatory drawing for *On Guard* bridges Homer's work during the war and after it. Here, a young boy perches atop a wooden fence and holds a stick as he gazes out into the distance (fig. 18). Homer created a related wood engraving, clearly derived from the drawing, to illustrate the poem "Watching for Crows" in the Boston children's magazine *Our Young Folks* in 1868 (fig. 19). However, Homer likely originally made the drawing as a study for the 1864 oil painting *On Guard*, a rare depiction of rural boyhood *during* the war (fig. 20). A lifelong admirer of the outdoors and keenly aware of contemporary tastes, Homer continued to center carefree children, industrious youths, wistful maidens, and laboring farmhands in his work from

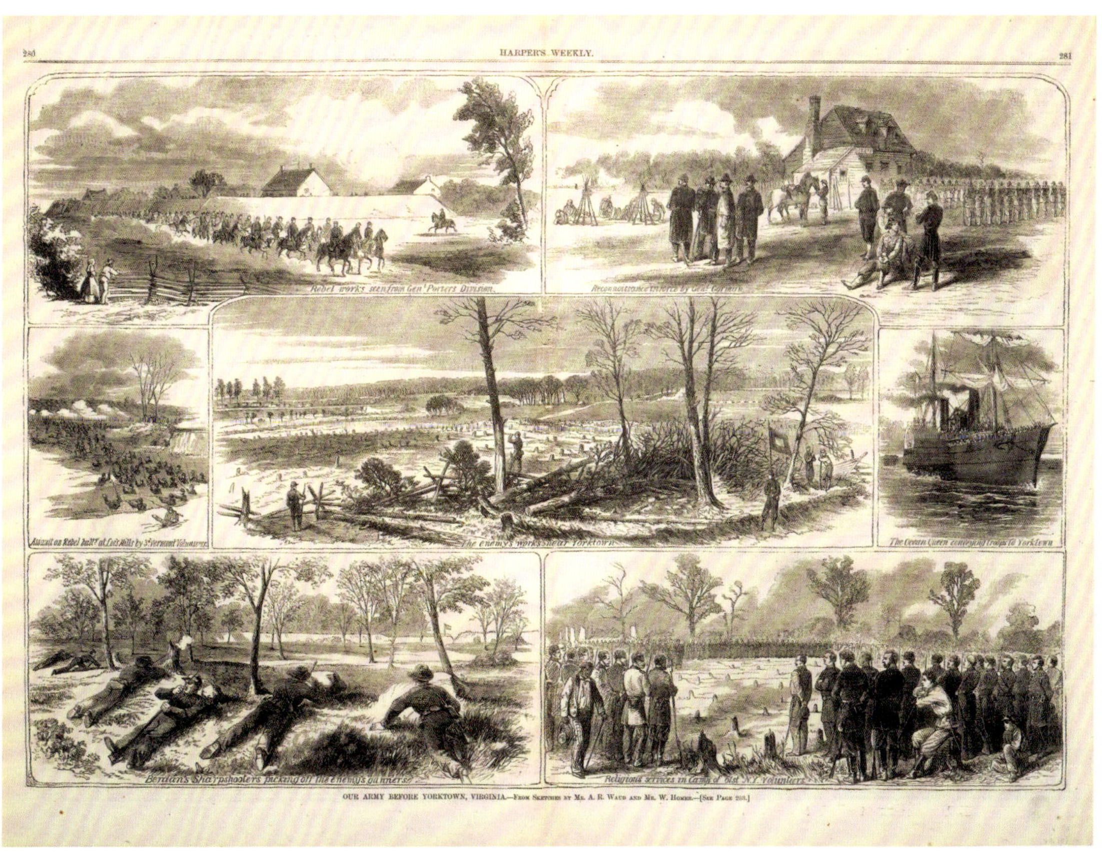

17. Unidentified artist after Winslow Homer, *Our Army Before Yorktown, Virginia*, 1862

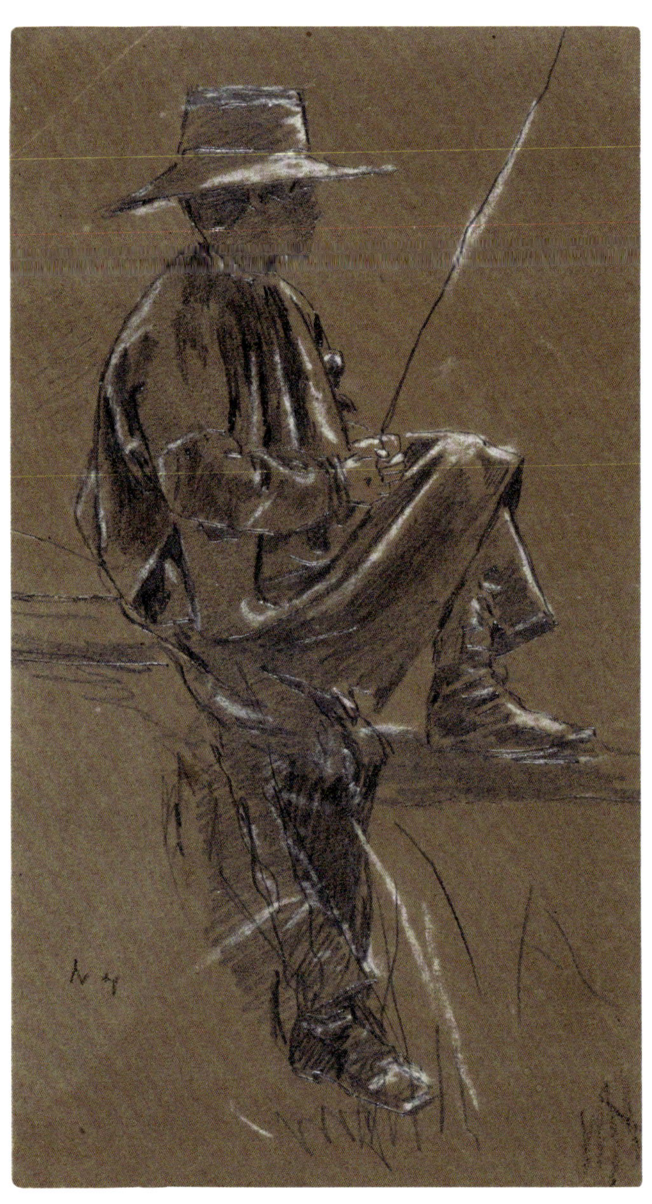

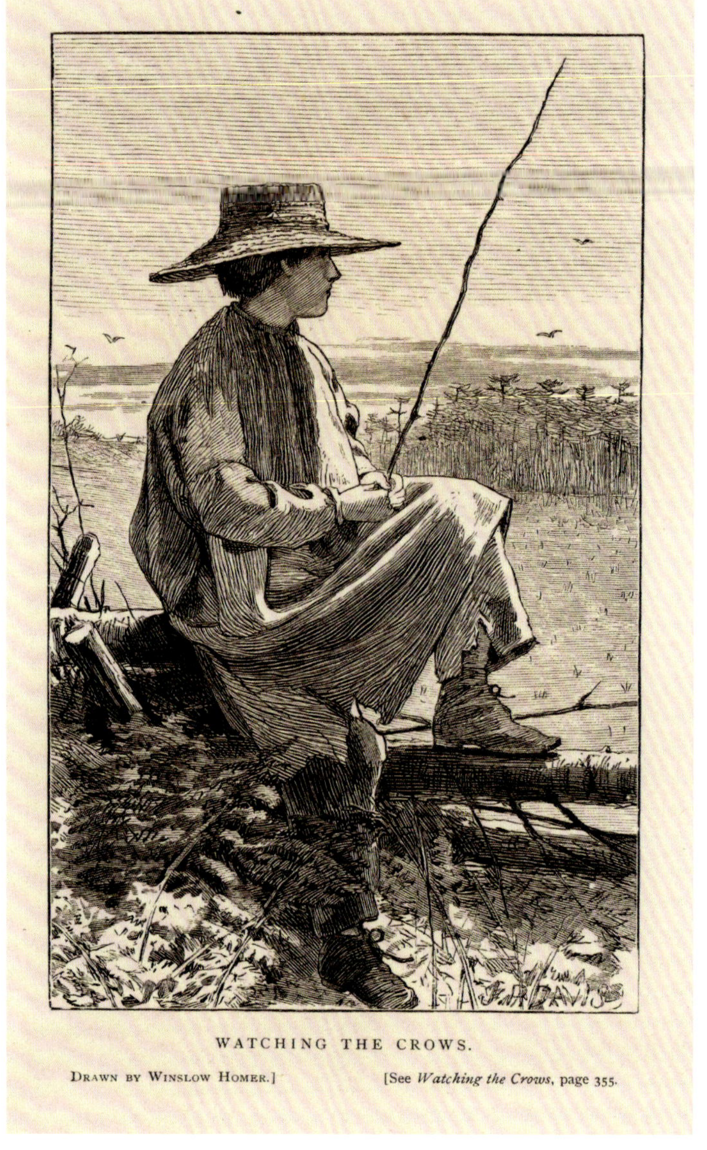

18. Preparatory drawing for *On Guard*, about 1864   19. *Watching the Crows*, 1868

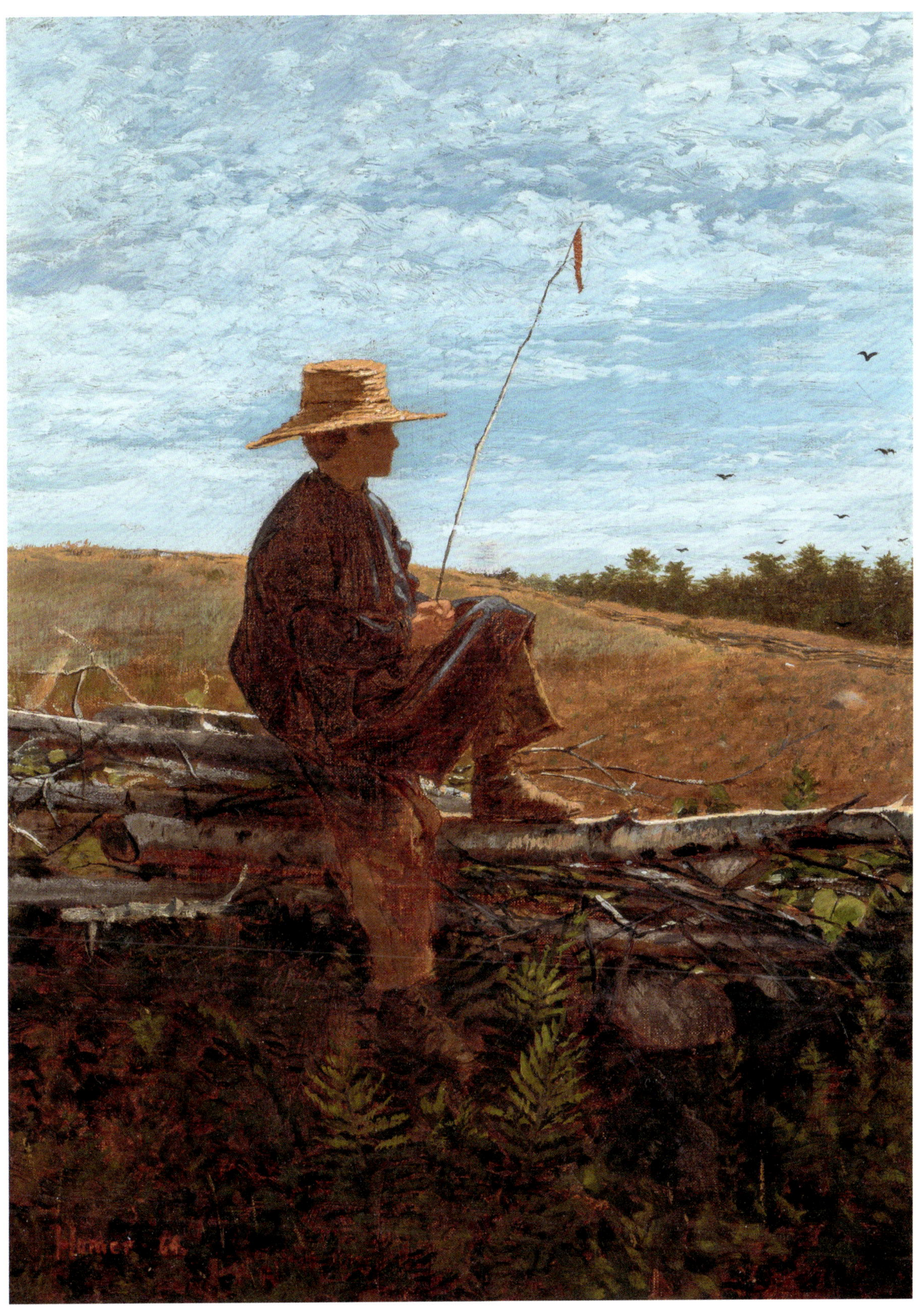

20. *On Guard*, 1864, Terra Foundation for American Art

the late 1860s and 1870s. *Boys in a Pasture* is a prime example of his work from this era and also of the relationship between his painting in oil and his painting in watercolor (fig. 21). The blades of grass articulated by individual brush-strokes and surrounding the seated figures recall a related technique (and subject matter) in the early watercolor *Boy and Girl on a Hillside* (see fig. 38). Homer also applied bright white highlights to the nearest boy's shirt to evoke illumination by bright sunlight; he does the same in the watercolor *"Bo-Peep,"* with a similarly positioned figure (see fig. 36).

Watercolor — previously associated with "amateur" artists, especially women, and dismissed by critics and tastemakers — rose in popularity and became professionalized precisely at the time that Homer began to work seriously in the medium.[10] This also coincided with the moment Homer began to focus on the sea, a subject he would return to repeatedly in his career. His first exhibited seascape, *Rocky Coast and Gulls*, was panned by critics when it made its debut in 1869 but was pivotal to his evolving style (fig. 22). The elevated horizon line was a shift in perspective that he would embrace in later works. Another important oil from this period, *Long Branch, New Jersey*, relates to his earliest forays into watercolor (fig. 23). His first watercolor known to be exhibited, *Women and Children on Beach at Long Branch, New Jersey*, appeared in the American Watercolor Society's exhibition in 1870, three years before he would take up the medium in earnest during a summer stay in Gloucester, Massachusetts (fig. 24).

The 1870s were a time of transition in Homer's life and art, but also in the cultural landscape of the United States. Homer continued to work across media, transferring compositions between drawings, oils, and illustrations. Homer's parents moved from Belmont, Massachusetts, to Brooklyn, New York, in late 1872. In 1873, Homer produced his first major series of watercolors, while his mother, Henrietta, exhibited her own watercolors for the first time. Henrietta would become a frequent exhibitor at the Brooklyn Art Association. Notably, by 1875, Homer stopped contributing illustrations to *Harper's Weekly*, though he occasionally contributed illustrations to books through the 1880s. In addition to the National Academy of Design, where Homer was elected a member in 1865, the growing network of art dealers and the recent establishment of public art museums (including the Museum of Fine Arts, Boston, founded in 1870) buoyed Homer's career.[11] The Boston gallery Doll & Richards gave Homer

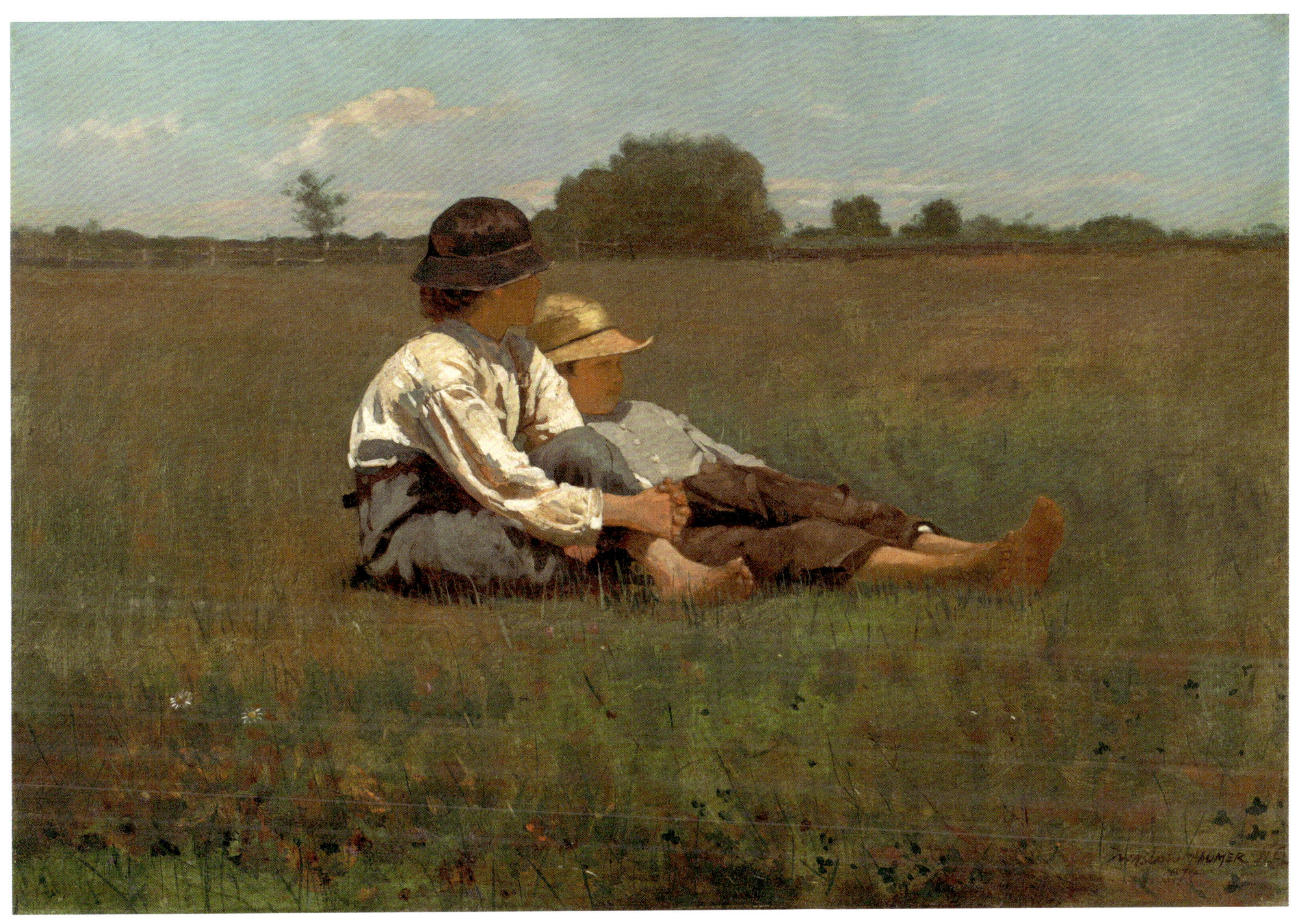

21. *Boys in a Pasture*, 1874

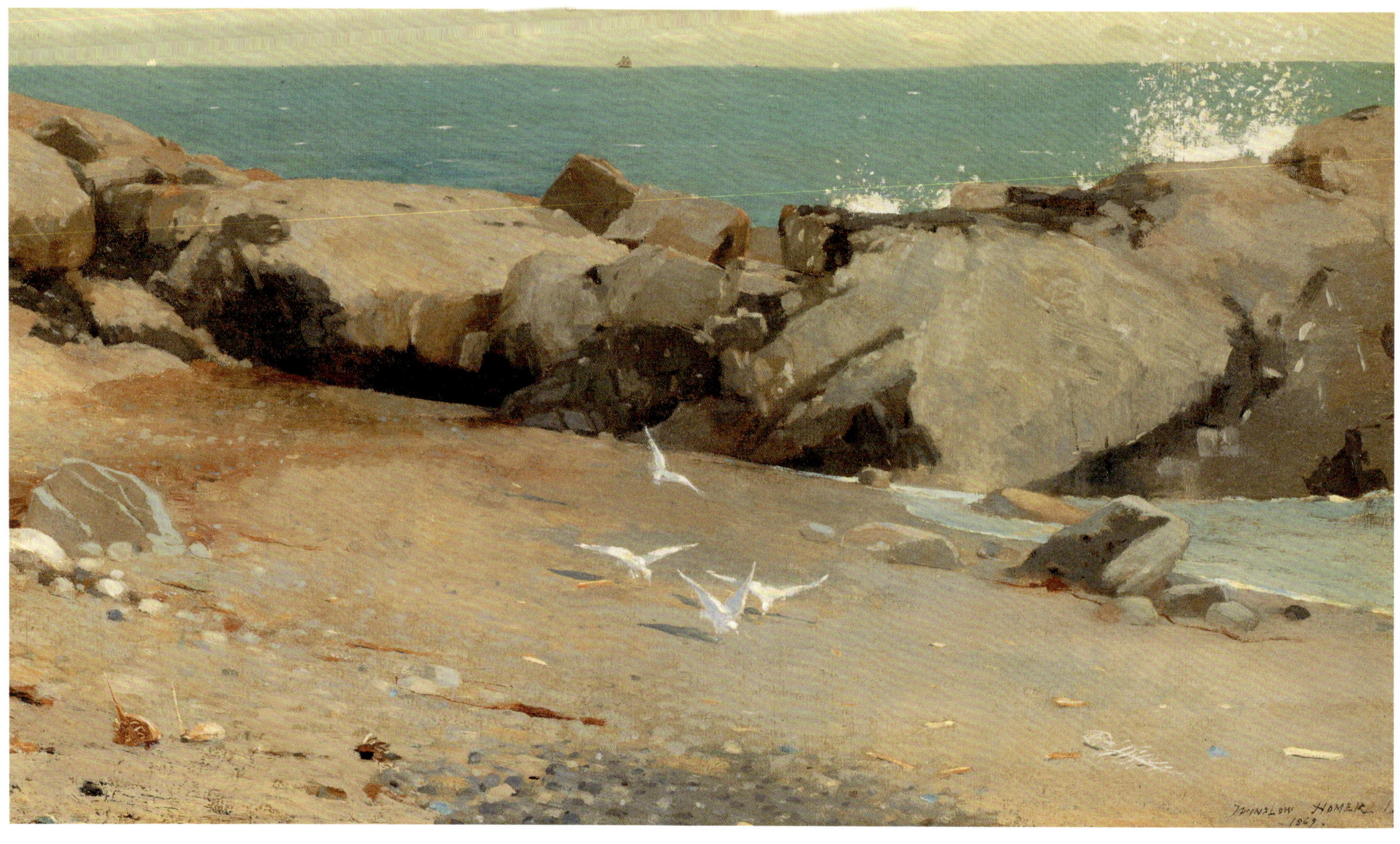

22. *Rocky Coast and Gulls,* 1869

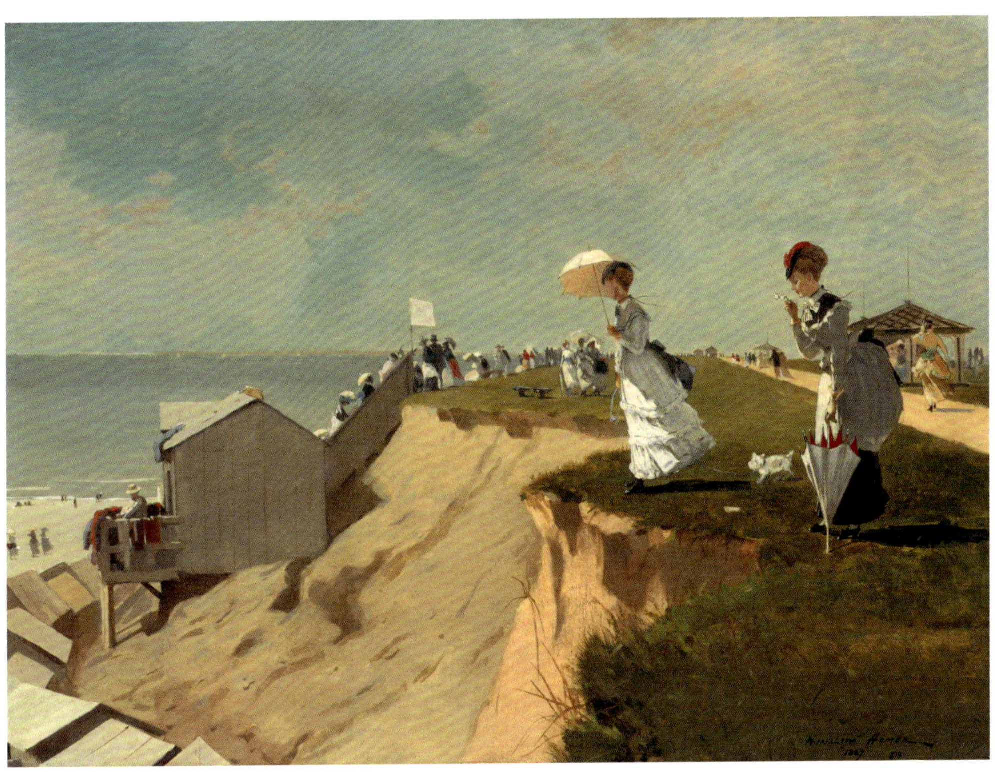

23. *Long Branch, New Jersey*, 1869

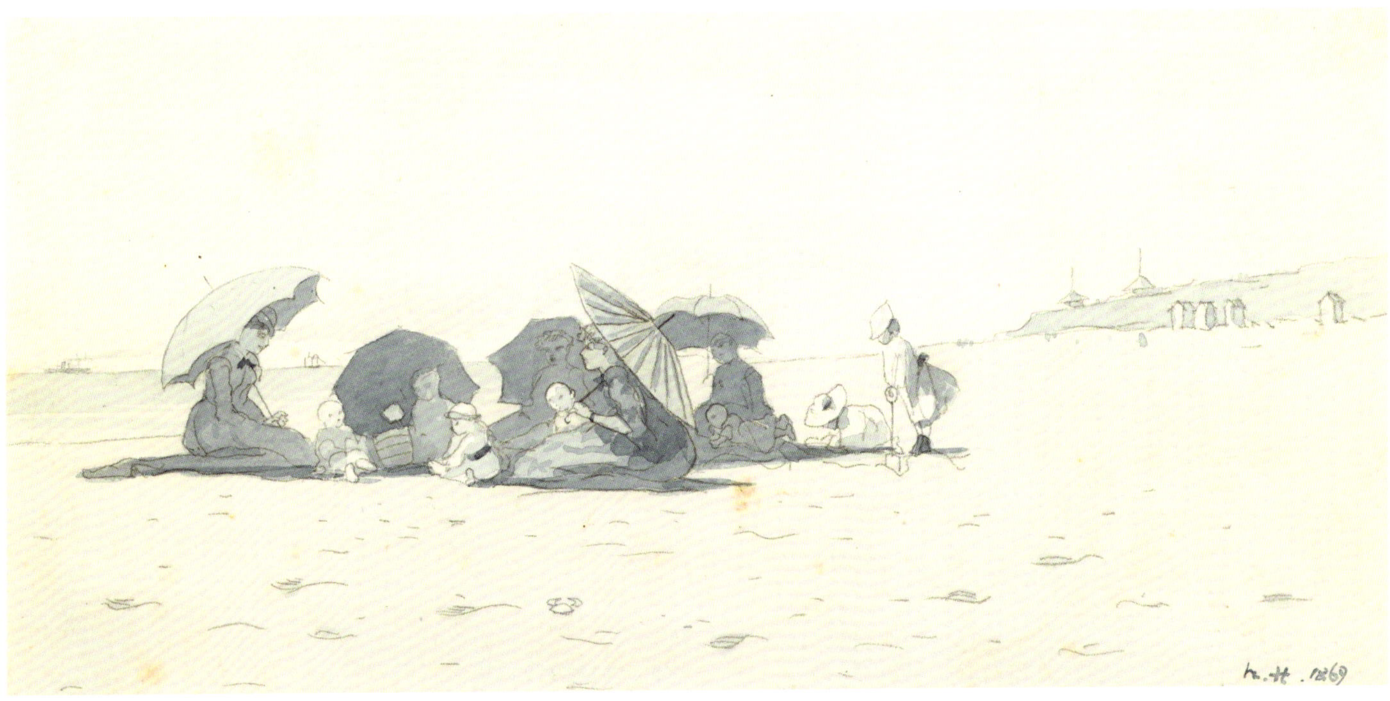

24. *Women and Children on Beach at Long Branch, New Jersey*, 1869, Yale University Art Gallery

his first one-man show, featuring a series of Gloucester watercolors, and continued to work with the artist for much of his career. Homer also cultivated relationships with several New York galleries, especially M. Knoedler and Company. By the mid-1870s, Homer had gained considerable notoriety as an artist and a reputation for creating work characterized by "freshness" and "truth" due to his keen powers of observation and straightforward realism. In 1875, author and critic Henry James wrote that "Mr. Homer has the great merit, moreover, that he naturally sees everything at one with its envelope of light and air. He sees not in lines, but in masses…Things come already modelled to his eye."[12]

From the mid-1870s on, watercolor became a critical medium in Homer's artistic practice (fig. 25). This book focuses on key geographic locations represented by Homer's watercolors in the Museum's wide-ranging collection. Rather than a comprehensive, chronological mapping of his output in watercolor, the remaining pages revel in the breadth and depth of the Museum's holdings while making connections between them. The following sections include: Gloucester, Massachusetts, the site of his first concentrated watercolor series in 1873 and later, in 1880, another career-defining series; central Massachusetts and upstate New York, where the artist explored the pastoral during a transitional period in his life and work during the 1870s; Cullercoats, England, the coastal town across the Atlantic where Homer stayed for eighteen months between 1881 and 1882, took inspiration from the working fisherwomen and their families, and refined his technique; the North Woods, encompassing the Adirondack Mountains and southeastern Canada, where Homer created some of his most innovative mature watercolors of the late 1880s and early 1890s; the subtropical and tropical locales of Florida and the Caribbean, including the Bahamas, Bermuda, and Cuba, that Homer visited periodically from the mid-1880s until the early 1900s; and Prouts Neck, Maine, his home for the last two and a half decades of his life (fig. 26). Select drawings by Homer in the Museum's collection have also been included in relevant sections.

As Annette Manick demonstrates throughout this volume, Homer utilized a wide array of techniques to create these dynamic works on paper in a famously unforgiving medium. Decades of dedicated work by conservators have revealed interesting discoveries in Homer's watercolors, as well as ensured their vibrancy and longevity. Watercolor is fugitive, with some pigments being especially light-sensitive, and what is lost cannot be recovered or repaired. One Homer

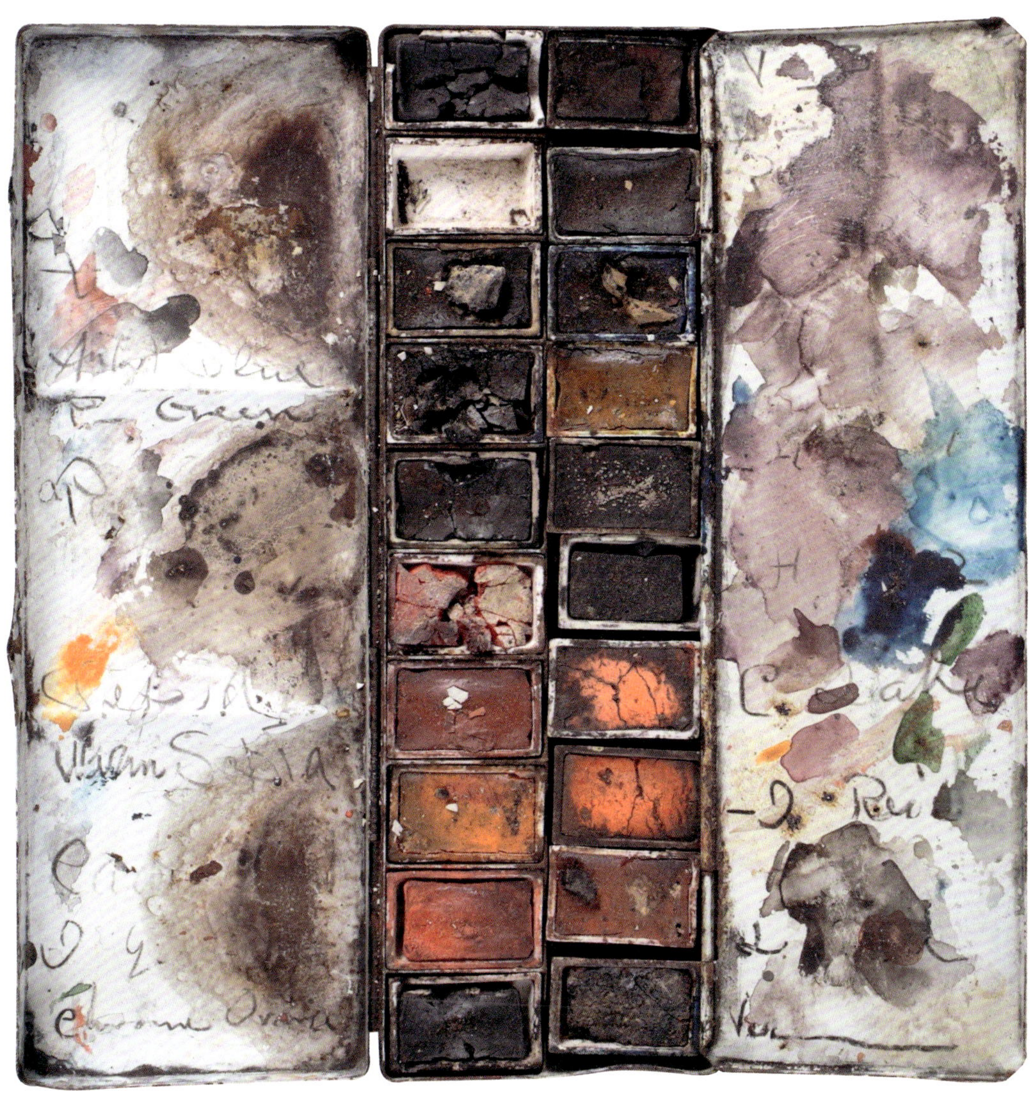

25. Homer's watercolor box, 1900–10, Bowdoin College Museum of Art

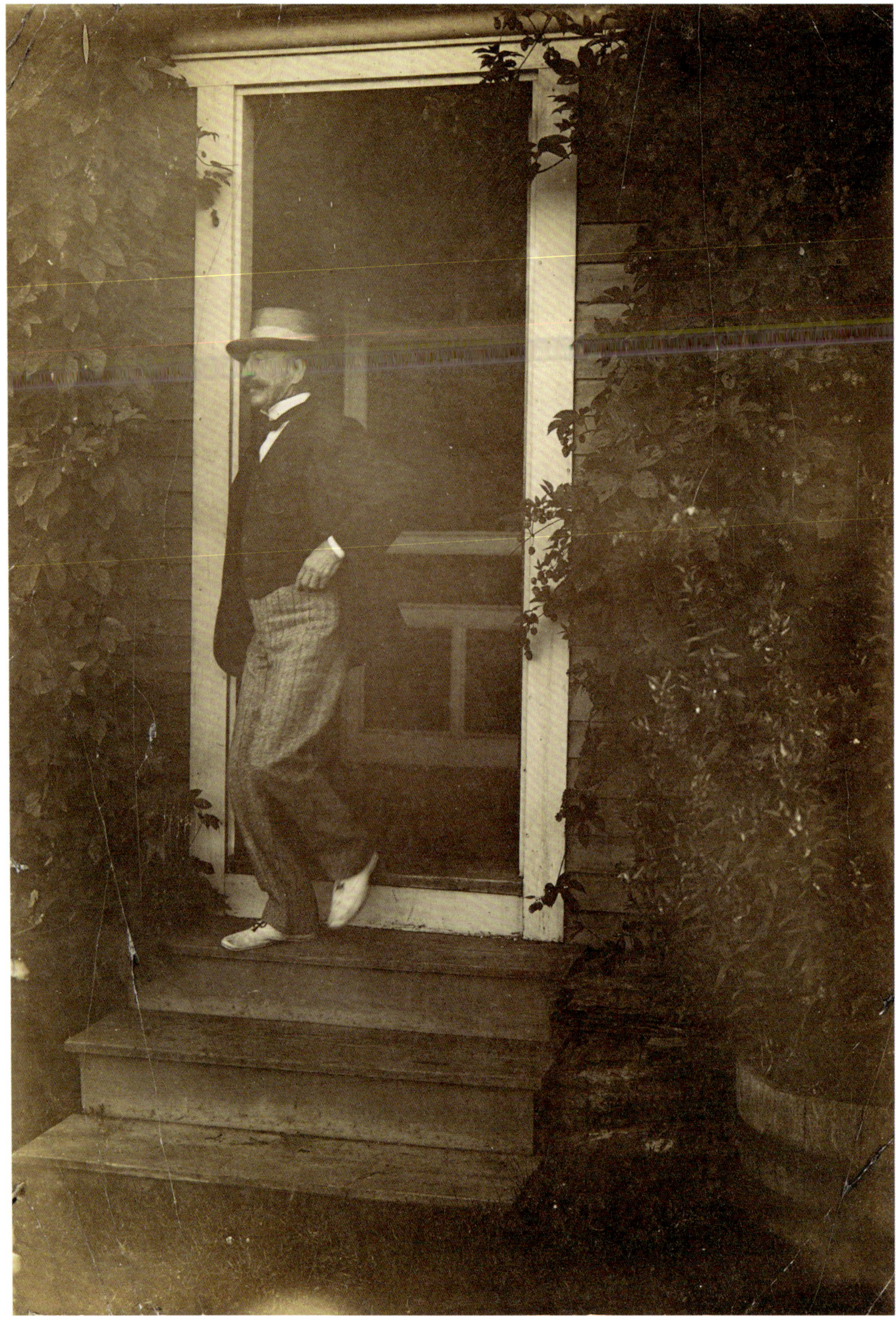

26. Lillian Baynes Griffin, Winslow Homer at the door of his studio,
Prouts Neck, Me., about 1907, Boston Athenaeum

watercolor in the Museum's collection is particularly instructive regarding both fading and Homer's penchant for cropping finished watercolors, especially during the late 1880s. *Clamming*, painted in 1887, is a quiet scene of coastal labor in Maine: a figure, recalling the fishwives of his Cullercoats series from a few years earlier, stretches down to retrieve clams burrowing in the sand beneath a muted beige sky (see fig. 82). Lifting the mat, however, reveals a number of surprises. Most immediately striking are the large Xs Homer added to the bottom of the paper. This instruction to the framers ensured the composition would be cropped to his liking, effectively bringing the person forward and further immersing the viewer in the scene. The other surprise is the amount of fading the watercolor endured prior to joining the Museum's collection by gift in 1965, evidenced by the stark difference between the exposed portions of the picture and the edges protected beneath the mat that retain the colors Homer intended. Most of the pigments lost are purples and reds, which tend to be the most fugitive. This loss occurred especially in the sky, which appeared more like a dusk or twilight scene than what instead reads as an overcast afternoon. While the material components of *Clamming* have faded over time, the subject it depicts has, too. In recent decades, the rising temperatures and acidity levels of the North Atlantic have negatively impacted the clamming industry in New England. When considered alongside ongoing environmental threats from climate change, Homer's watercolors take on a new resonance, underscoring the fleetingness and vulnerability of the natural world and the medium of watercolor, then and now.

Homer died in 1910 at his Prouts Neck, Maine, house and studio and is buried at Mount Auburn Cemetery in Cambridge, Massachusetts. Late in his career, Homer famously said to a friend, "You will see, in the future I will live by my watercolors." Indeed, Homer's work in watercolor not only immortalized him as an innovative painter, but continues to influence artists to this day.

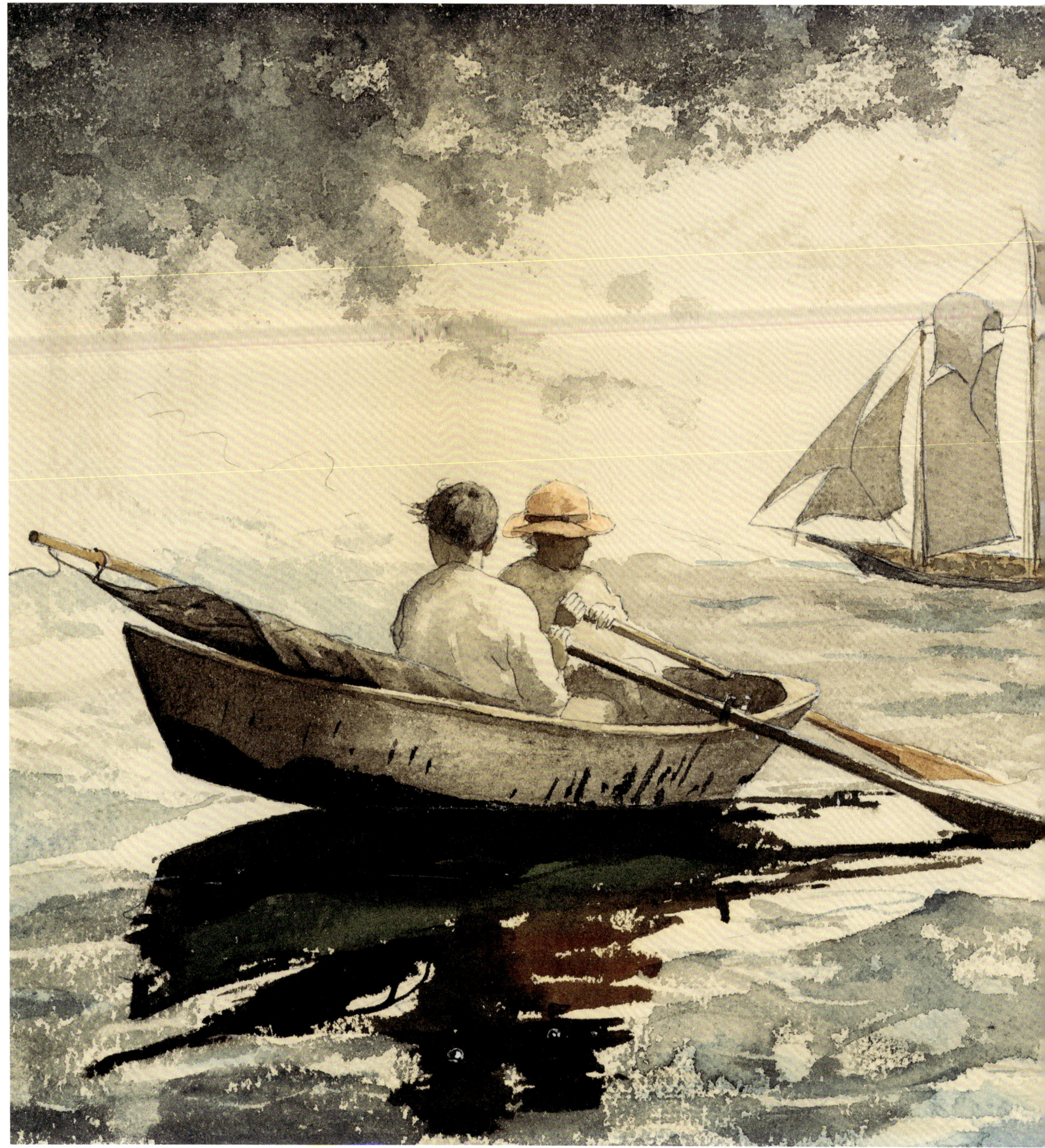

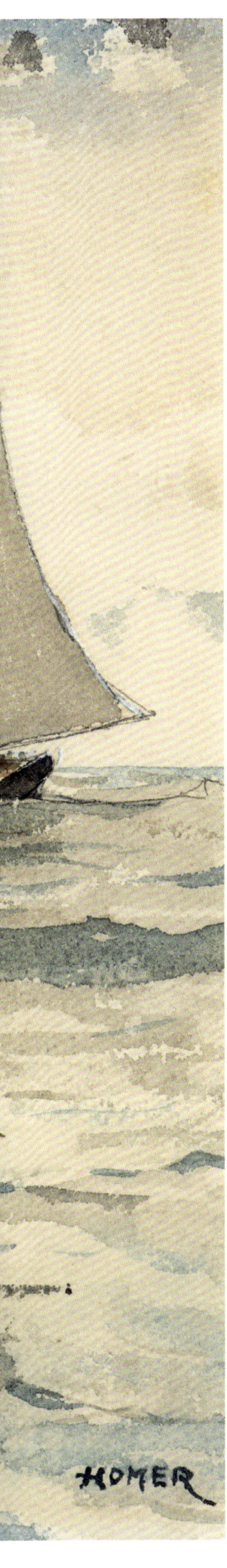

Gloucester, Massachusetts

In 1873, Winslow Homer summered in Gloucester, Massachusetts. Between July and late August of that year, the artist produced his first series of watercolors. Gloucester, some thirty miles north of Boston and one of the oldest seaports in North America, offered Homer a bustling harbor and charming local subjects. Foreshadowing his work in Cullercoats, England, in the early 1880s, the majority of Homer's output that summer focused on local children playing near the shore, docks, and shipyards as they awaited the return of their fathers' fishing fleets. The watercolors are characterized by opaque, saturated color, applied in a manner similar to that of an oil painting. This pivotal moment in the artist's career is represented in the Museum's collection by the highly finished drawing *Three Boys on a Beached Dory*. Here, Homer uses black chalk and white highlights to articulate a moment of calm as three boys in broad-brimmed hats perch on an overturned boat and look toward sailboats coasting along the horizon. Homer found the drawing so successful that he adapted it into an oil painting and a watercolor. Many of Homer's other compositions from that summer later appeared as illustrations for *Harper's Weekly*, whose readership reveled in the seaside adventures of his youthful subjects.

Seven years later, in the summer of 1880, Homer returned to Gloucester and created another extensive watercolor series. This time, he stayed in the lighthouse on Ten Pound Island in Gloucester Harbor and produced over a hundred works in just two months. His watercolor techniques had evolved since 1873, and he began to embrace looser brushstrokes and broader, more evocative washes of color. Local youth still featured prominently in his compositions, but this series demonstrates an increased interest in the effects of light and in people braving the elements of nature, qualities that would come to define his work later in the century. In *Two Boys Rowing*, a composition reminiscent of his later oil *The Fog Warning* and other Prouts Neck work, the titular subjects navigate a small boat on churning seas as a schooner with billowing sails rocks in the distance. Beneath ominous storm clouds, the reflections of the boys and their boat dissolve into agitated waves, an effect masterfully achieved by Homer's more experienced brush.

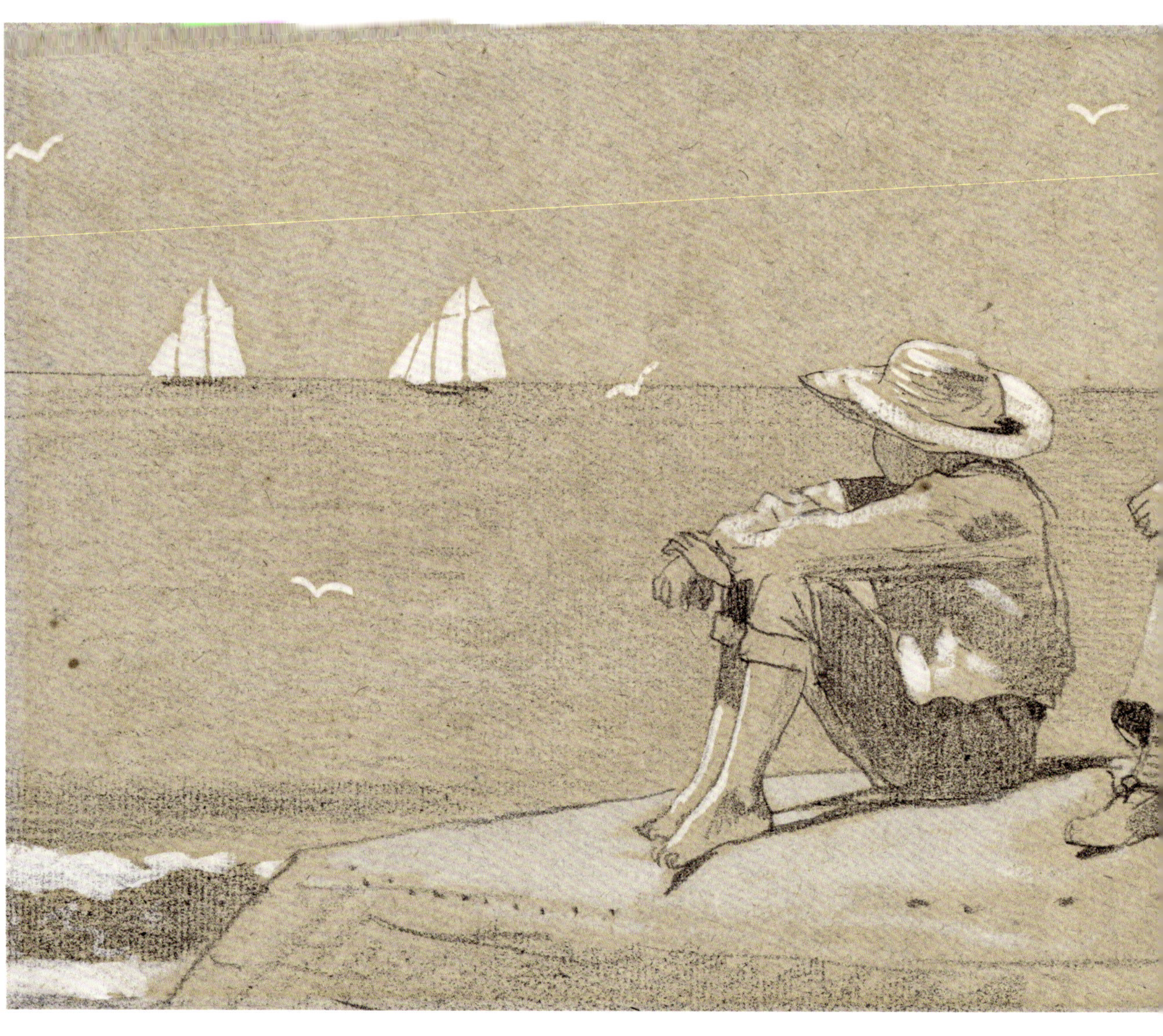

27. *Three Boys on a Beached Dory*, 1873

White Watercolor Pigments / Homer preferred painting with Zinc White, likely aware of the disadvantages of other white watercolor pigments. Lead White, valued for its opacity, was known to discolor, and Constant White, regarded as more stable than Lead White, was difficult to use. Instructional manuals pointed out that the opacity of Constant White changed as it dried, making it challenging to judge its effect on value. Zinc White provided sufficient covering power and was considered "unquestionably permanent."[13] Zinc White also sold as Chinese White, and Constant White as Permanent White, Blanc Fixe, or Barium White. Zinc White responds to ultraviolet radiation in a distinctive way, reemitting energy in the visible light range, appearing yellow, as recorded in the detail image. — AM

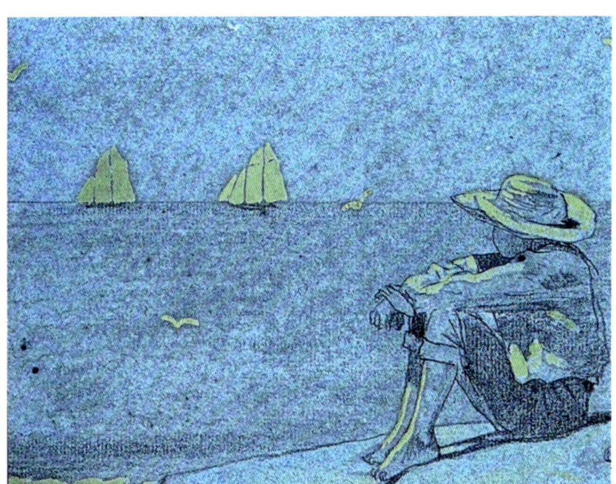

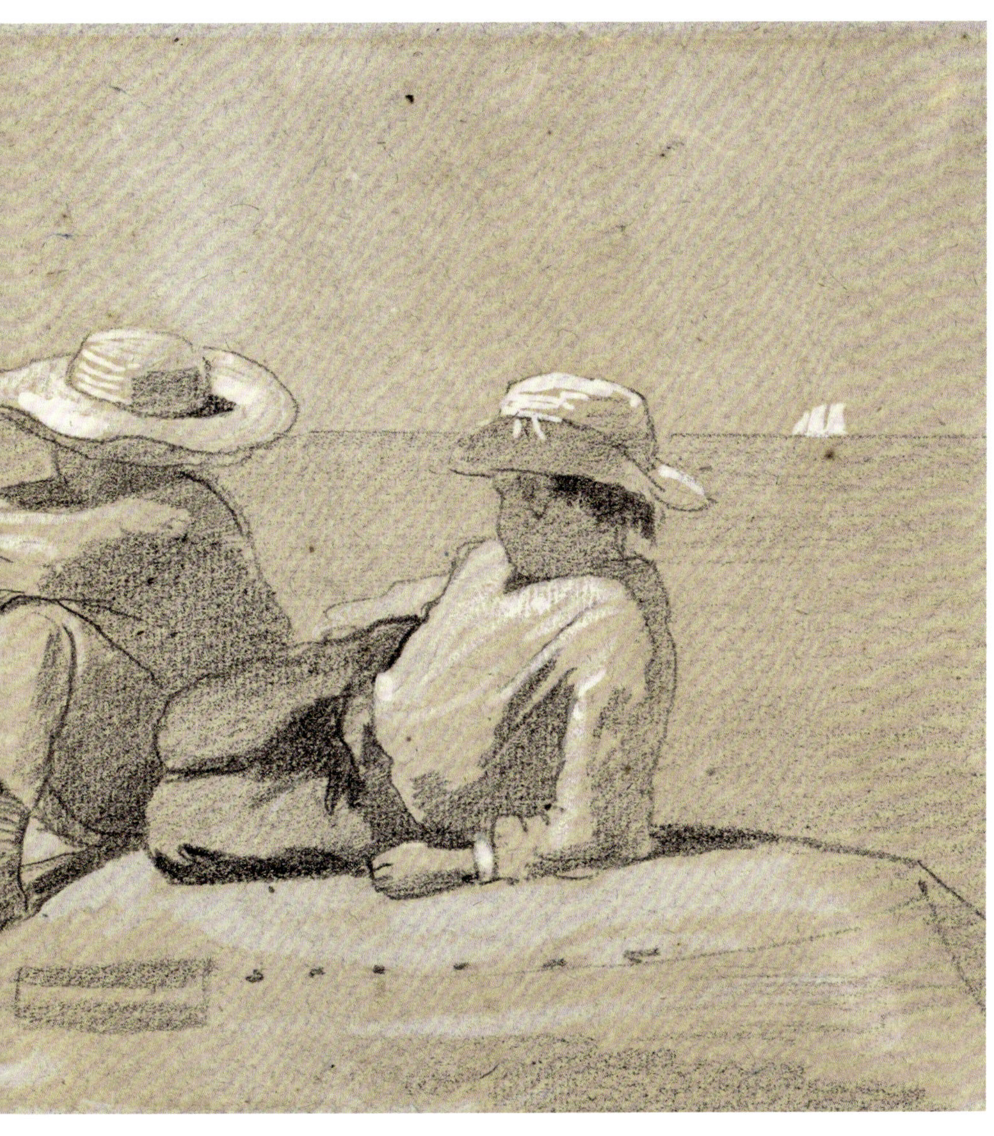

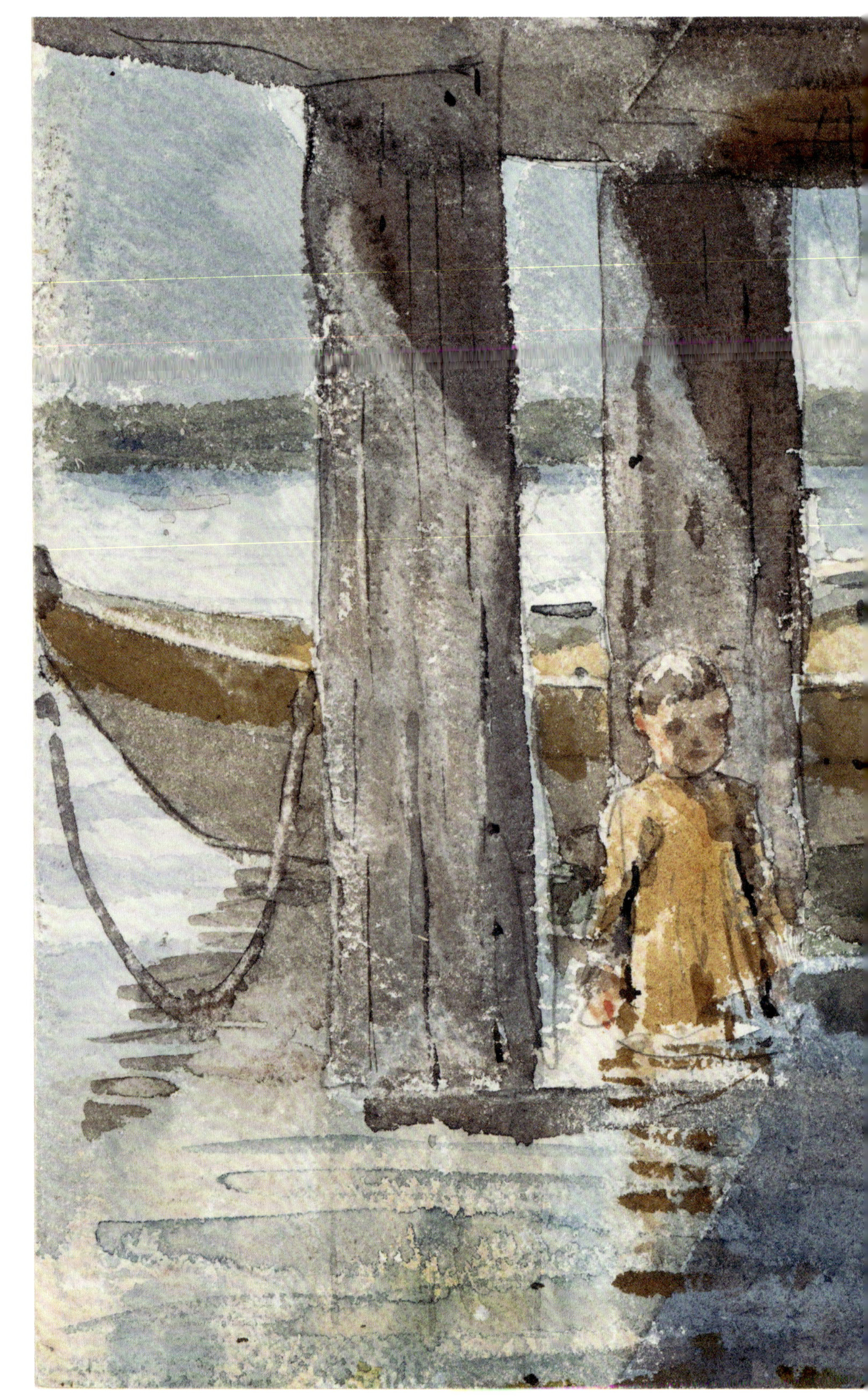

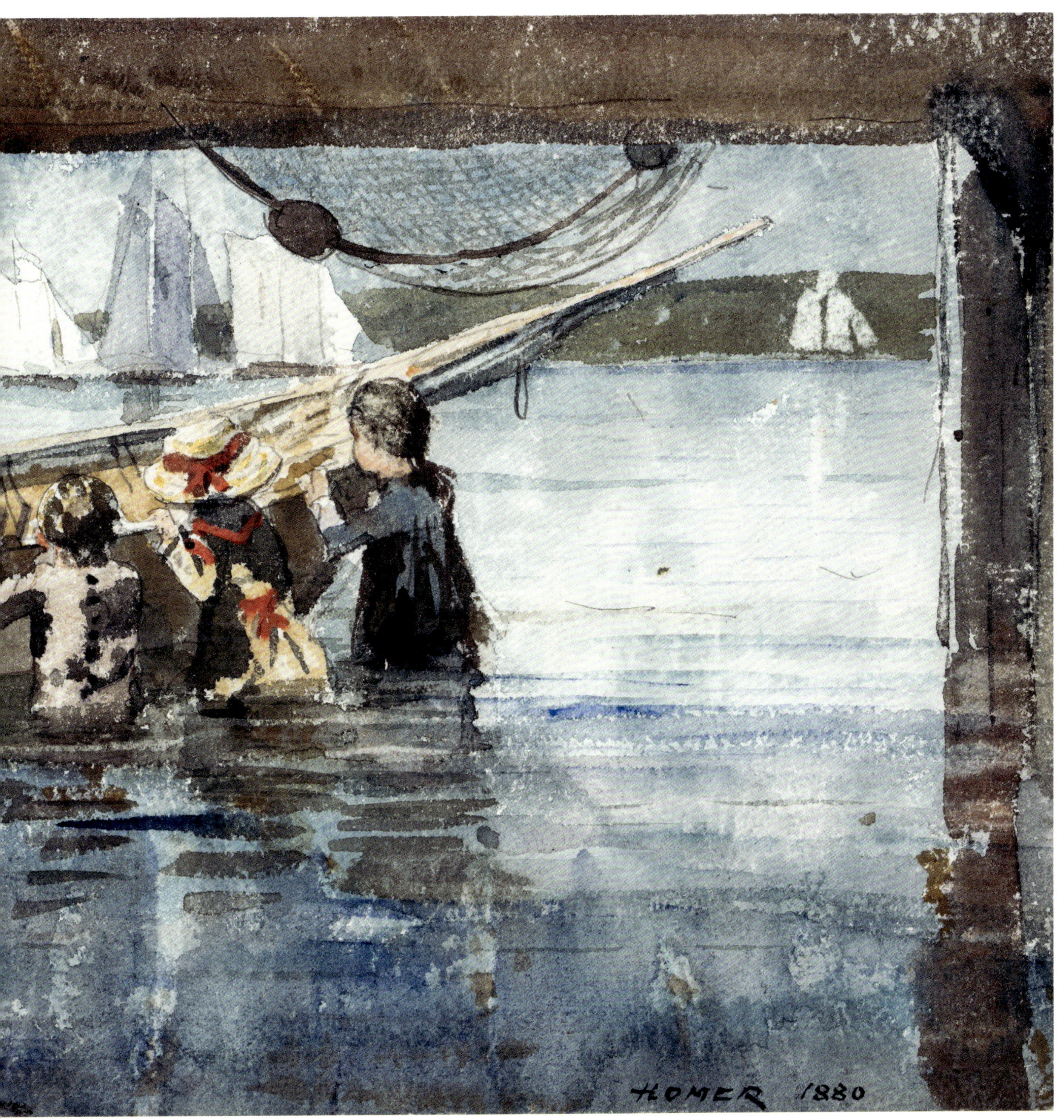

28. *Children Playing under a Gloucester Wharf,* 1880

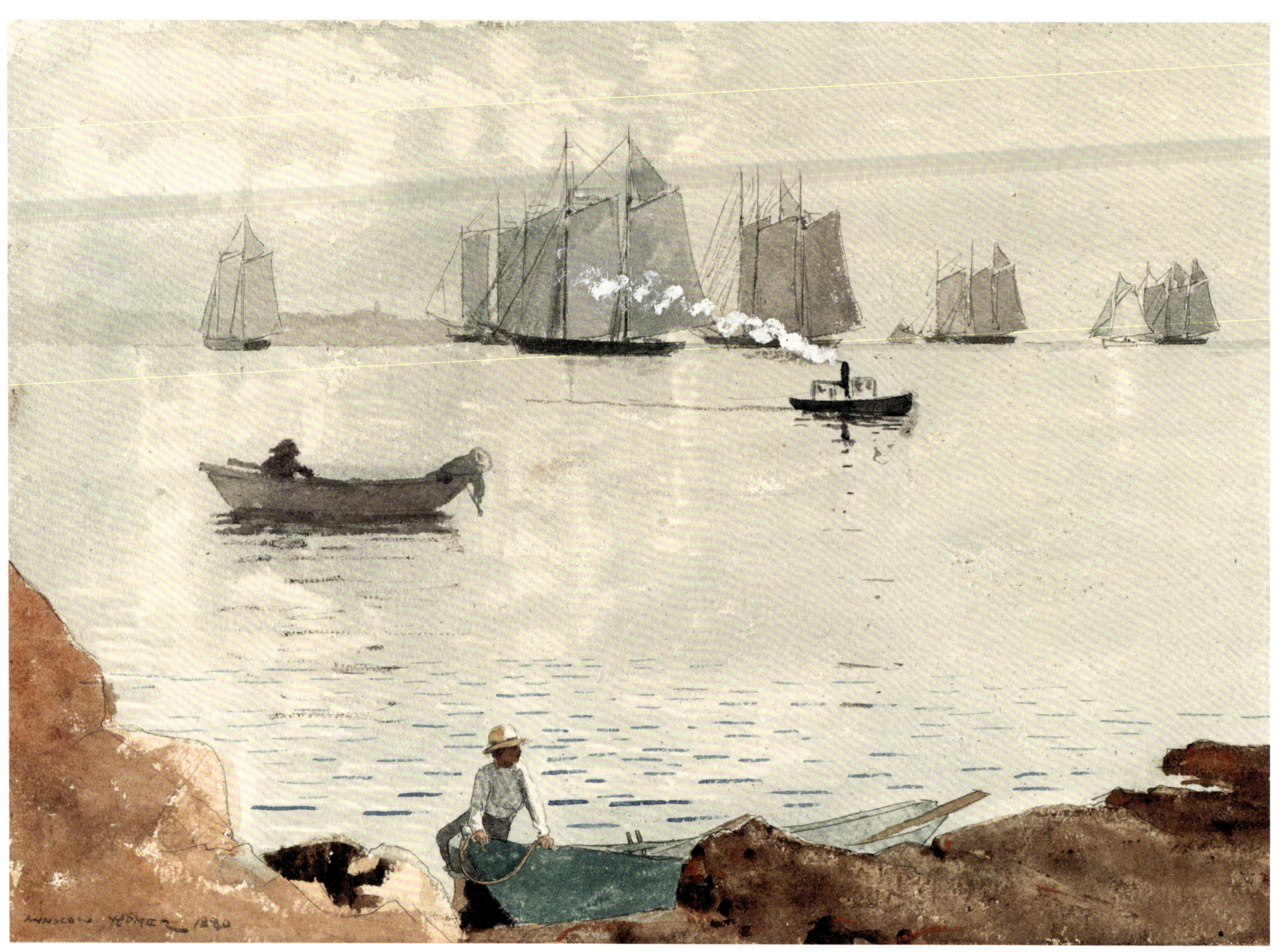

29. *Gloucester Harbor*, 1880

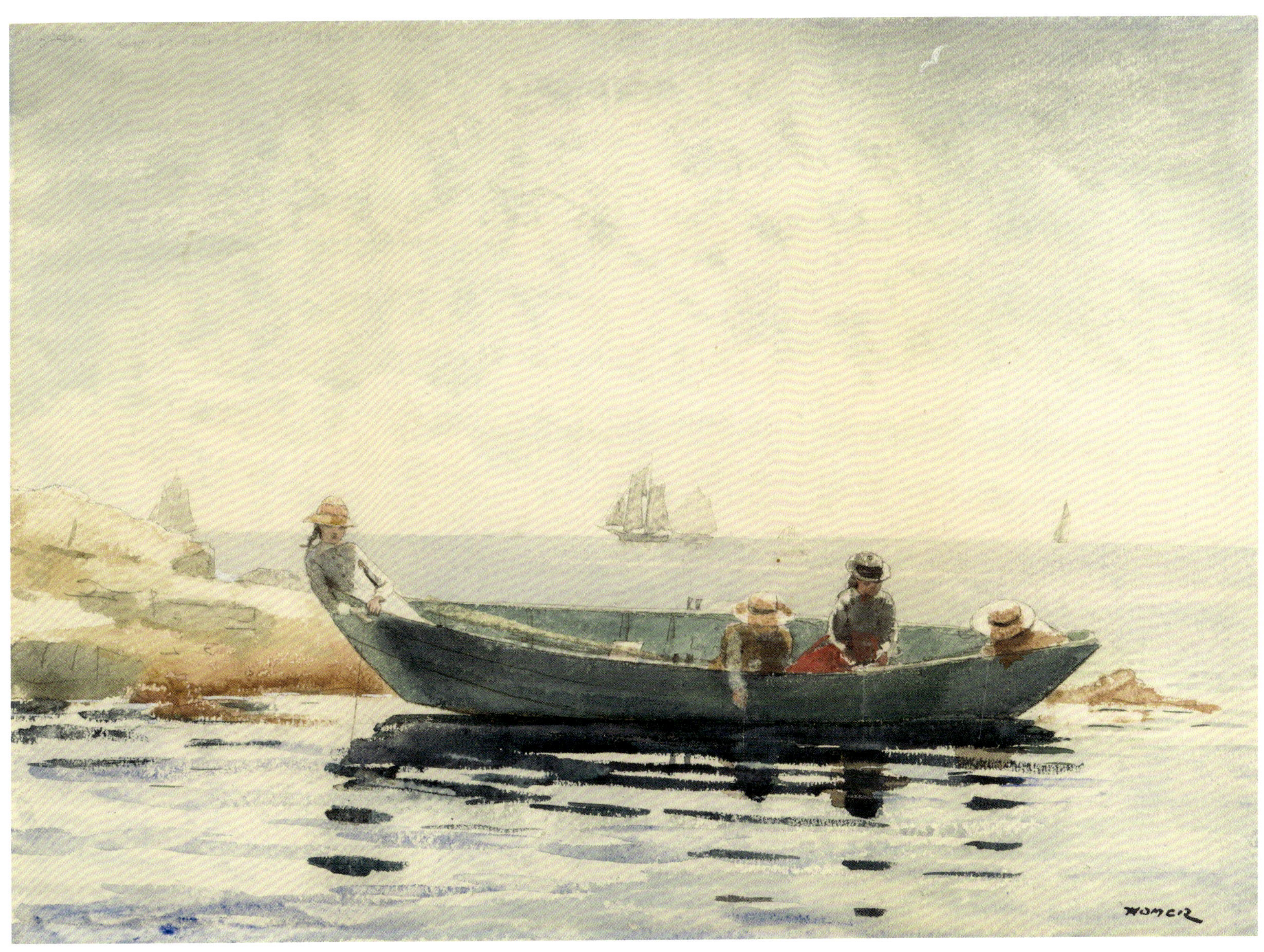

30. *The Green Dory,* 1880

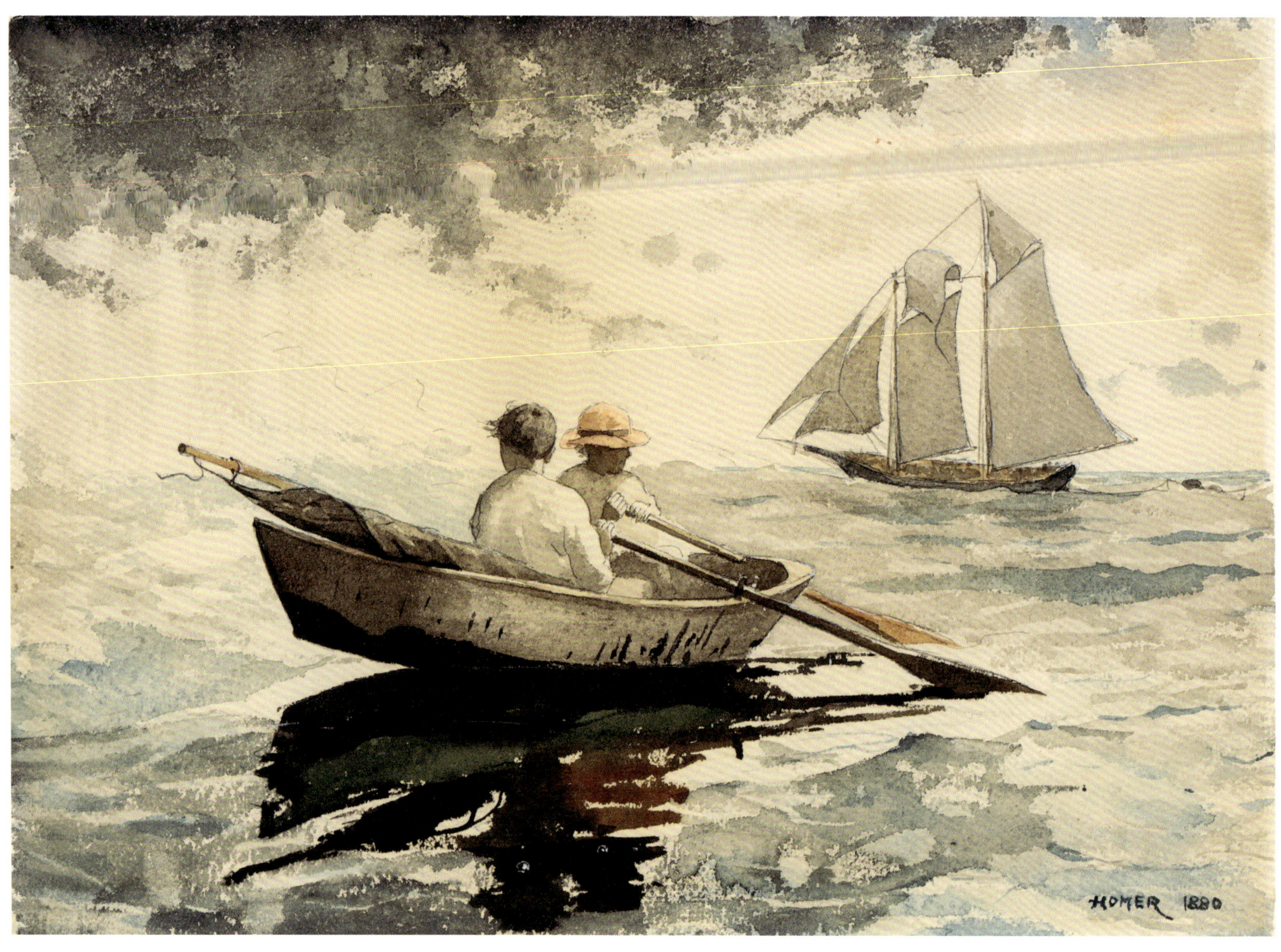

31. *Two Boys Rowing*, 1880

Carbon Paper / Originally made by coating paper on one side with pigmented wax or similar material, carbon paper placed between sheets of paper provides a means of making duplicates. Pressure on the top sheet in the form of typing, writing, or drawing transfers the colored coating of the center sheet to a bottom sheet, creating a copy. Although carbon as a colorant is black, carbon papers were available in several colors, including blue.

Blue lines in the detail below correspond to the main outlines in the composition and suggest Homer created the "bones" of this watercolor by copying from another drawing using carbon paper. Homer then reinforced the transferred blue with graphite, the black lines in the detail. Together, the carbon paper and graphite lines provide the underdrawing, or compositional guide, for the watercolor. Homer likely valued the efficiency of utilizing this and other copying techniques he may have learned while working as an illustrator. —AM

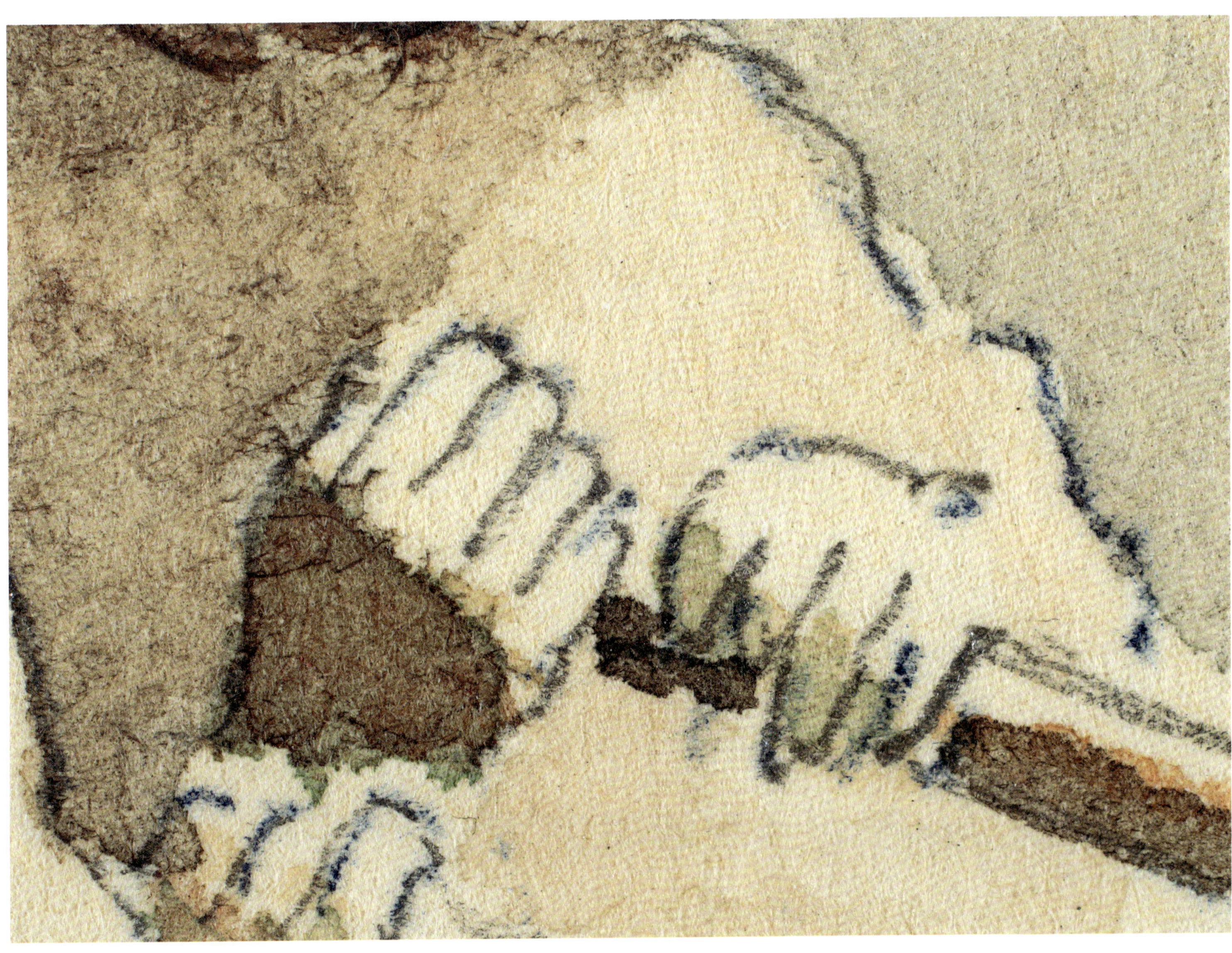

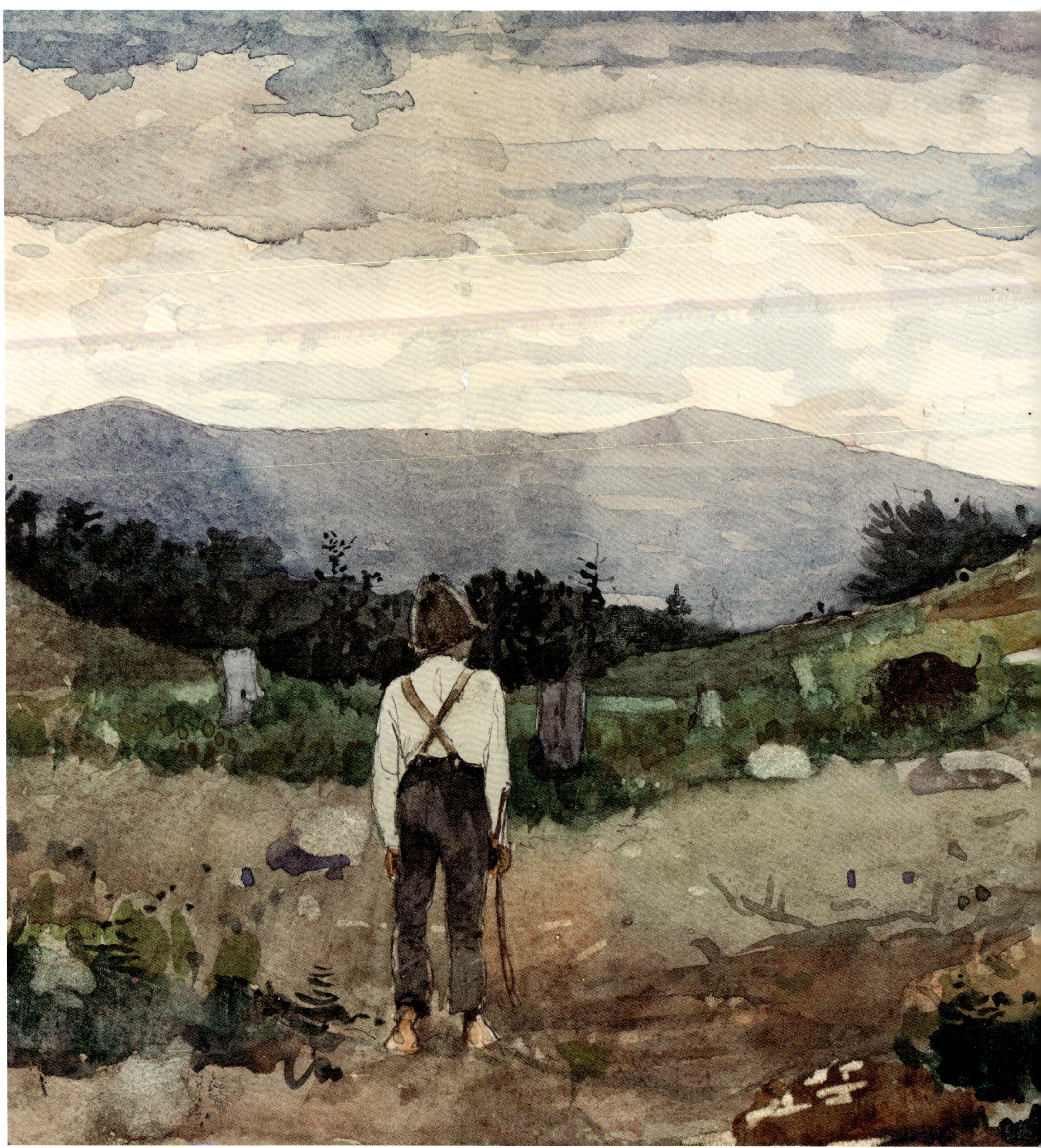

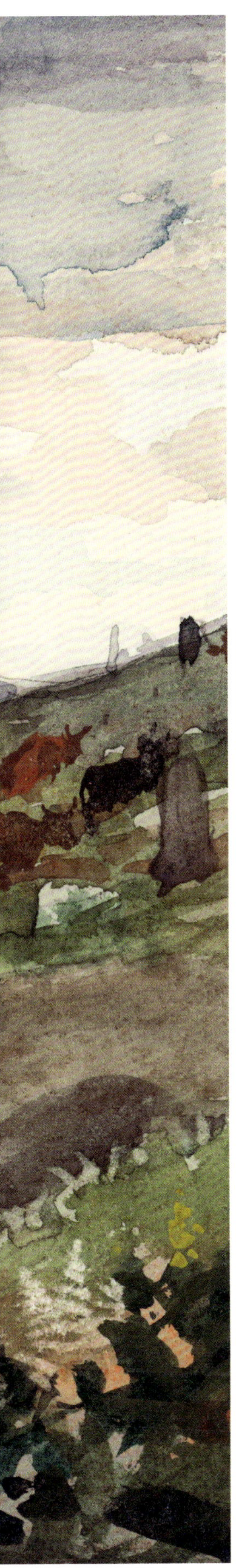

Central Massachusetts and Upstate New York

During the 1870s, Homer made frequent trips to the countryside. The resulting work from this decade is defined by quaint representations of pastoral life tinged with nostalgia in the wake of the Civil War. From pensive shepherdesses and barefoot youths to rolling hills and roving farm animals, Homer's brush blended bucolic ideals with naturalism. As one critic reflected, "Never was any painter more rurally minded. …But while landscape elements are very prominent in his work, humanity is rarely absent, and is usually his chief concern. But it is rustic humanity always. The rural American of his earlier pictures is shown with a persistence, a sympathy, and an artistic clearness and directness of speech quite unequaled in our art."[14]

In 1867, Homer's older brother Charles married Martha (Mattie) French from West Townsend, Massachusetts, where the couple stayed frequently. *Driving Cows to Pasture* and *Boy and Fallen Tree*, along with the drawings *Going Berrying* and *Girl on Swing* (both of which were studies for watercolors), were created during Homer's visits here. Houghton Farm, near Mountainville, New York, also proved to be a critical site in Homer's growth as a watercolorist. The property was owned by his childhood friend from Cambridge, Lawson Valentine, who also employed Homer's older brother Charles as a chemist at his varnish manufactory. As in the 1873 Gloucester series, Homer used more opaquely applied watercolor to render his posed figures. *"Bo-Peep" (Girl with Shepherd's Crook Seated by a Tree)* is an extreme example of this, almost resembling an oil painting in its thickly applied dabs of color. *Boy and Girl on a Hillside*—visually similar to the dynamic *Girls on a Cliff* painted just three years later in England— maintains some stiffness but is softened by looser brushstrokes and subtle washes applied within the lines of his pencil underdrawing.

By the late 1870s, Homer's watercolor practice began to evolve and embrace features unique to the medium, moving from rigid and opaque to fluid and transparent. *Driving Cows to Pasture* stands out as a turning point for Homer's work in the medium and evinces a more conscious shift to landscape from figure study. The boy in the foreground is a departure from the models of previous posed works. With his back turned to the viewer, he assumes the pose of a *rückenfigur* (a figure seen from behind), a compositional device that Homer would return to in later works (see *Driftwood*, fig. 4, for example). The boy, seemingly rooted to the ground, is nearly consumed by unruly flora. Walking stick in hand, the boy seems the youthful counterpart to the central figure in Homer's later *The Guide and Woodsman*, while the immersive landscape presages that of his later masterwork *The Blue Boat* (see figs. 63 and 67). The cows, rendered as brown blobs on the hillside, would be easily missed were it not for the title. Here, Homer embraced abstraction as well as some advanced watercolor techniques, removing pigment through scraping and lifting to create rough rocks and ghostly ferns.

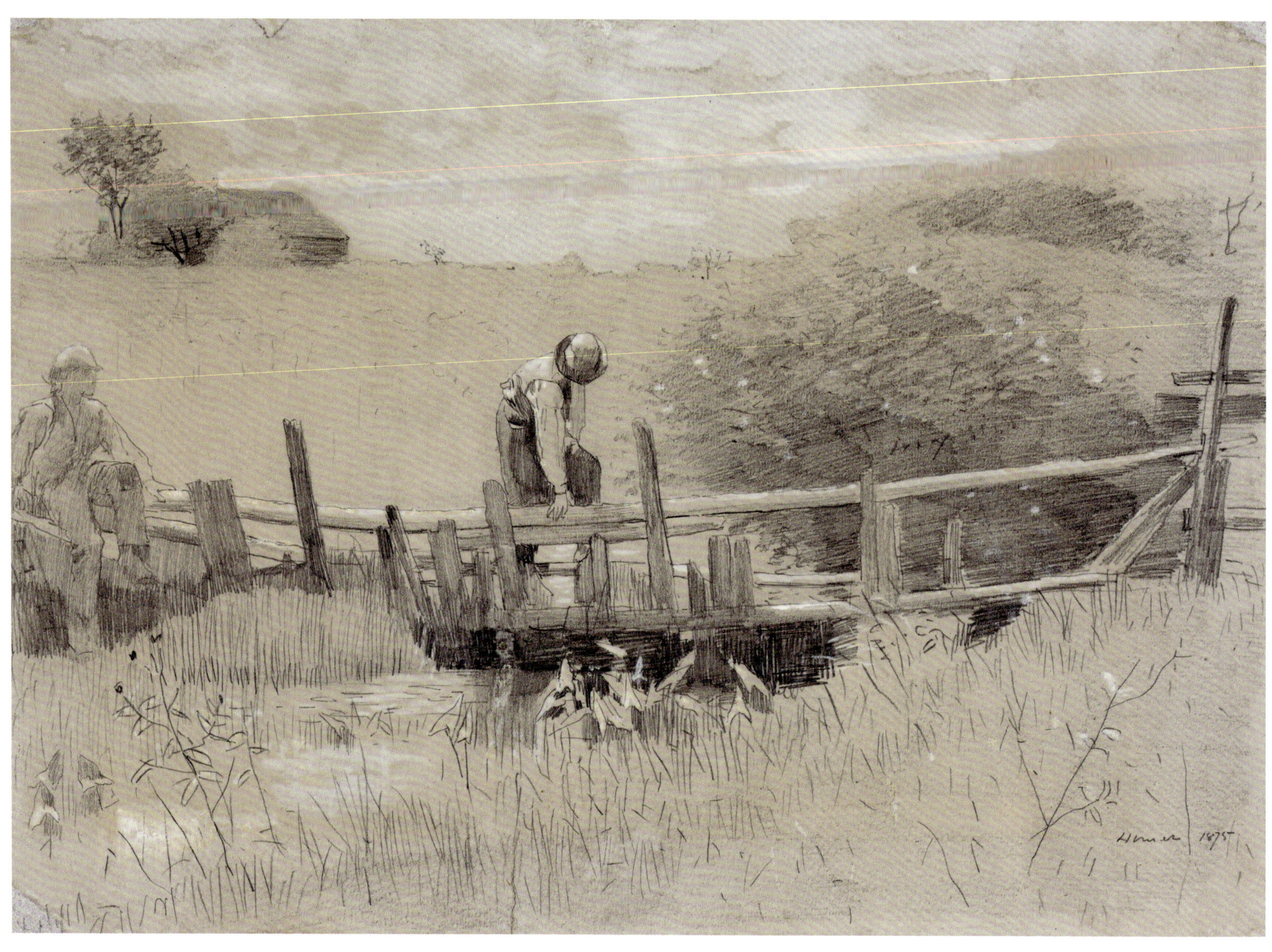

32. *On the Edge of the Farm,* 1875

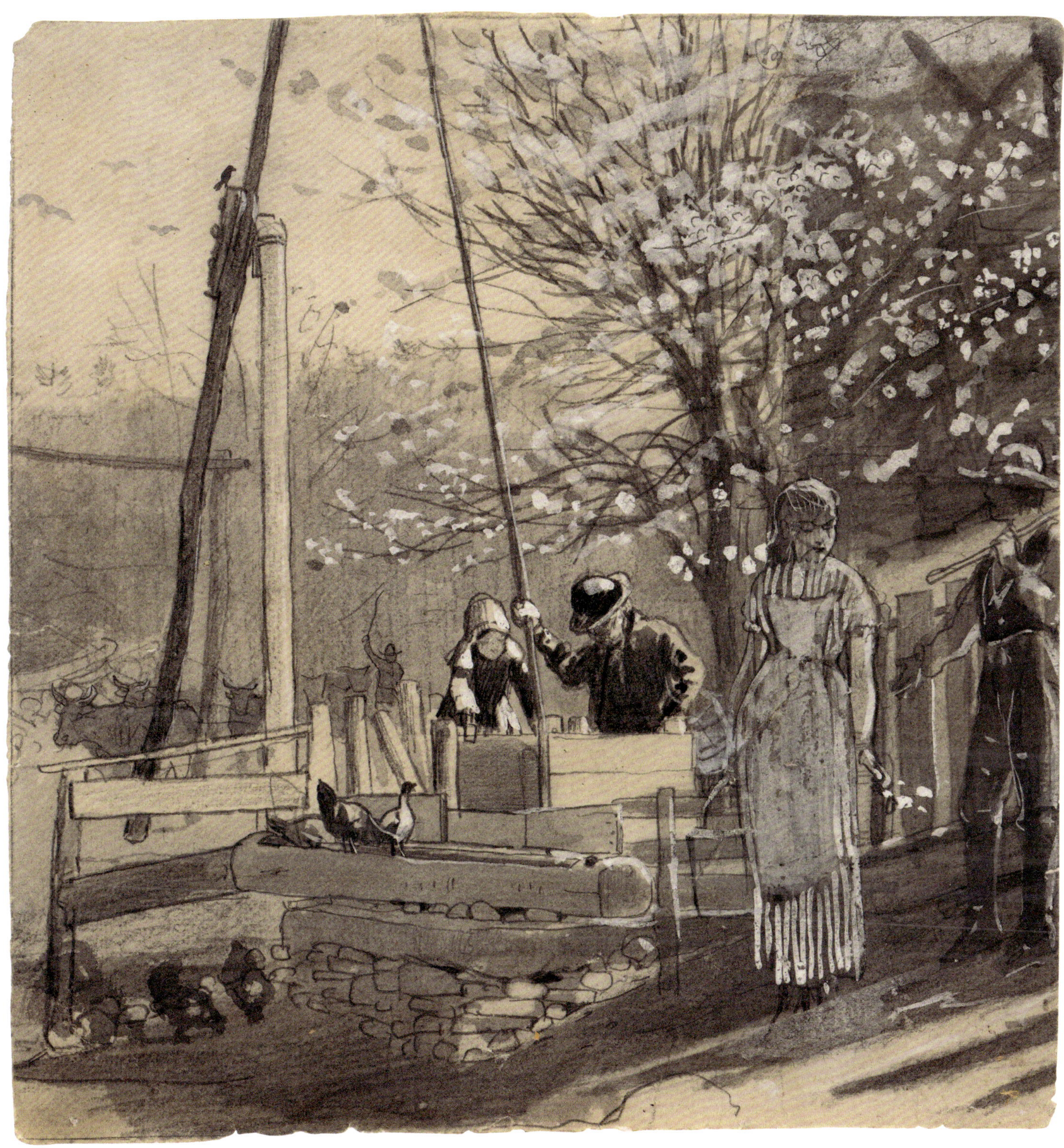

33. *Spring (Women and Men at Well)*, about 1875

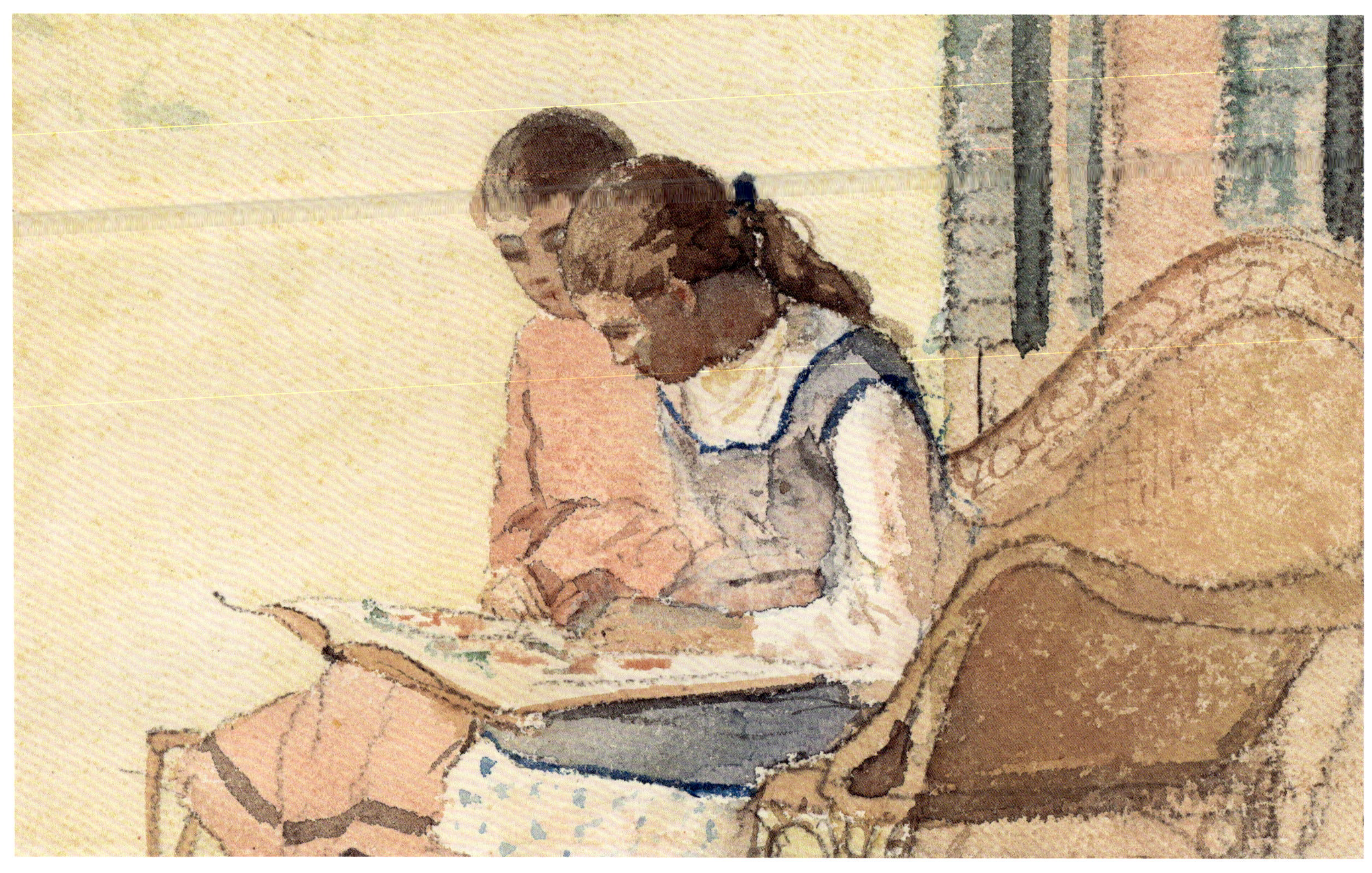

34. *Two Girls Looking at a Book*, about 1877

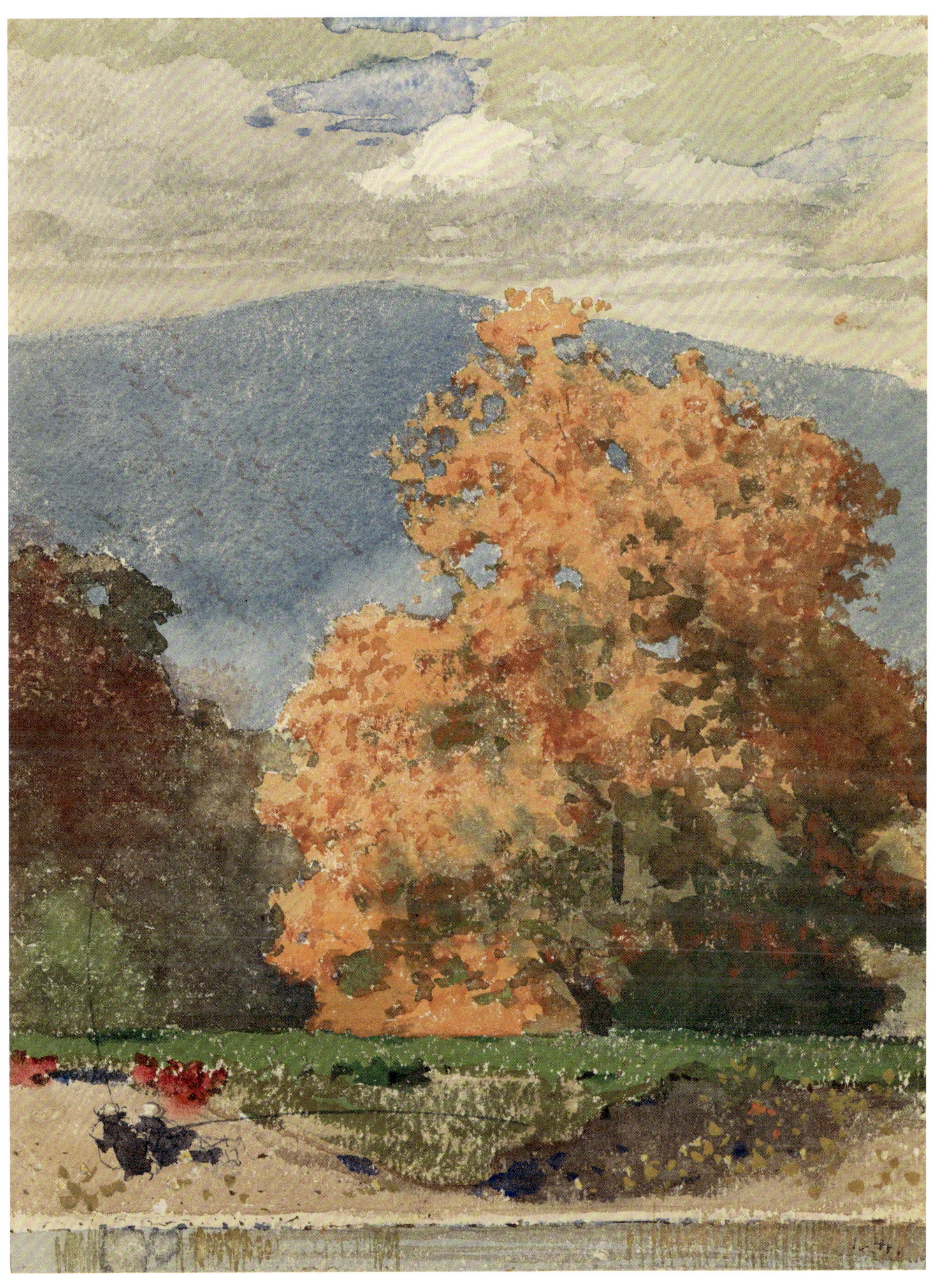

35. *Autumn Foliage with Two Youths Fishing*, about 1878

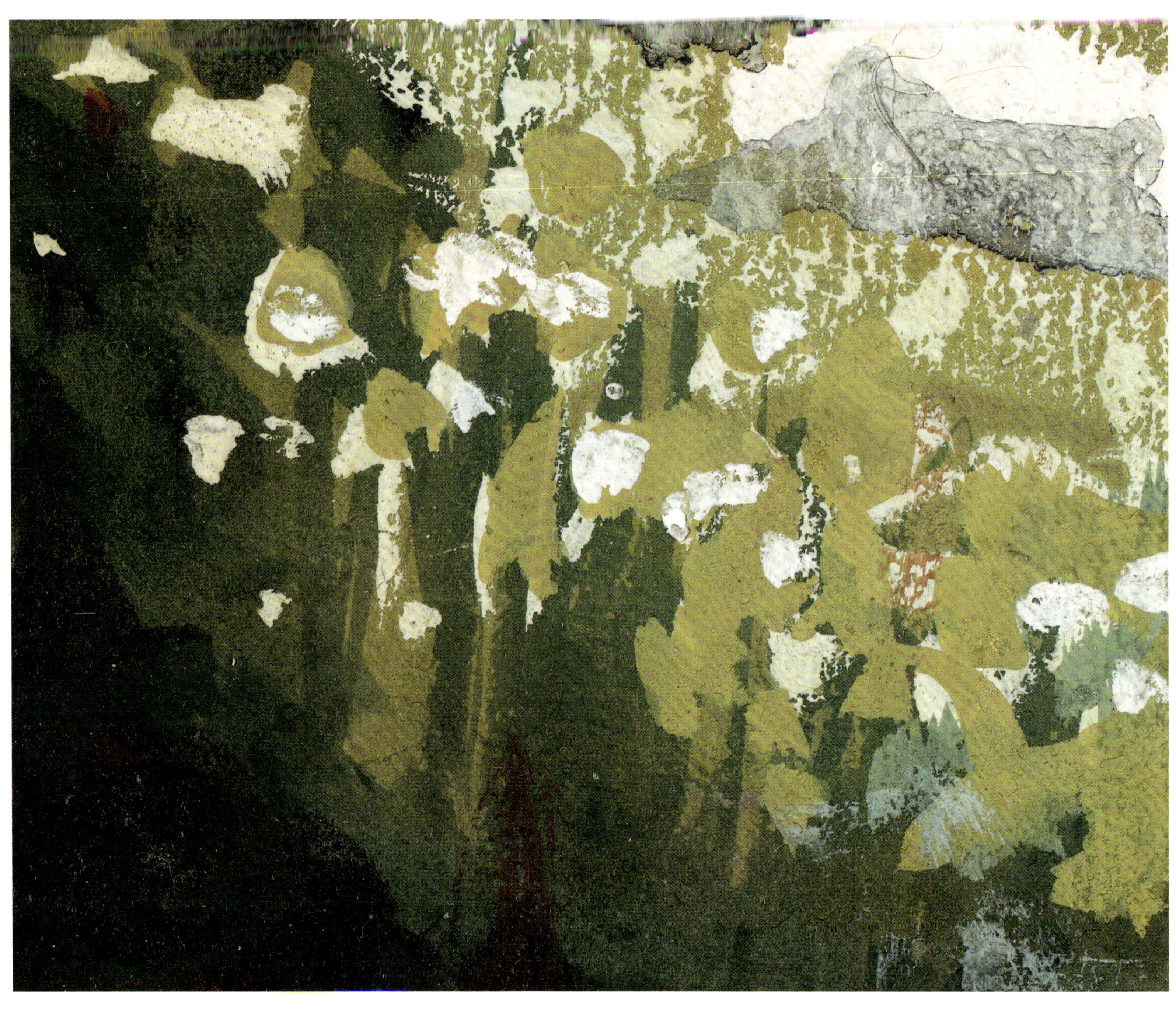

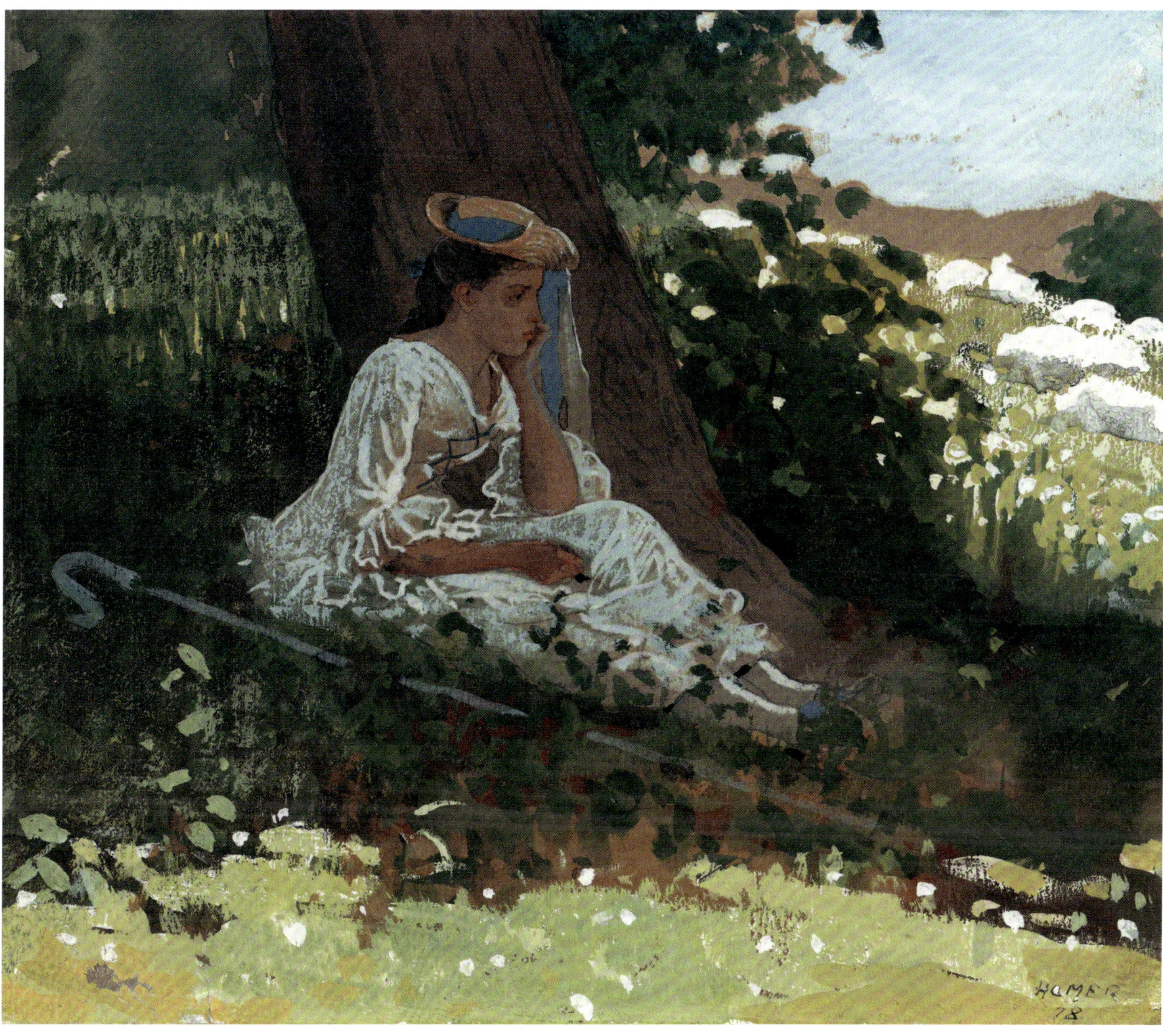

36. *"Bo-Peep" (Girl with Shepherd's Crook Seated by a Tree)*, 1878

Opaque Watercolor / Opaque watercolor covers and conceals whatever is below it. Some colors are naturally opaque, while other colors are made opaque by adding white to the paint. One usually works from dark to light when painting with opaque colors. Pure white, if used, is typically added last. — AM

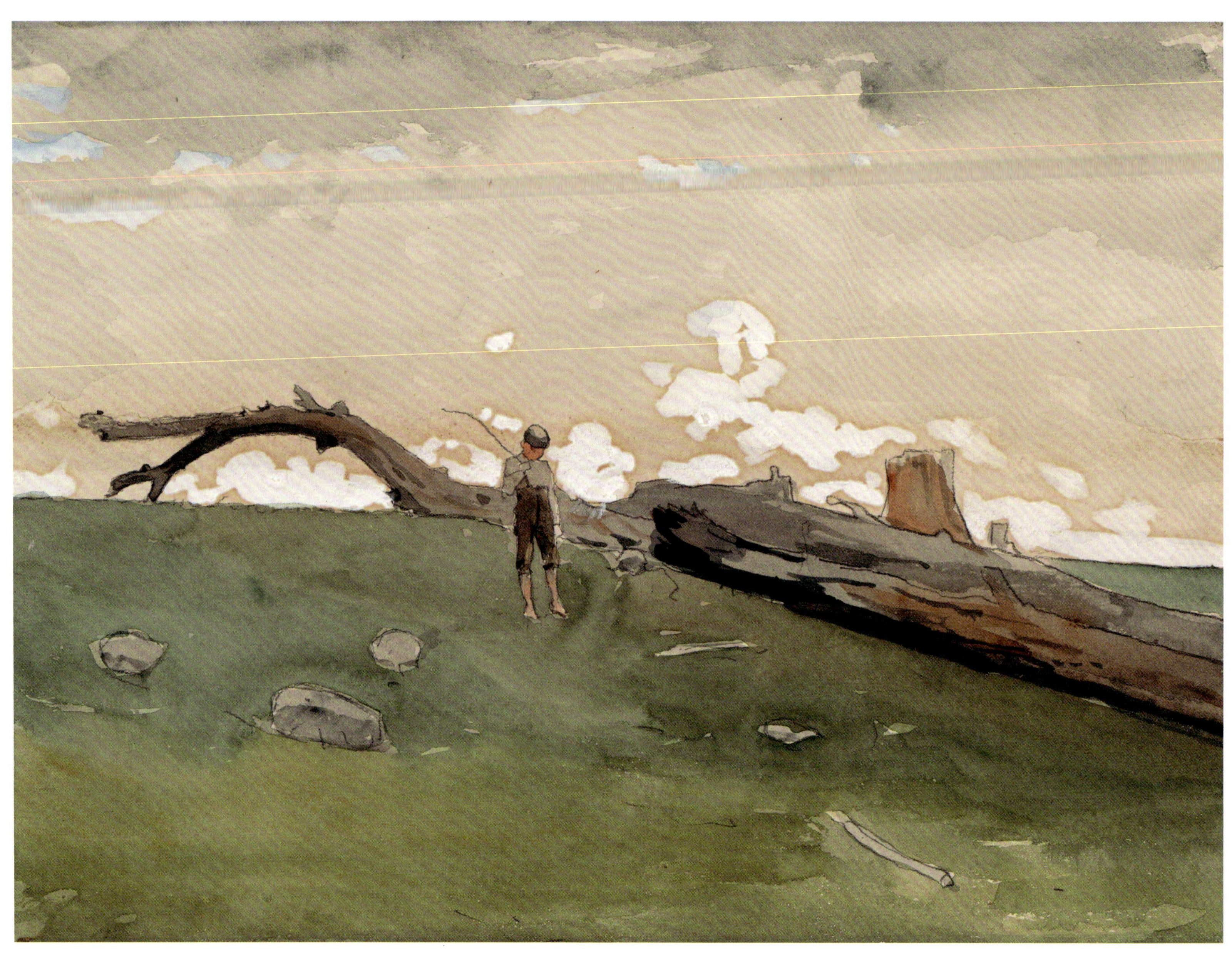

37. *Boy and Fallen Tree*, 1879

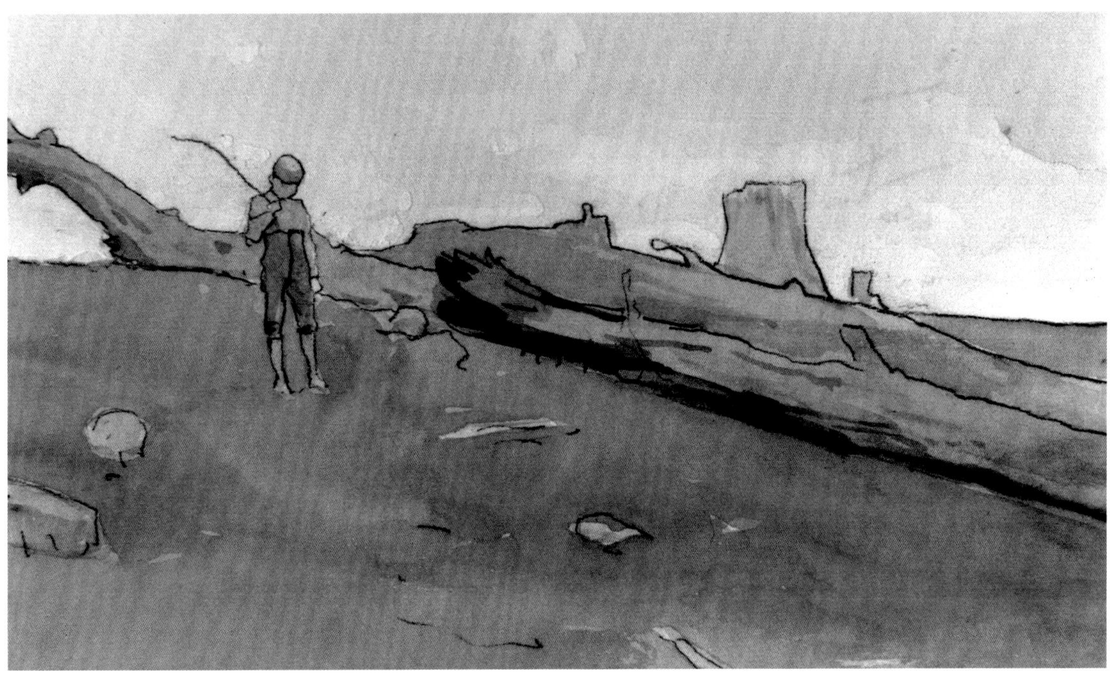

Underdrawing / A drawing created as a compositional guide for subsequent work is called underdrawing. An underdrawing represents an artist's early thoughts about a design. It can vary from highly detailed to very simple. Depending on the artist's process or compositional need, it may be scrupulously followed or largely dismissed. Meant to be covered by later media, it is often difficult or impossible to see much of this source work in a finished painting.

Infrared imaging can reveal underdrawing if the drawing is made from a material that absorbs infrared energy more strongly than the covering paint layers. The dark lines in the gray scale image seen here indicate strong infrared absorption and represent the underdrawing. Microscopic examination identified these lines as graphite, a drawing material favored by Homer. —AM

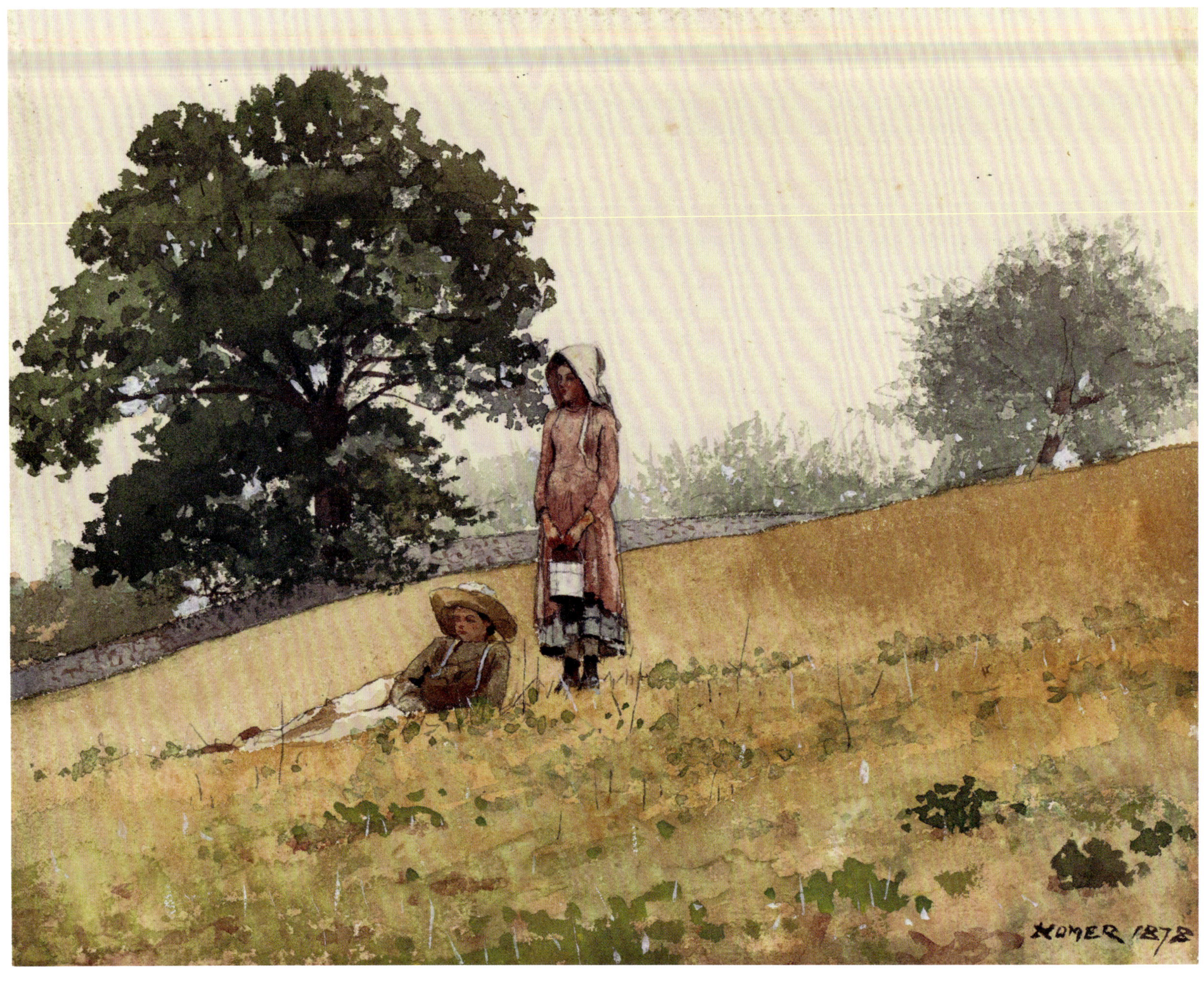

38. *Boy and Girl on a Hillside*, 1878

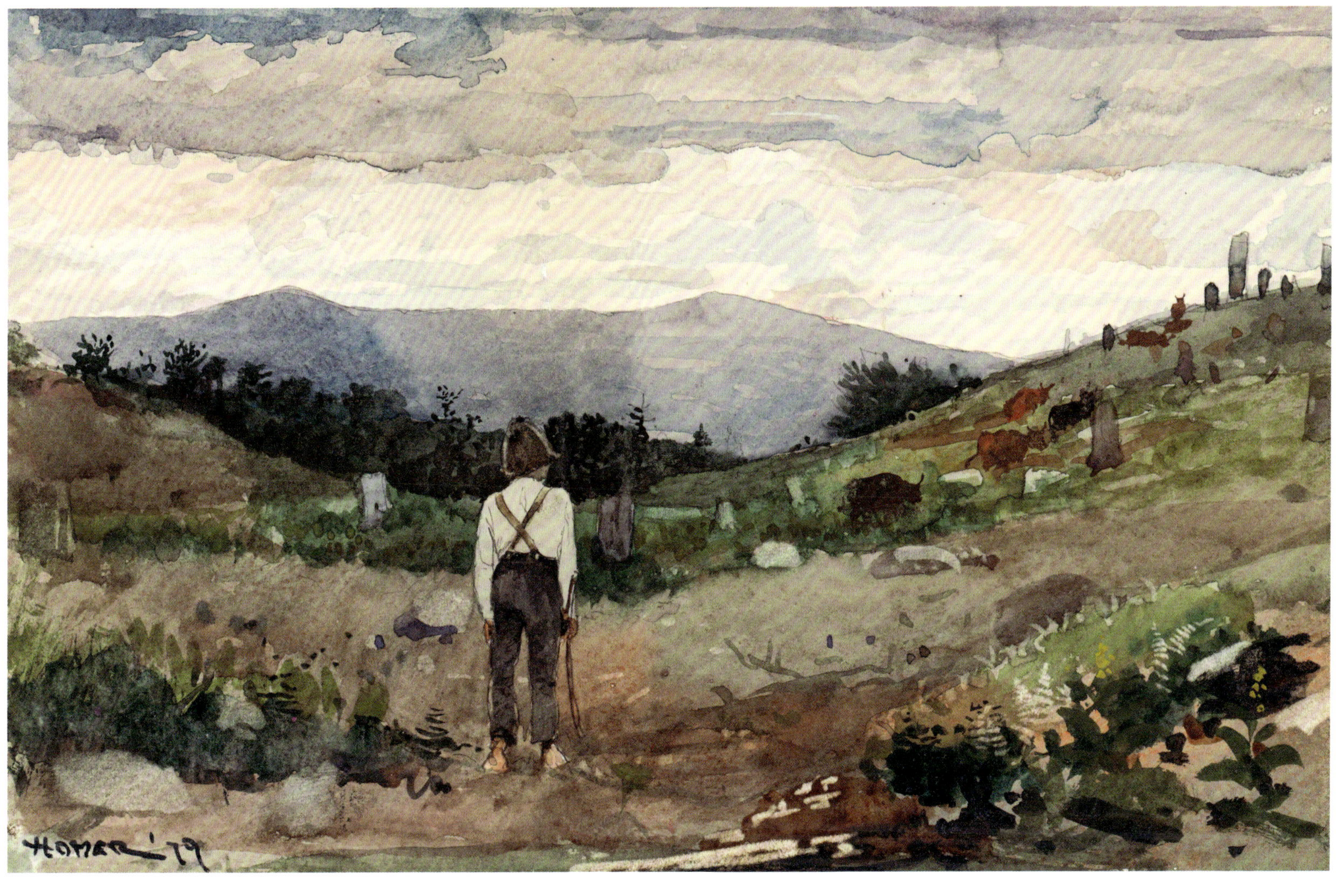

39. *Driving Cows to Pasture*, 1879

Graphite / Homer began this watercolor with a graphite drawing. Graphite is found in the common pencil and has a distinctive silvery black appearance. Homer covered most of his drawing with washes of color, but not all. The boy's shirt, prominent in the composition, remains defined by Homer's original graphite lines. —AM

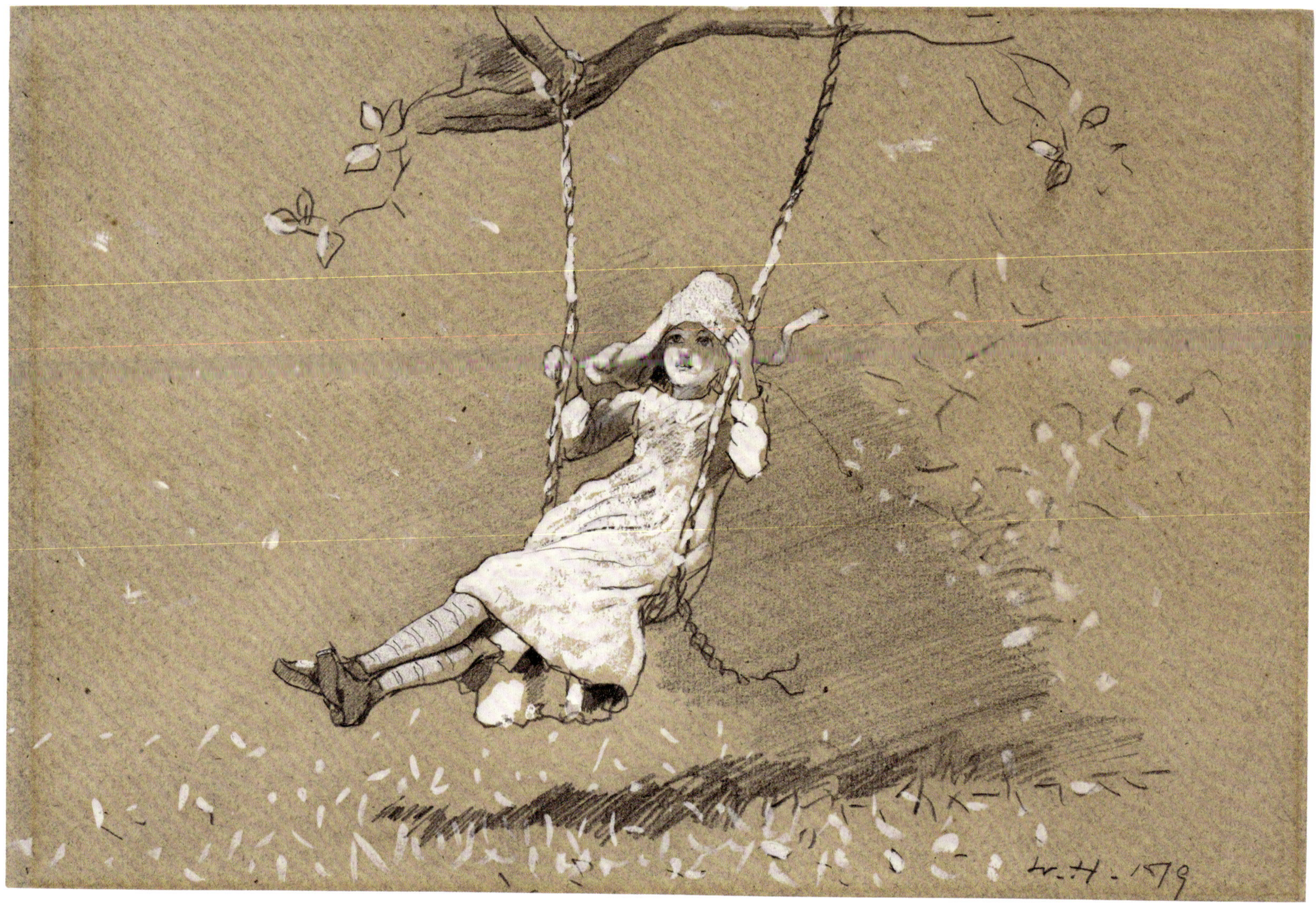

40. *Girl on Swing*, 1879

Overdrawing / Homer used graphite pencil to compose this pastoral scene. He then added brushy washes of white watercolor to give substance to the figure and flicks of white to suggest grass and foliage. To reestablish critical features lost under the watercolor layer and to add details, Homer drew on top of the white paint with graphite. This can be seen in the girl's face, dress, and stockings. —AM

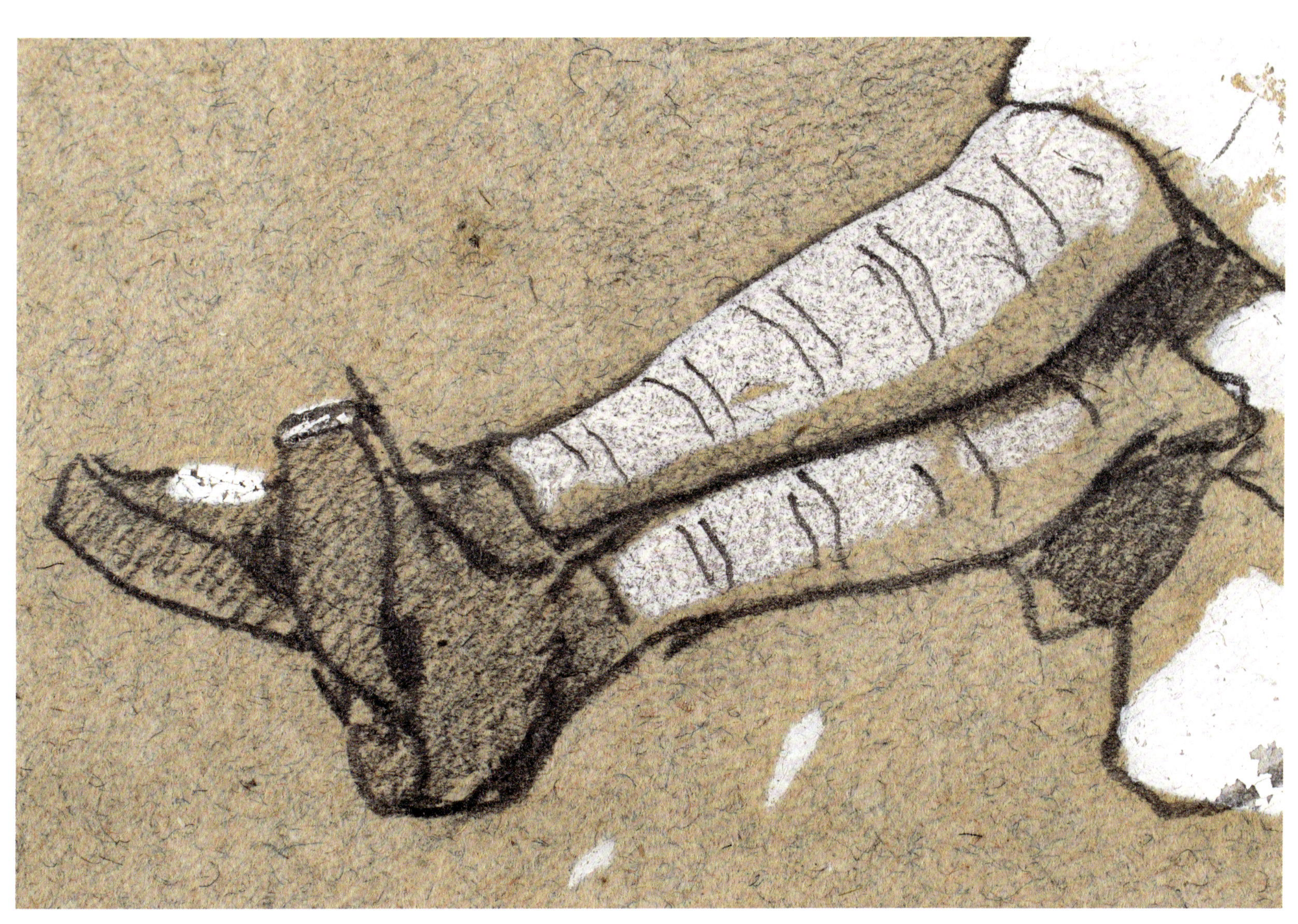

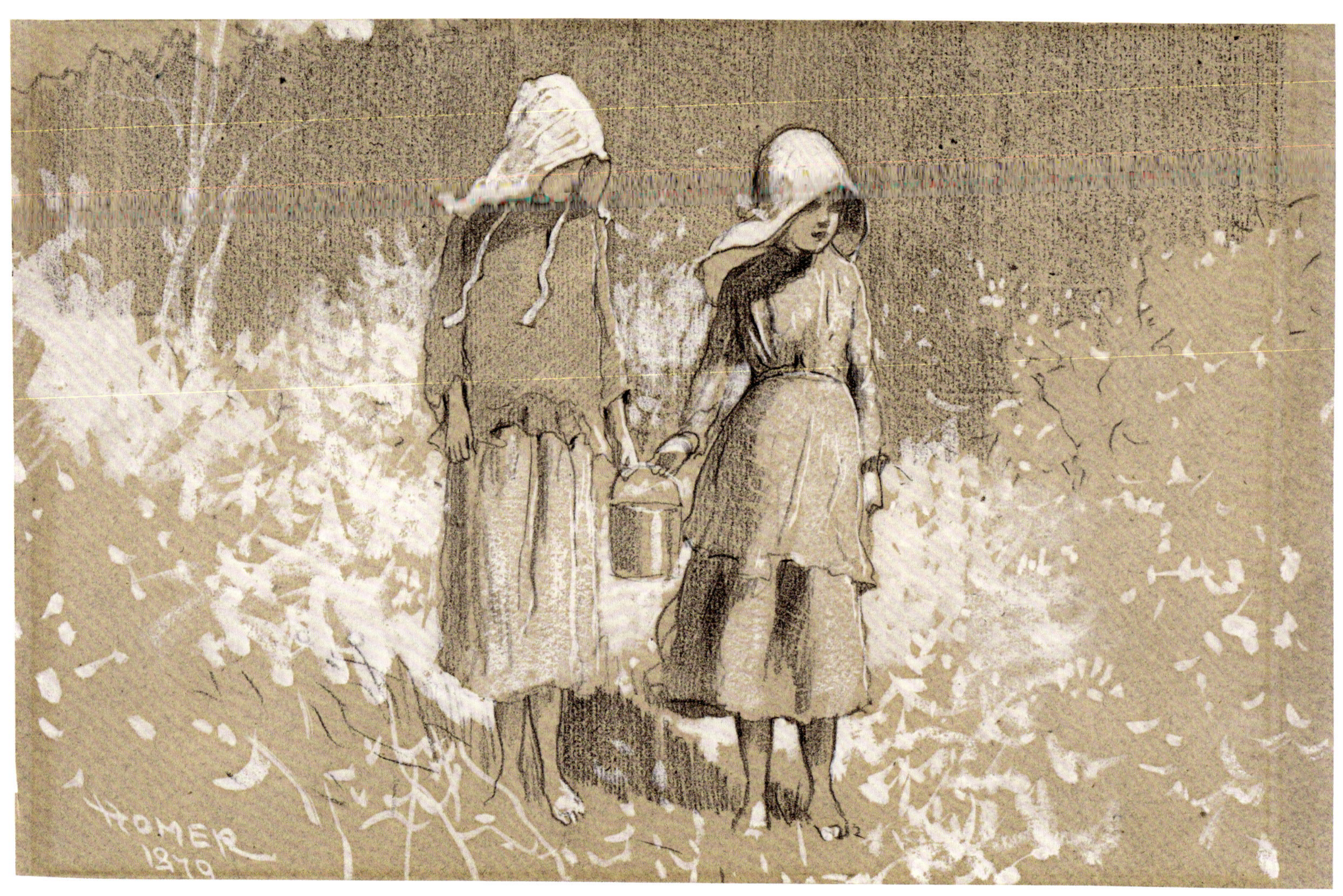

41. *Going Berrying,* 1879

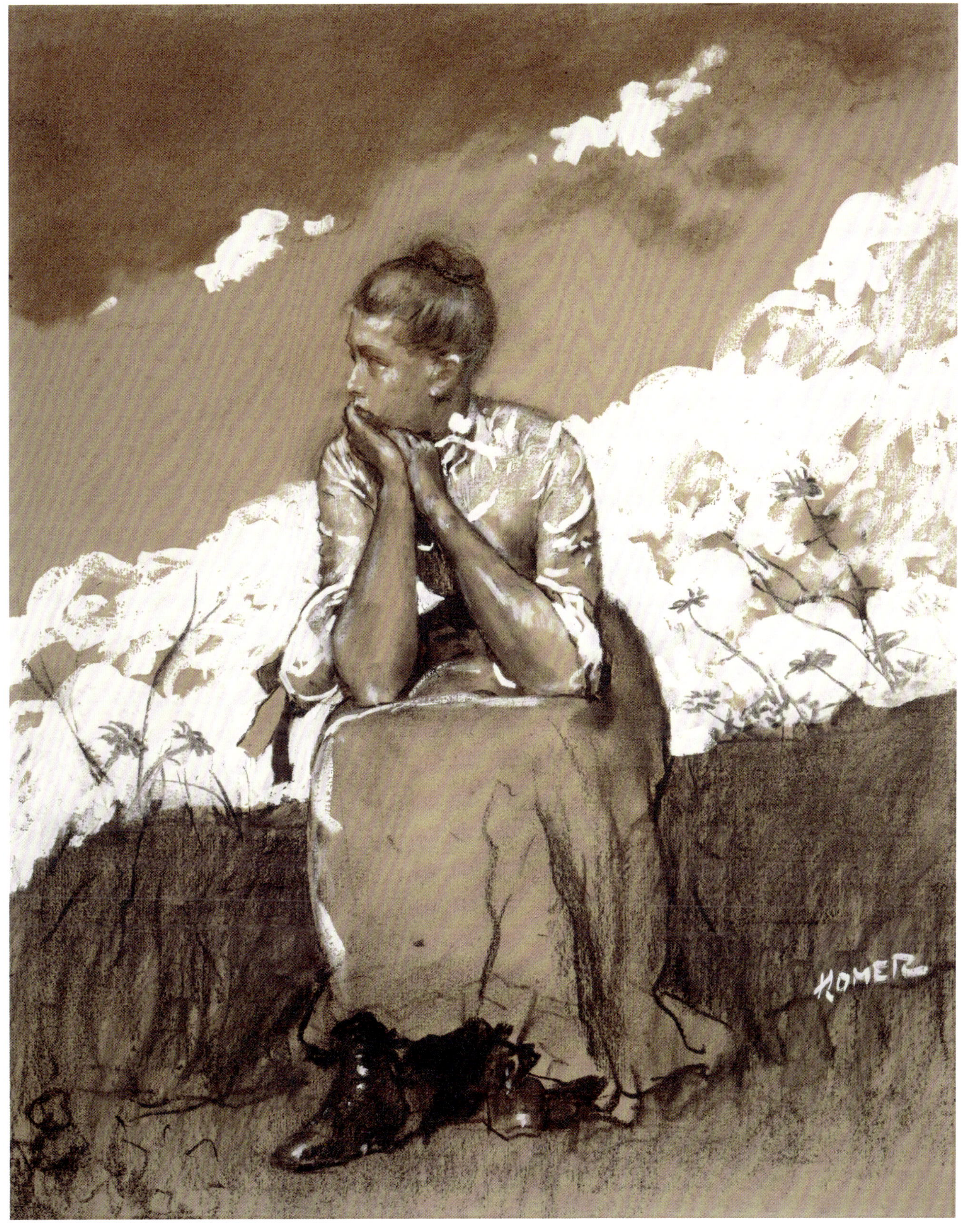

42. *Girl Seated*, 1880

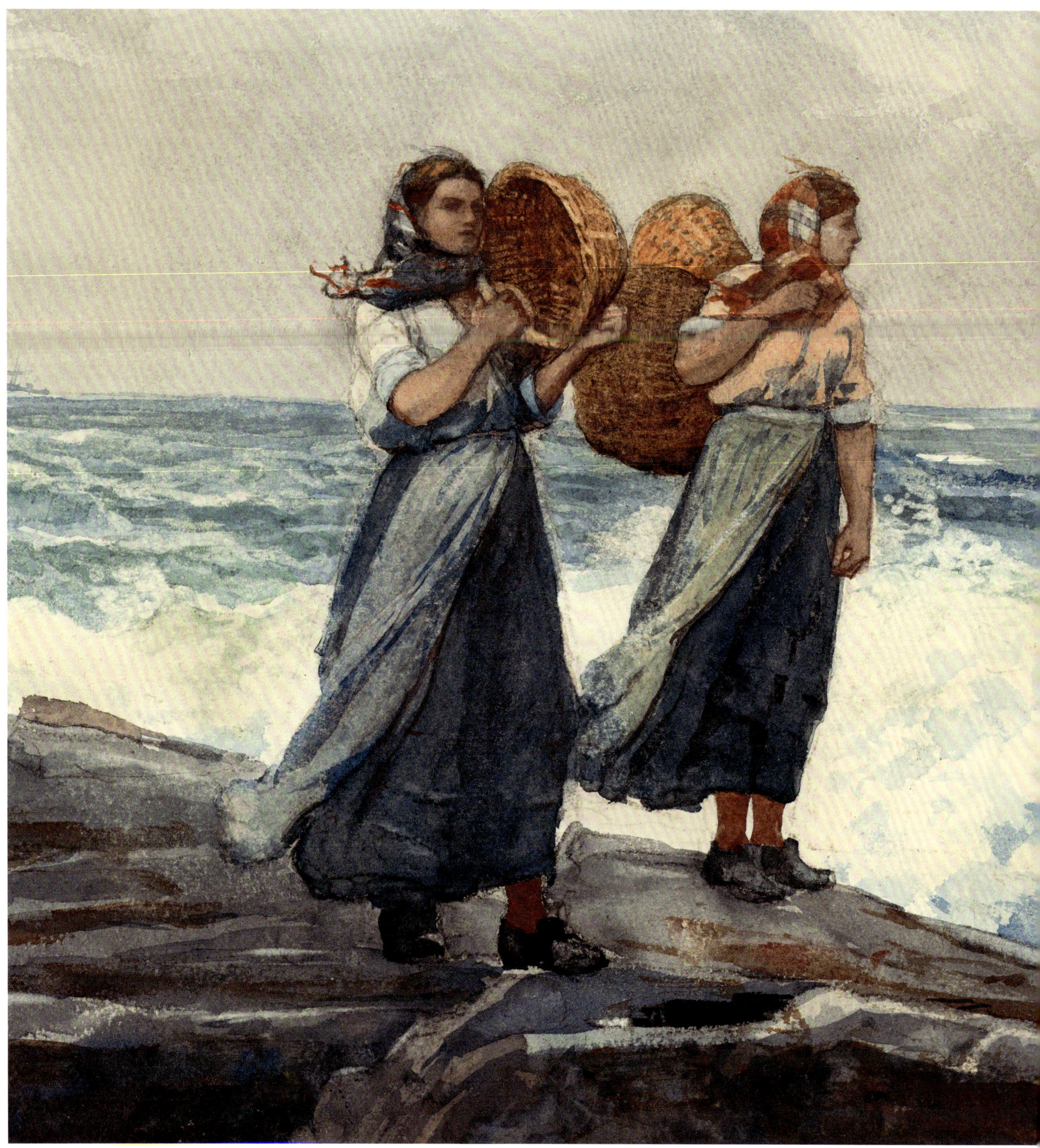

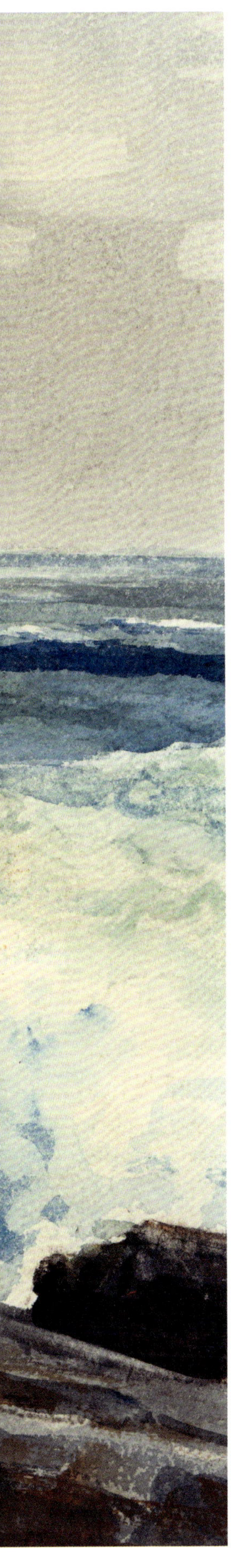

Cullercoats, England

Following the success of his 1880 Gloucester series, Winslow Homer found inspiration in another fishing village. This time, during the spring of 1881, he traveled across the Atlantic to England, settling in Cullercoats, an active port and artist's colony near the resort town of Tynemouth on the Northumberland coast. Staying for eighteen months, he painted primarily in watercolor and made arrangements to send many of the works to his dealers in Boston for sale and exhibition. Homer's Cullercoats work is in many ways an amplification of the themes nascent in earlier work—figures, women or children, laboring or lingering in rural or coastal landscapes. Homer explored these subjects more explicitly in his depictions of the English fishermen's families working on the shore or awaiting their return. Most feature the young women who gathered and then sold the recent catch, as men of the village fished at night and rested during the day. When the waters were too choppy for fishing, men stayed on land and joined the Tynemouth Volunteer Life Brigade, an early model for today's coast guard. Some scenes, such as *Storm on the English Coast (W. H. Flamborough Head),* show these volunteers braving the elements mid-rescue. In contrast, *Girl with Red Stockings (The Wreck),* captures one of the fisherwomen gazing up at a ship as it founders on the rocks, ocean spray overtaking its masts. The drama and uncertainty of everyday life in coastal Cullercoats made a lasting impression on Homer as a marine painter, and a fascination with human relationships to the natural world would characterize his work for the rest of his career.

During this period, Homer still relied on an under-drawing, keeping it visible in the finished work. However, he also began to further embrace the atmospheric capabilities of layered washes and the wet-on-wet technique, where pigment is applied to a wet area of paper, allowing it to spread, blend, or "bloom." All of these qualities are present in his striking *Fisherman's Family (The Lookout),* where wisps of hair and thread flutter in the breeze while the same fine line is used to define jagged edges in the cliffside. In these same areas of rock, Homer dabbed and overlaid washes of brown, orange, and gray to suggest a rough texture. A column of smoke, achieved through the flooding of a wet brush, billows from a vessel in the distance. Though critics were initially unsure of Homer's Cullercoats work, art critic Mariana Griswold Van Rensselaer later praised the series, writing, "The dignity of these landscapes and the statuesque impressiveness and sturdy vigor of these figures, translated by the strong sincerity of his brush, prove an originality of mood, a vigor of conception, and a sort of stern poetry of feeling to which he had never reached before."[15]

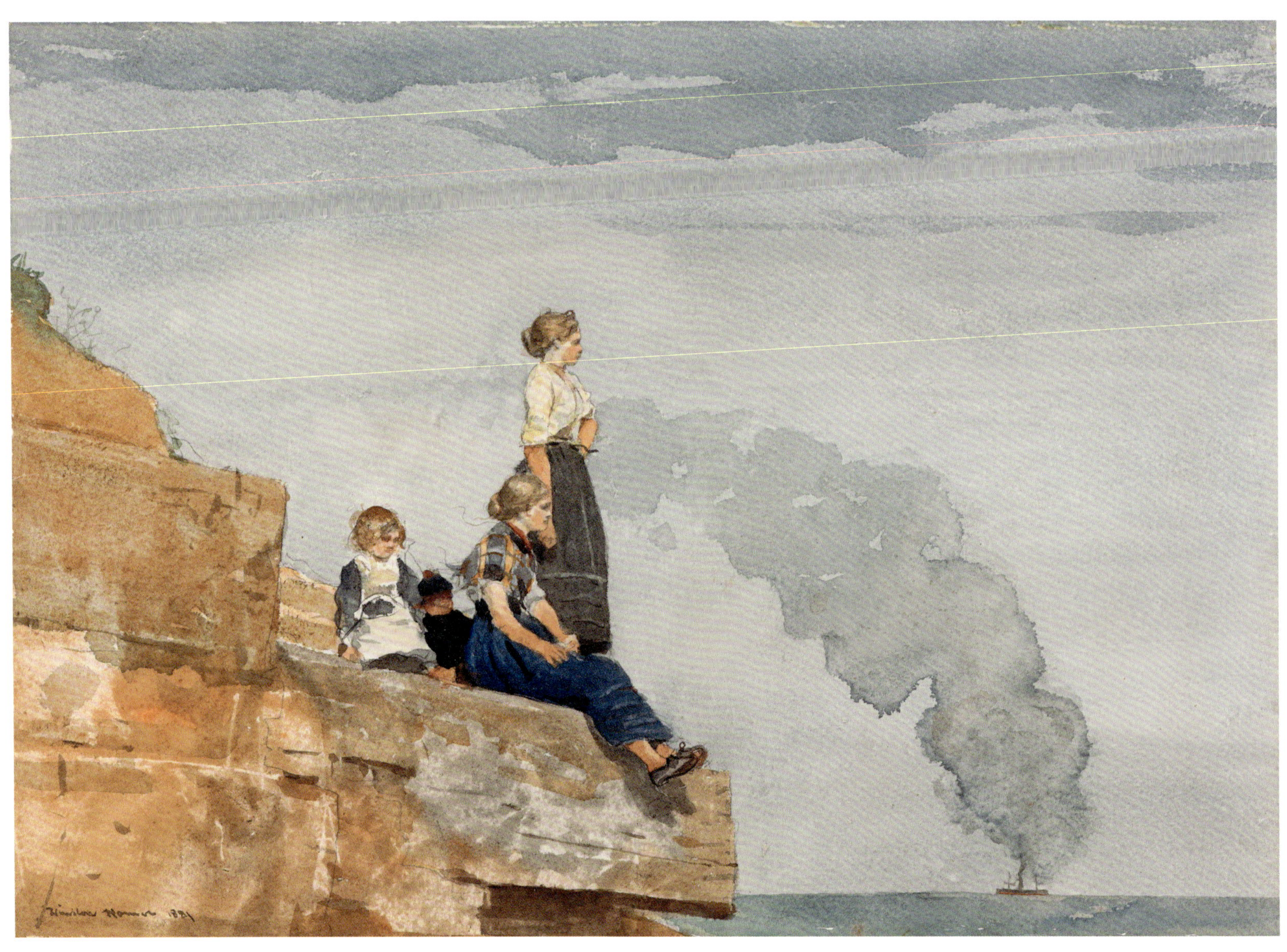

43. *Fisherman's Family (The Lookout)*, 1881

Flat Wash and Drying Lines / Flat washes generate uniform expanses of color and are often employed to represent sea or sky. A flat wash is typically created by applying paint in even strokes across dampened paper beginning in a top corner and working one's way down. A successful flat wash requires the proper amount of moisture in the paper, an adequate quantity of paint on the brush, and unfaltering and swift application. Dampened paper takes color more evenly than dry, allowing passes of paint to merge and form an even layer. Paper that is too wet or brushes that are over-charged with paint may cause color to run. If the paper is too dry or the brush is overloaded and timing is slow, one risks forming drying lines. Drying lines are the dark outer edges of a wash that form when pigment accumulates on dry-ing. While undesirable in a flat wash, this effect can be used to great advantage.

Here, Homer created an expansive backdrop for the waiting family by laying a flat wash of blue sky only to disturb it with billowing discharge from a passing ship. The passage of darker blue along the top edge together with the narrow band of sea below frame the scene.

The detail shows the meandering edge of a drying line, perfect for portraying the discharge near its source. In keeping with the vaporous nature of the subject, Homer softened some still wet edges by blotting and allowed the shape to dissolve into the sky in its upper reaches. —AM

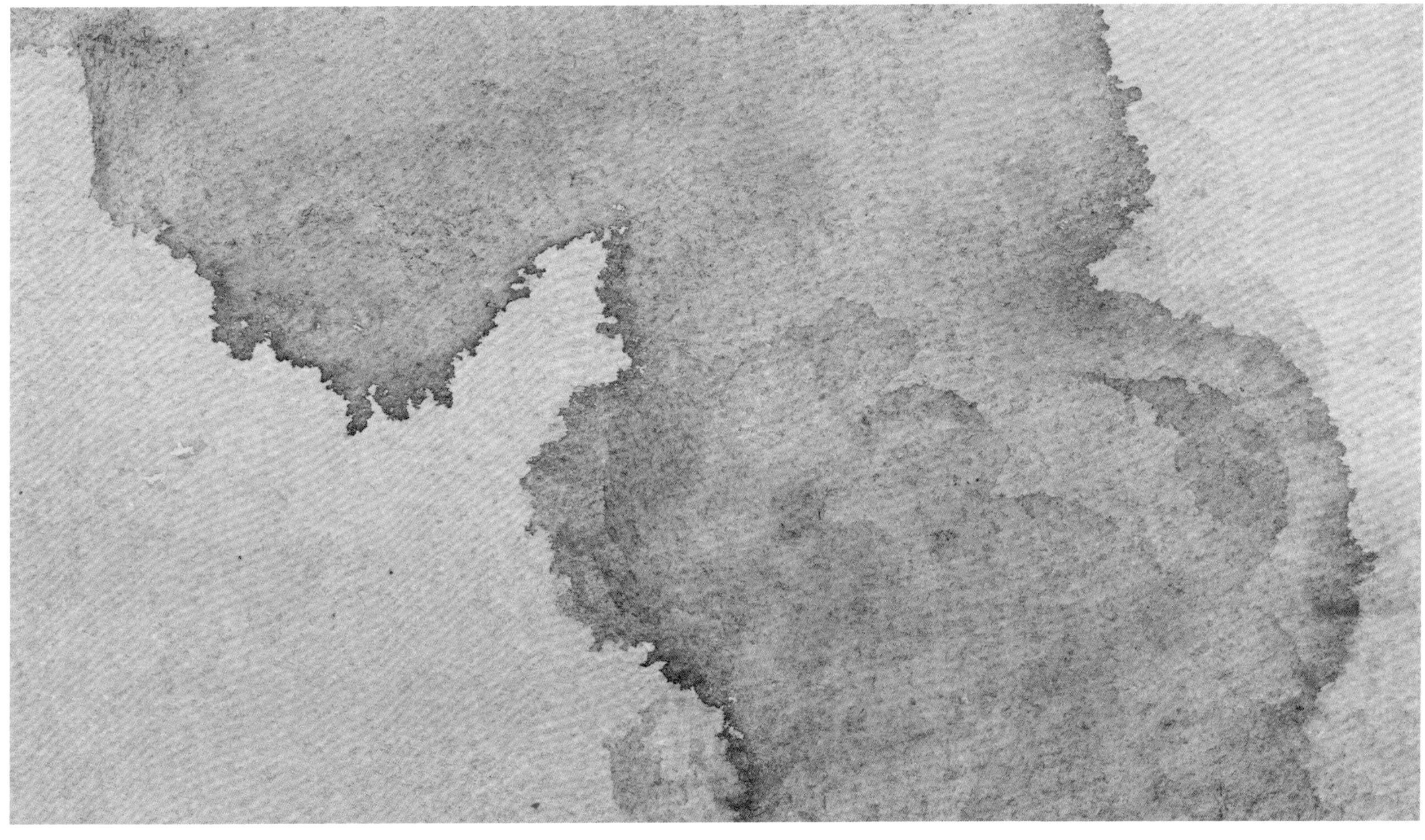

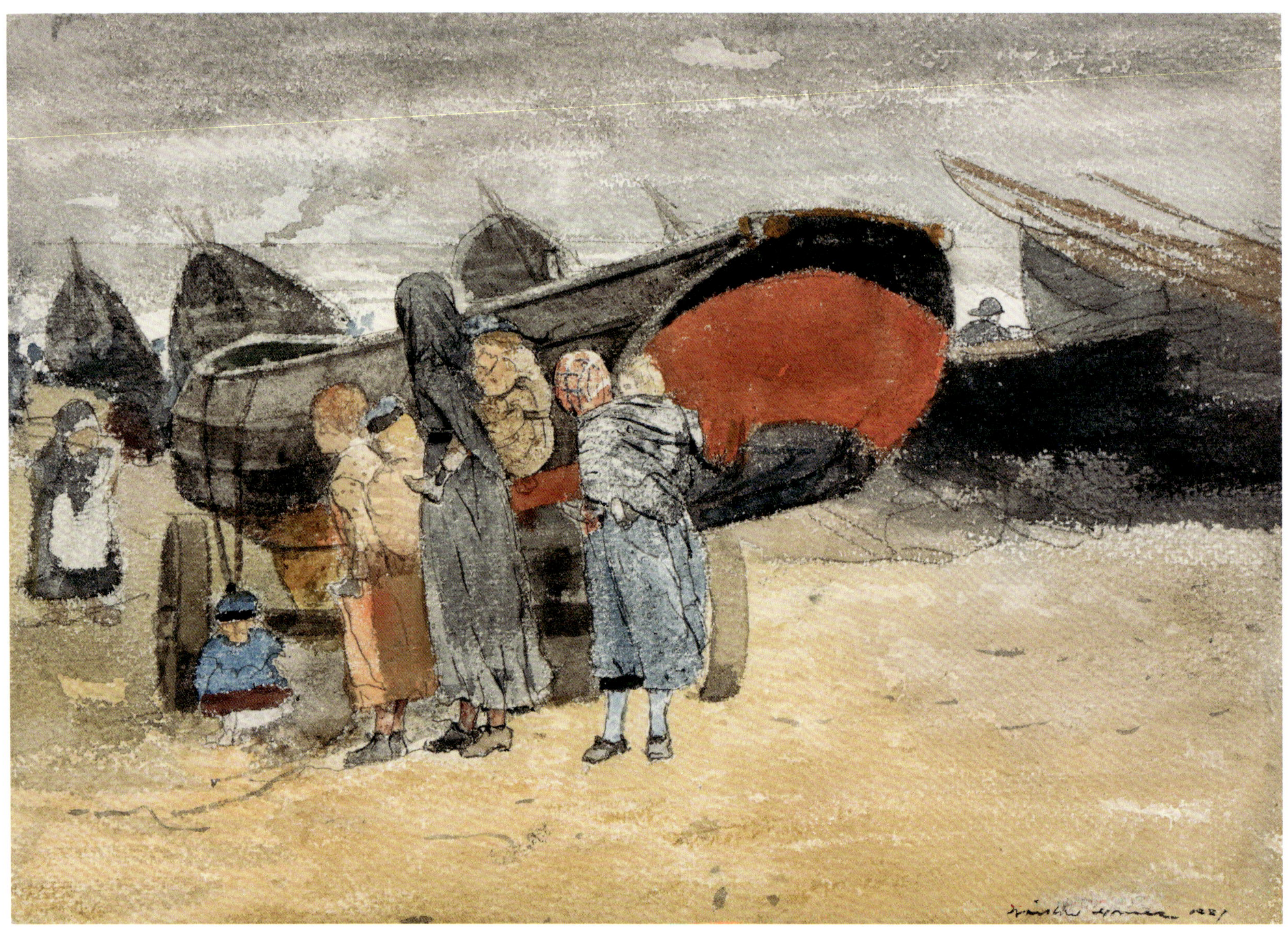

44. *Coast Scene, with Boats on the Beach*, 1881

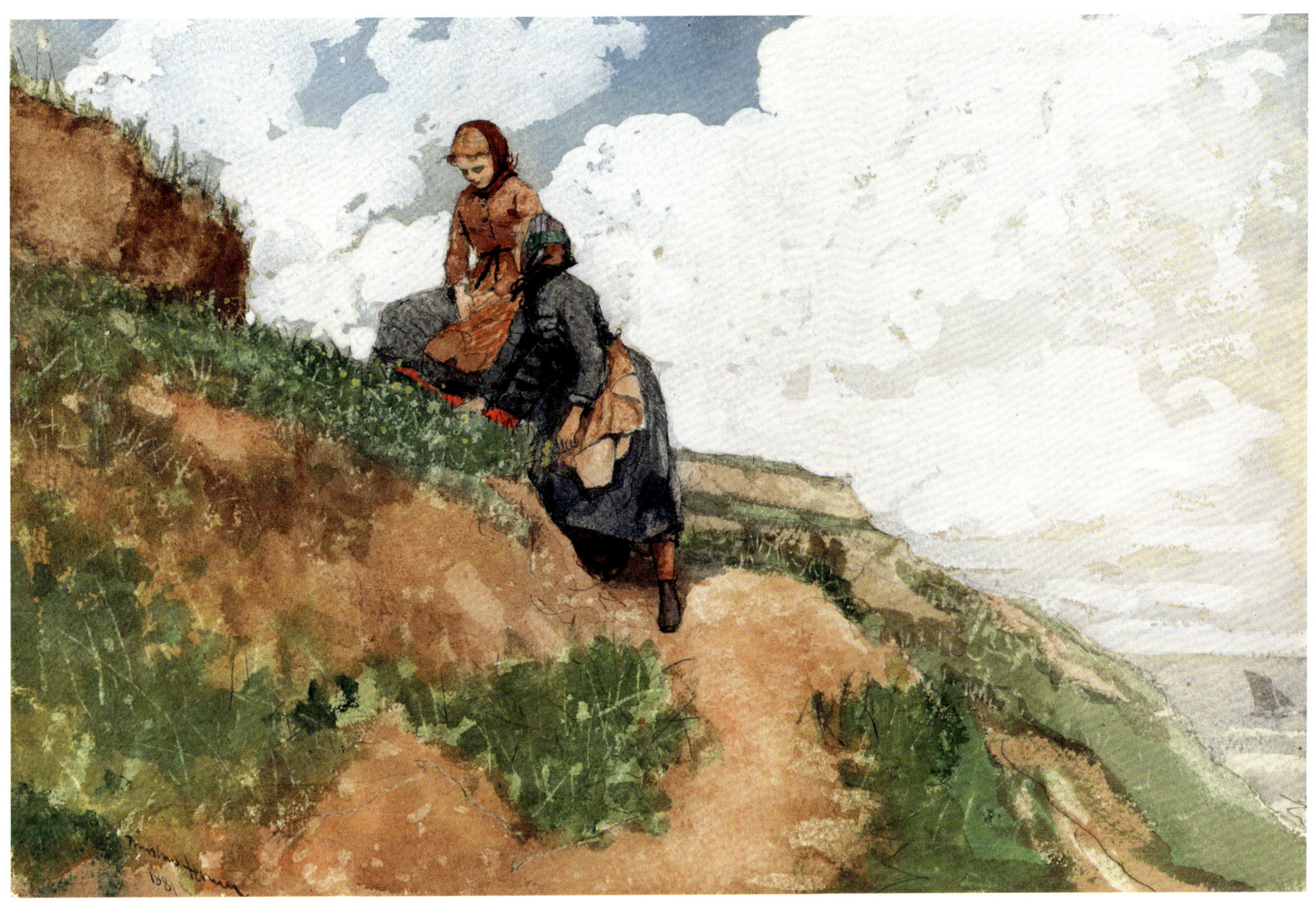

45. *Girls on a Cliff*, 1881

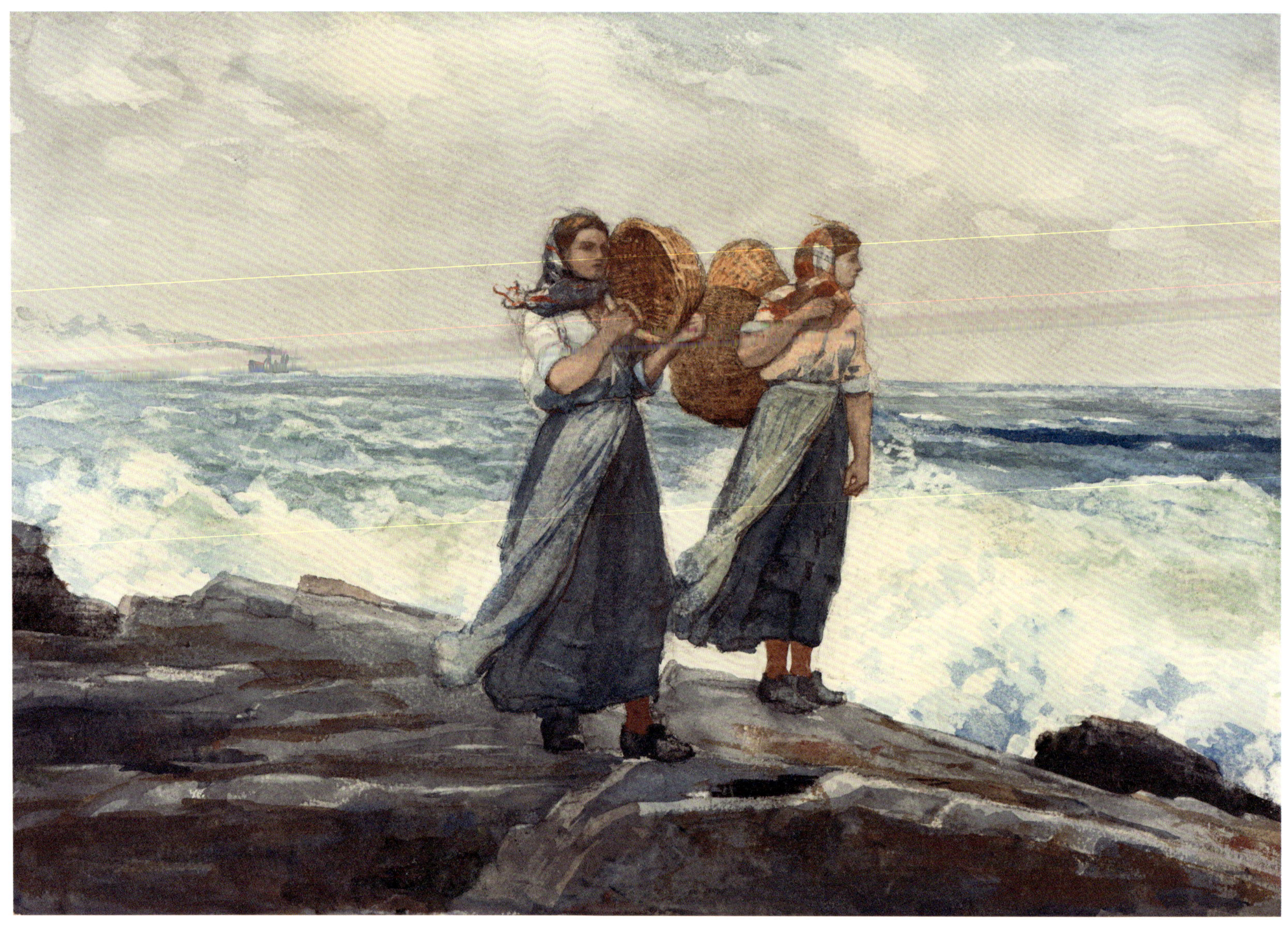

46. *A Fresh Breeze (Fishergirls, England)*, about 1881

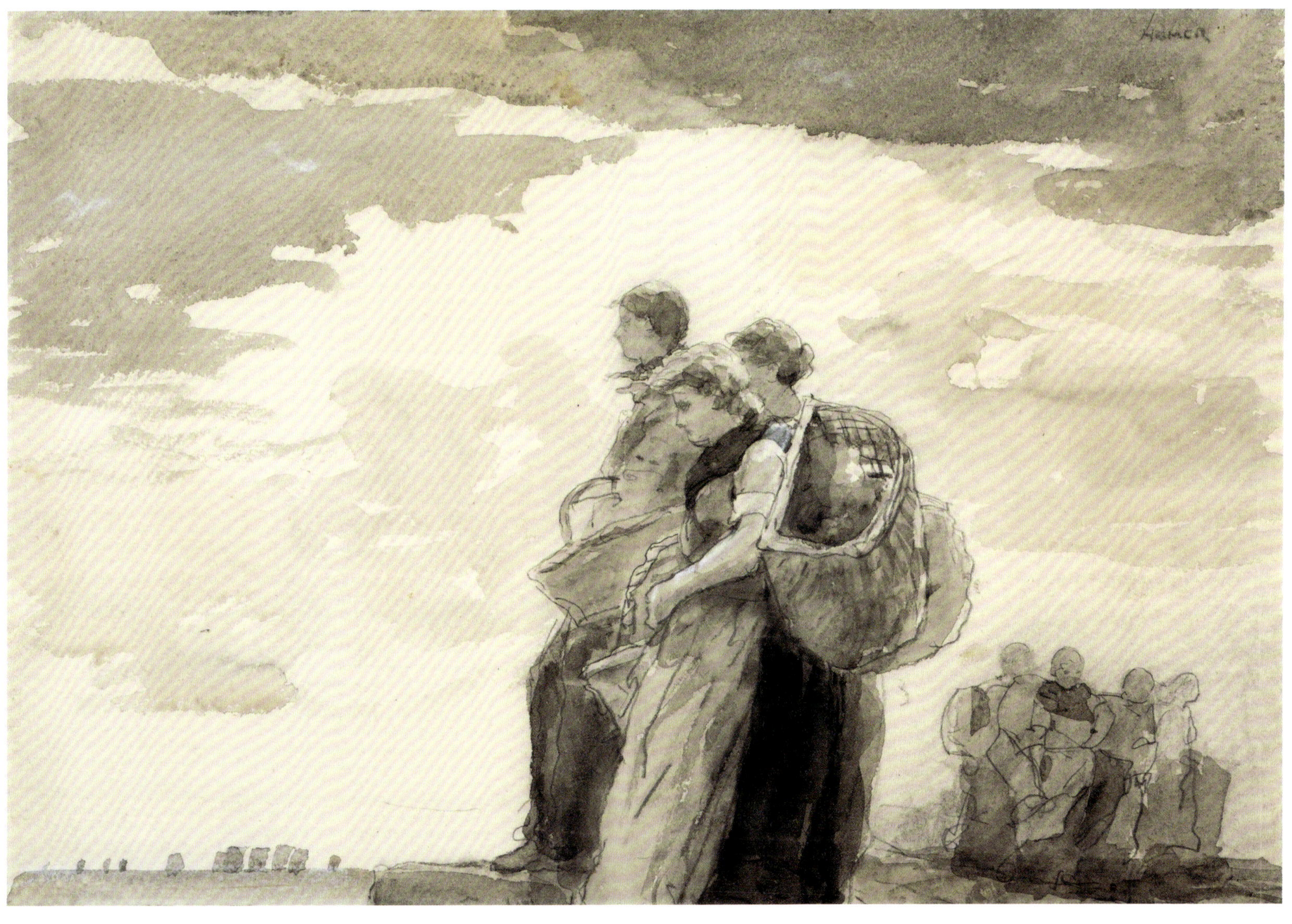

47. *Fisherwomen*, 1881–82

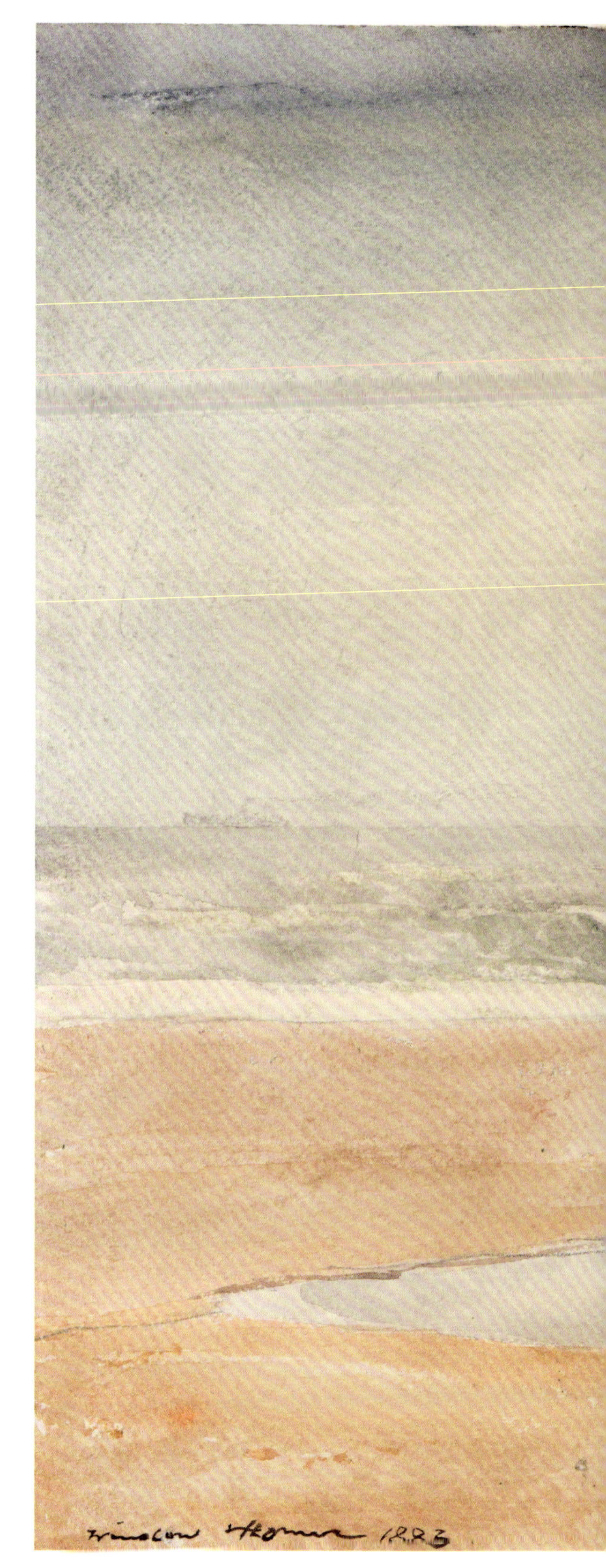

Winslow Homer 1883

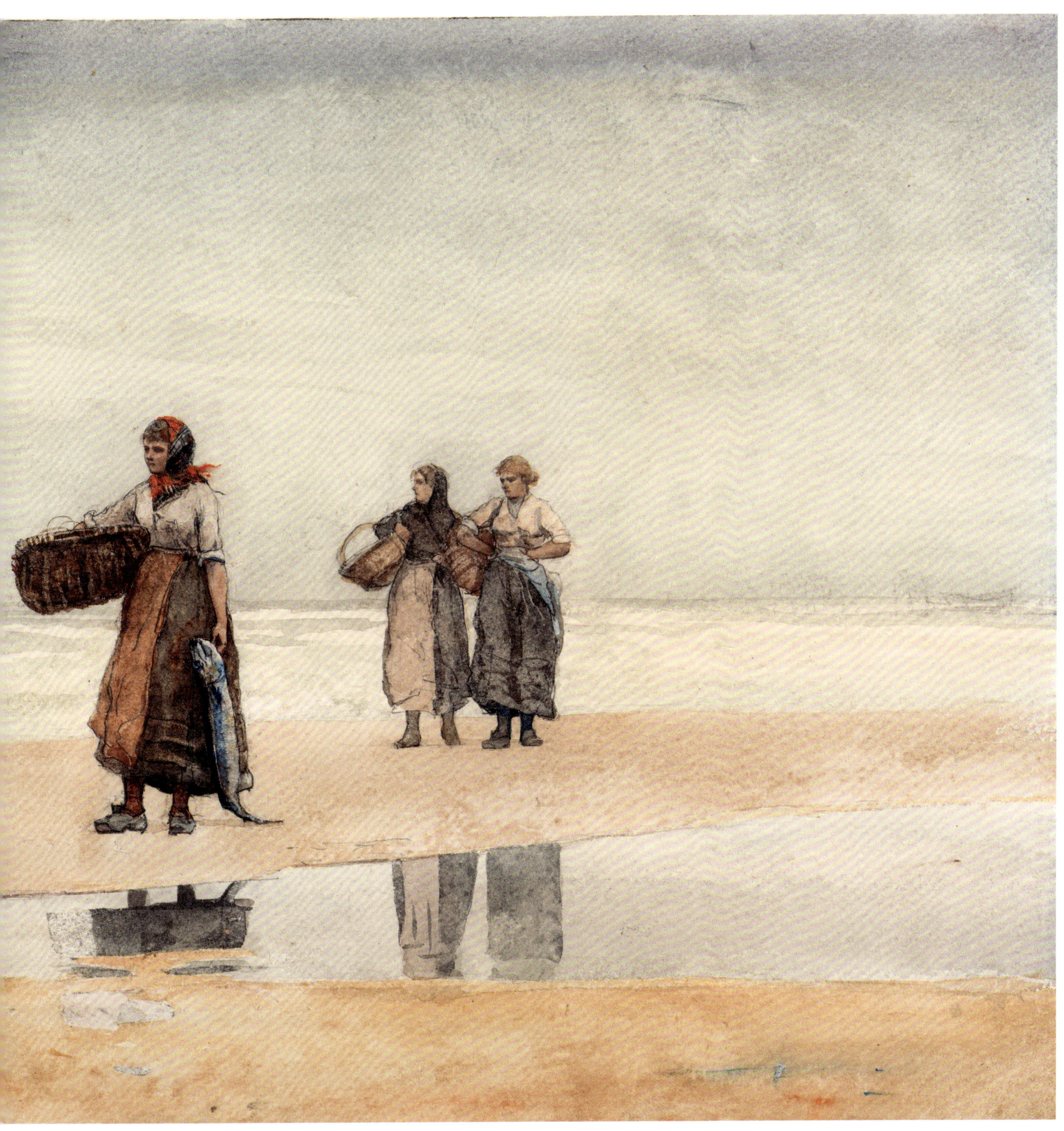

48. *Tynemouth Sands*, 1881–82

Charcoal / Homer visualized his work within the framework of value relationships; he understood the power of black and white. Early training in lithography and experience drawing for the printed illustrations of weekly magazines likely sharpened this awareness and skill, but discussion of the foundational function of black and white could also be found in 19th-century instructional manuals.[16]

In this stark and striking drawing, Homer used conventional media for the whites: chalk in the sky, and watercolor in the reflected light of the landscape. Unusual are the wet washes of black charcoal that define the figures and landscape.[17]

Charcoal is a common dry drawing material, but here Homer used it to create a type of ink or paint. The improvised medium is easily made by combining crushed charcoal with water in a vessel. It can also be generated directly on paper by manipulating a dry charcoal drawing with a water-laden brush. Homer may have found the charcoal paint an expedient, as well as expressive, medium. The quick execution of the drawing, a study in black and white, is evident in the simple representation of forms and the running together of wet passages of black and white media, an effect descibed in period manuals.[18]

Close inspection of the coarse utilitarian paper used for this drawing reveals another surprise: numerous embedded black lumps. The material was analyzed in the 1980s and found to be coal! —AM

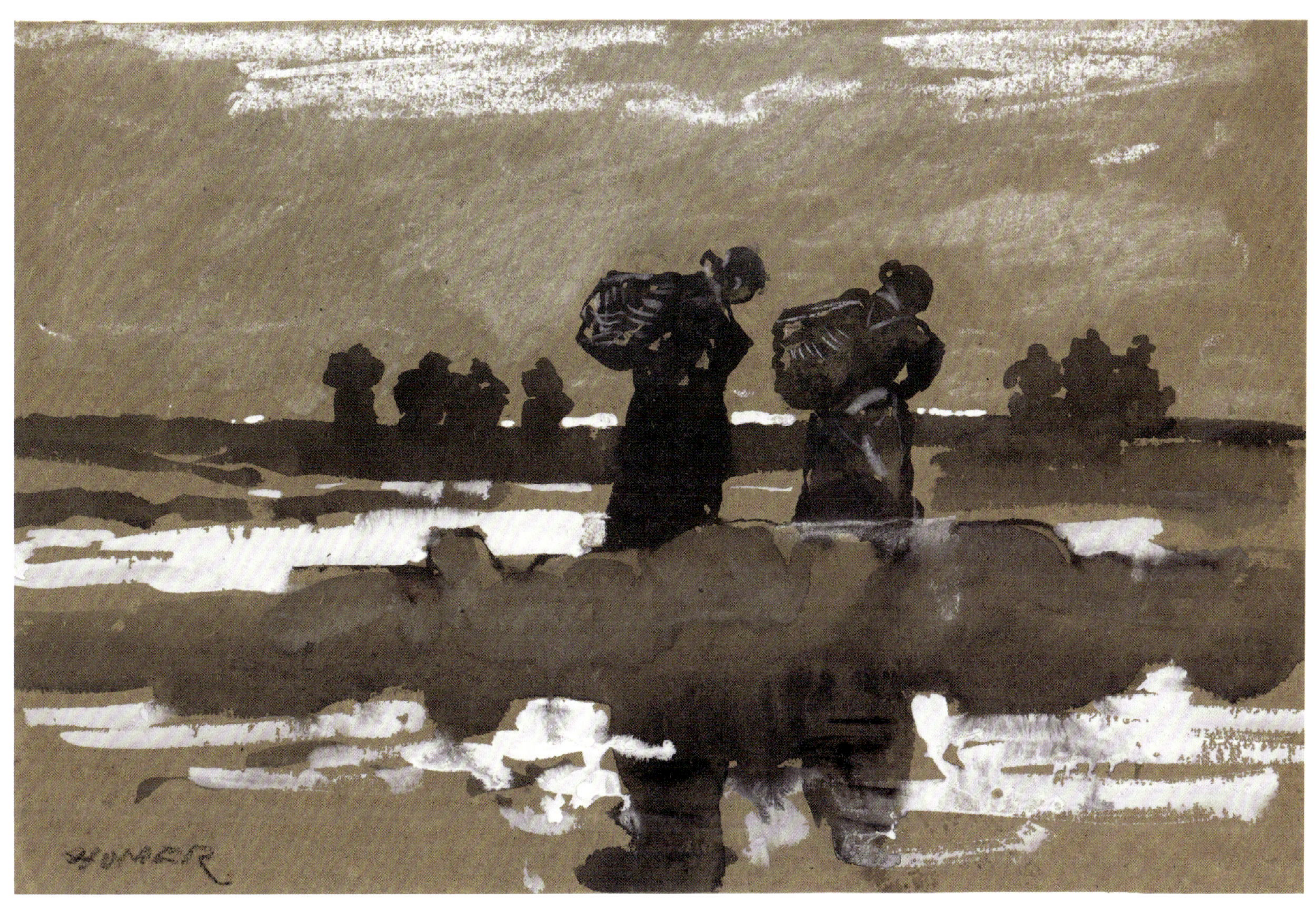

49. *Women on the Sands (Mussel Gatherers)*, 1881–82

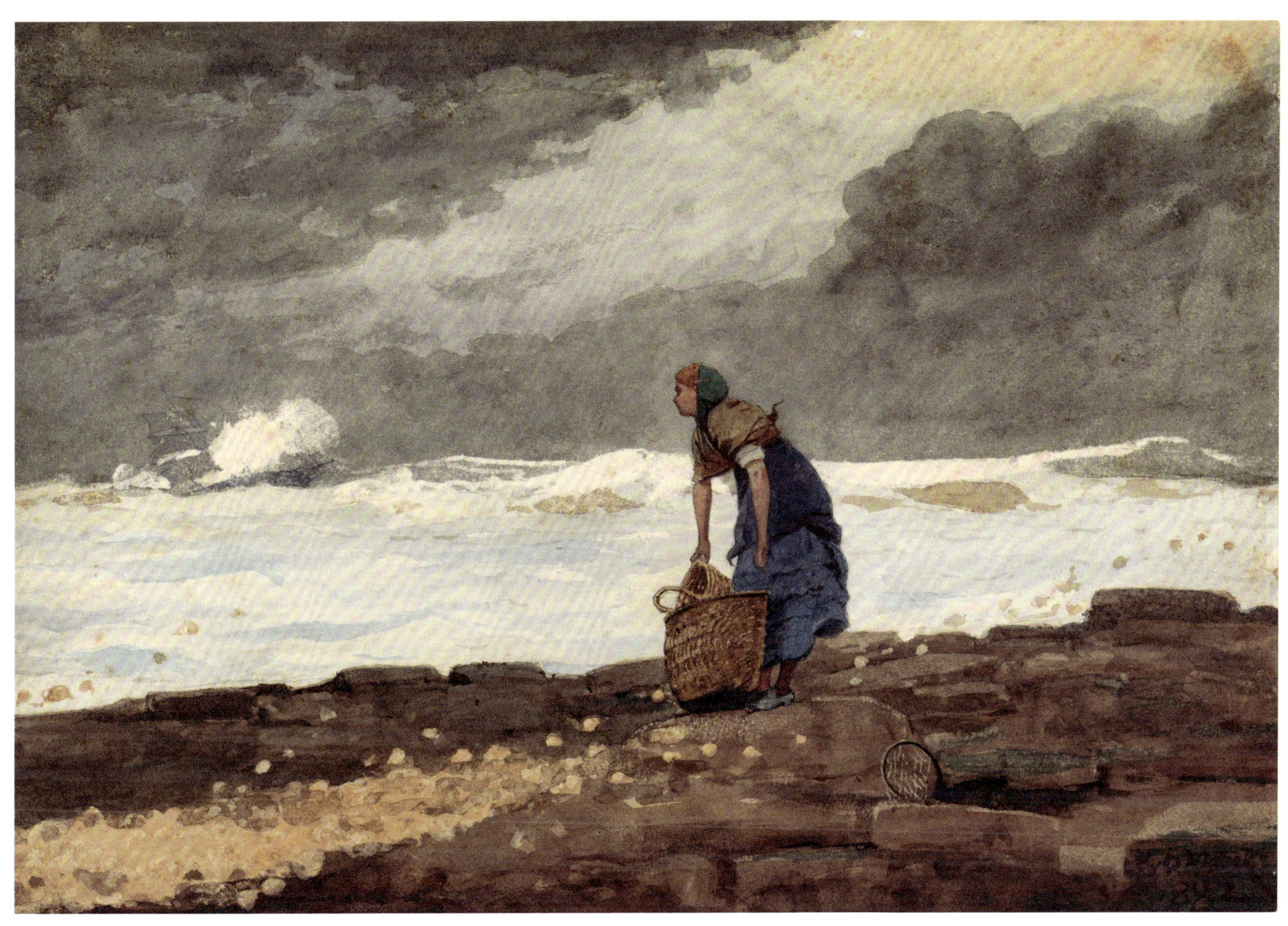

50. *Girl with Red Stockings (The Wreck)*, 1882

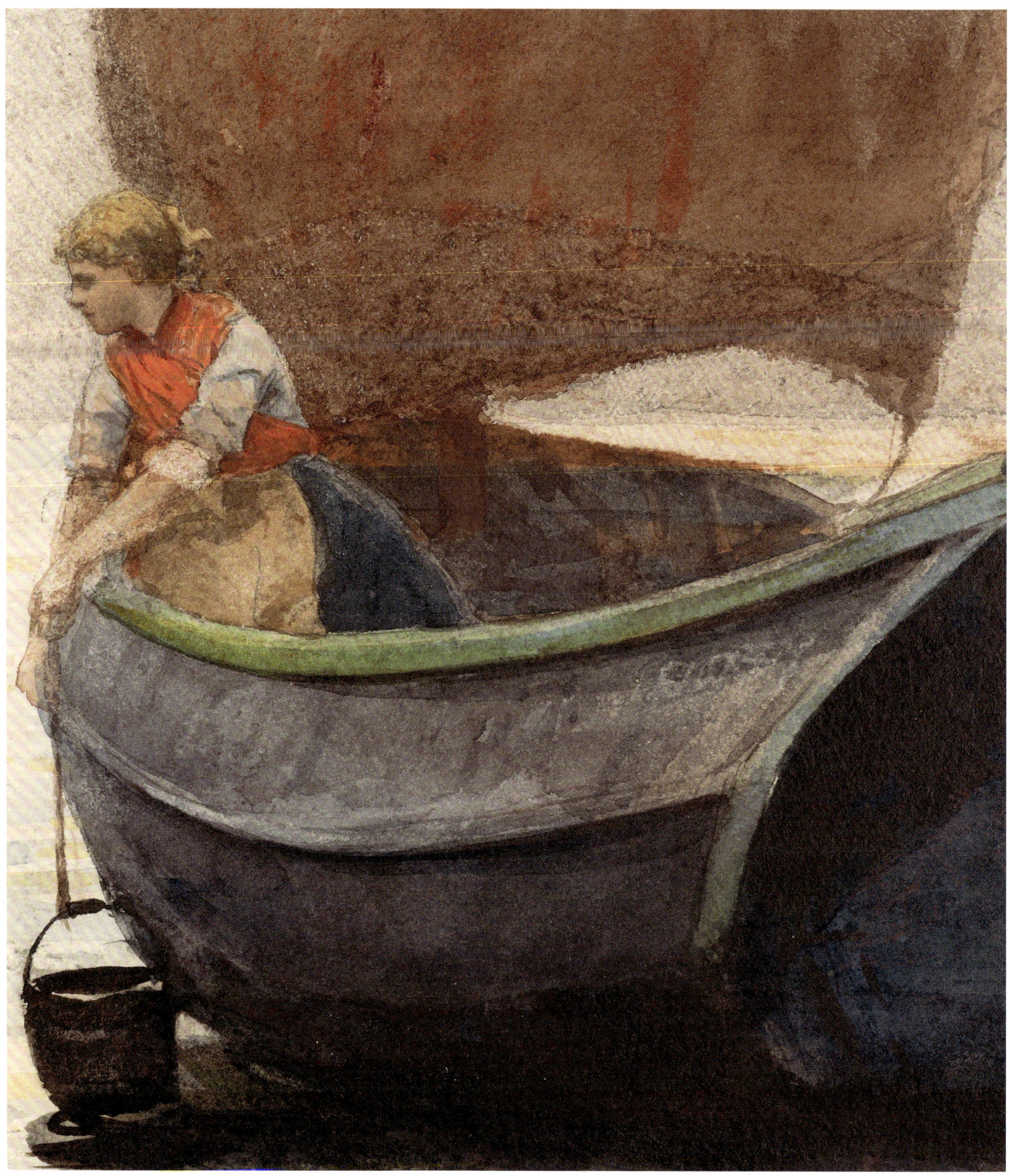

Scraping / Homer modified the sail featured in this detail by scraping away previous work with a sharp tool. Scraping changes paper texture, causing subsequent watercolor to sit differently on the altered surface. Note the slightly different color as well as the coarser, more granular appearance of the red at the bottom of the sail.

Some art manuals of the era recommended burnishing to "fix" roughened paper.[19] Burnishing compresses lifted paper fibers, providing the artist a smoother surface for further painting— a practice Homer seems not to have followed here. — AM

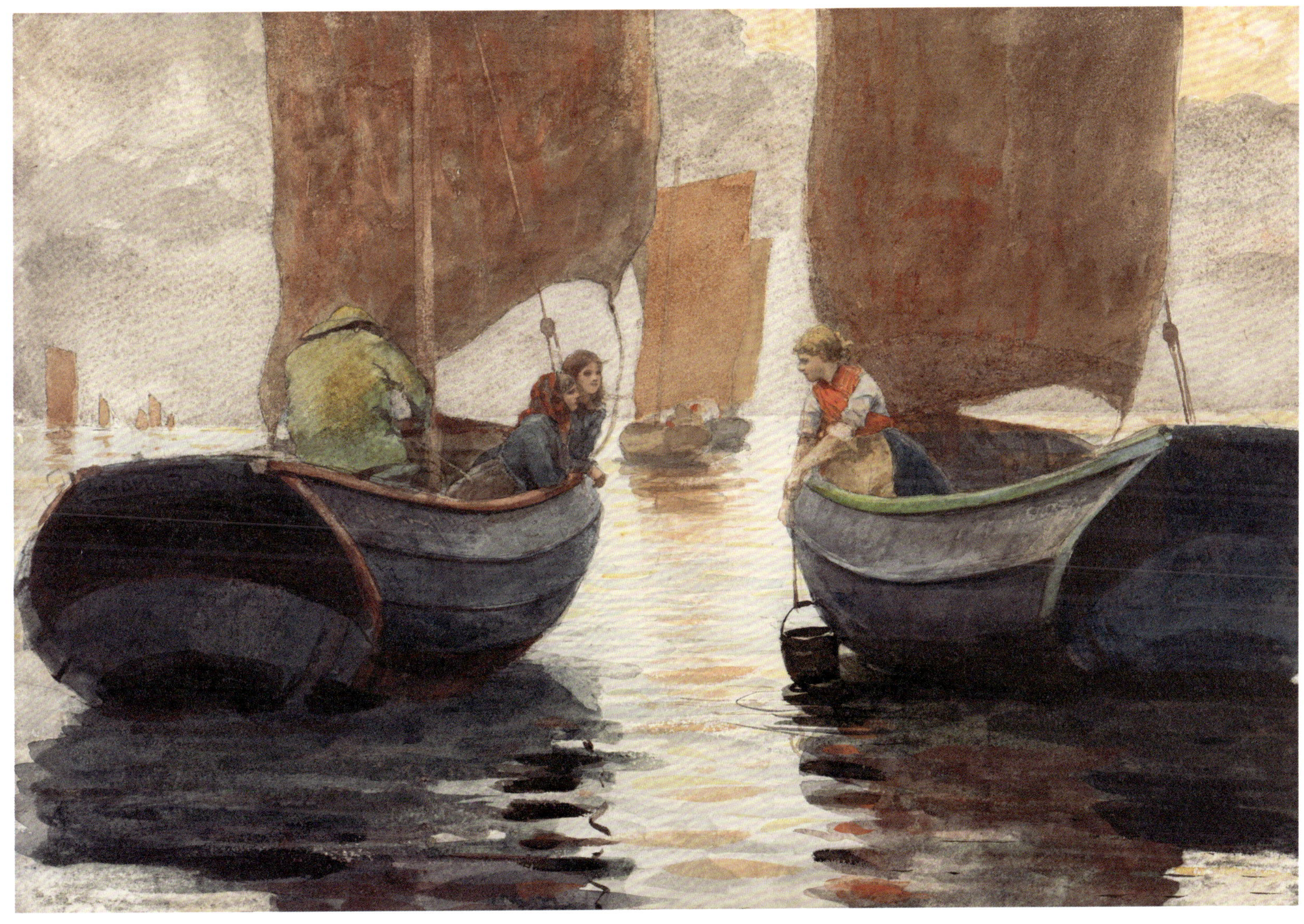

51. *An Afterglow*, 1883

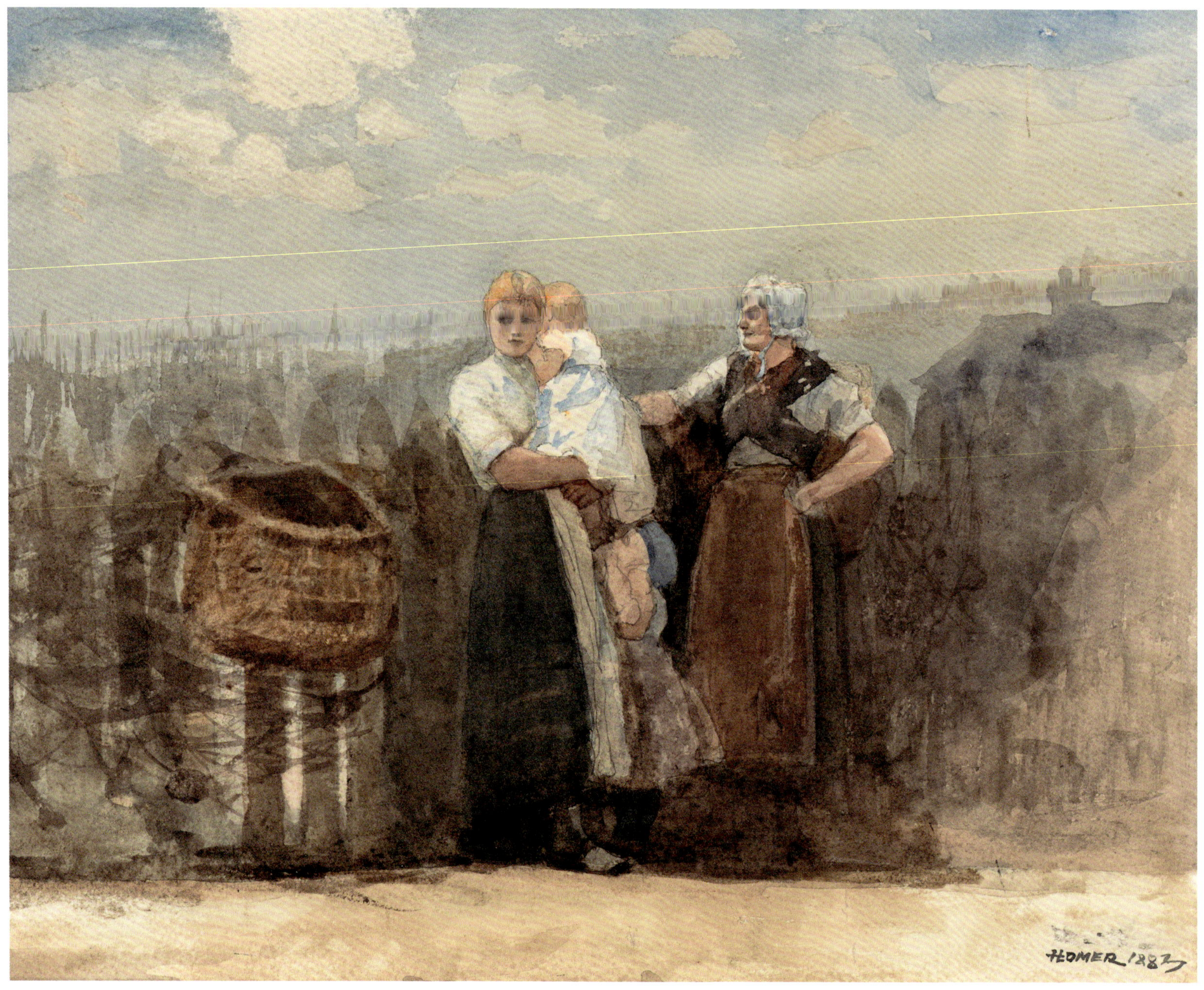

52. *Bridlington Quay*, 1883

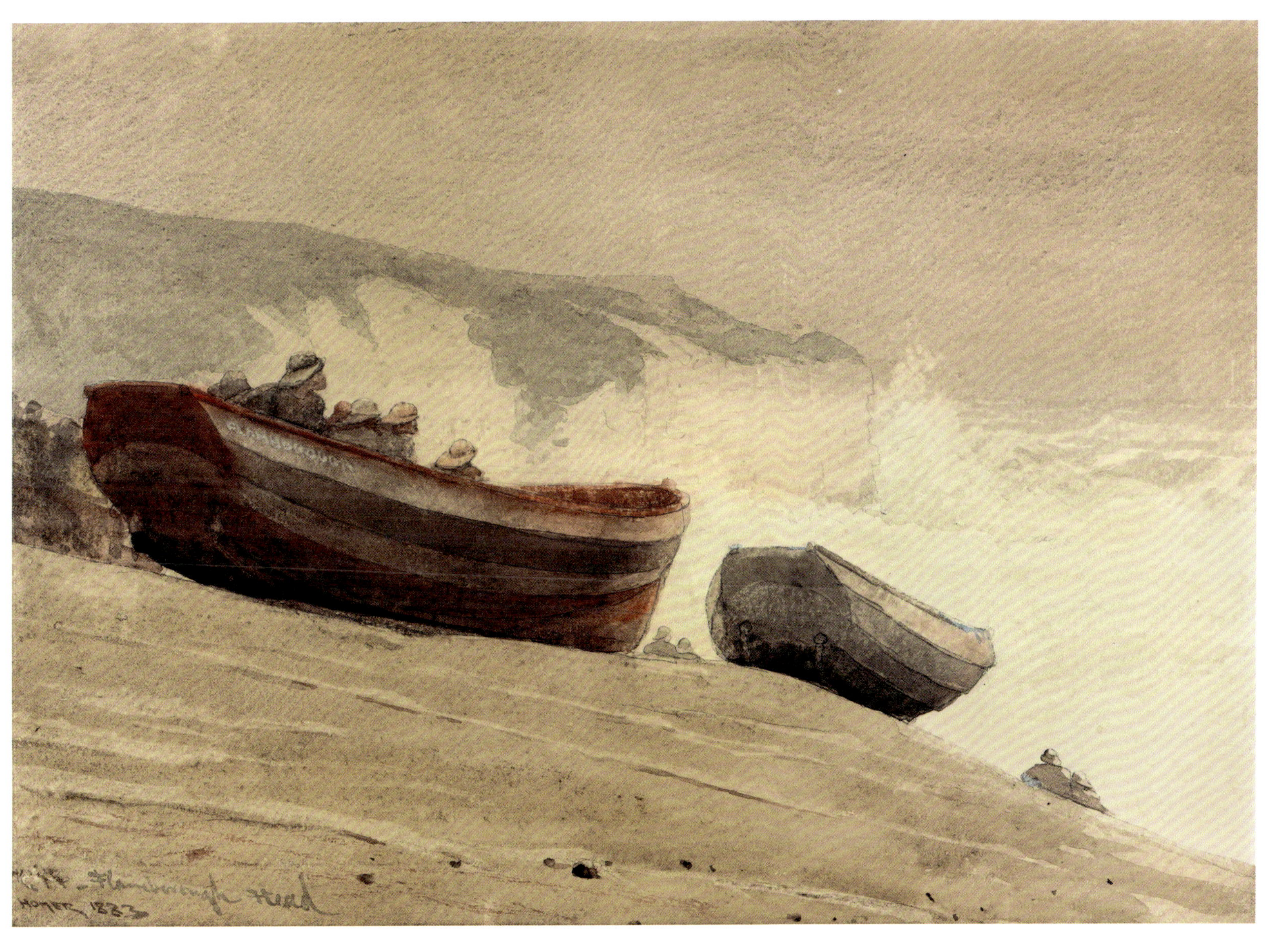

53. *Storm on the English Coast (W. H. Flamborough Head)*, 1883

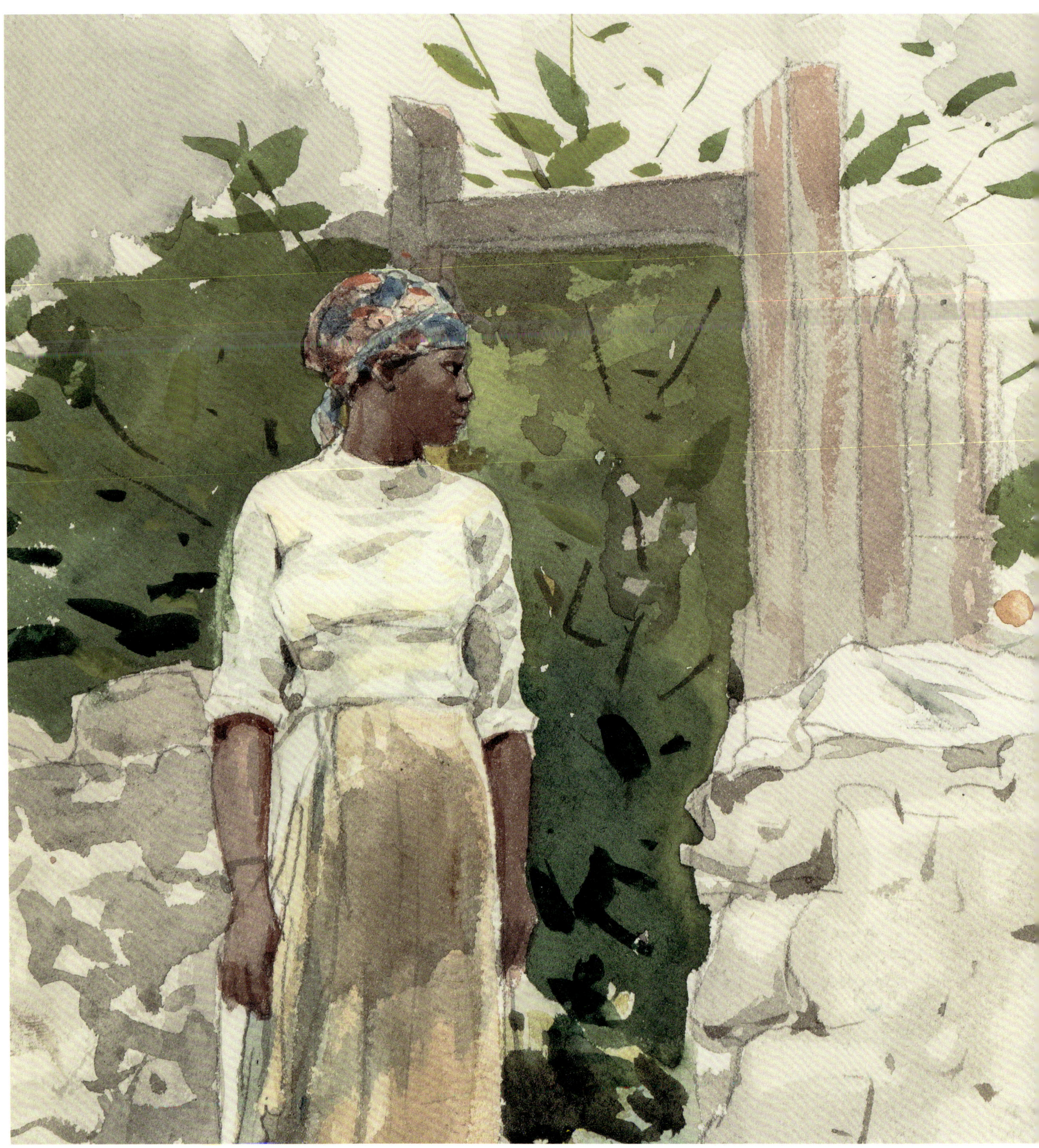

Florida and the Caribbean

During the mid-1880s, and again at the turn of the century, Homer traveled to a number of tropical locations. Alternating with summers spent in New York's Adirondack Mountains, Homer visited the Bahamas, Bermuda, Cuba, and Florida. Earlier literature has referred to these trips as "working vacations" for the artist, where he would create watercolor series in between or during fishing excursions. Recent scholarship, however, has investigated more deeply the implications and motivations of Homer's time in the tropics, examining his work through contexts such as the legacies of the transatlantic slave trade, colonialism, and empire.[20]

What is clear is the importance of the medium of watercolor to Homer's work in the tropics. Unlike his work from other regions, he painted very few oils during or inspired by these trips, preferring instead to render these locales in watercolor. Portable and quick-drying, watercolor is ideal for travel. Even more than that, Homer's mastery of the medium's translucence made it especially apt for capturing the crystal-clear waters of the Caribbean, while his confident brushwork and vibrant palette brought Florida's spiky palm trees and sun-drenched shores to life.

In the winter of 1884–85, not long after the death of his mother, Homer and his father traveled to Nassau, an emerging tourist destination in the Bahamas. While there, Homer made a concerted effort to leave other white visitors and residents out of his pictures, despite being surrounded by them. Instead, he focused on the Black men and women who lived and labored on the islands, such as the subjects of *Fox Hill, Bahamas* and *Harbor Island, Bahamas* observed during tours of Black neighborhoods such as Fox Hill or scenic boat rides out to sea.[21] He would revisit similar themes during a return trip in 1898–99, in a series that includes *The Sponge Diver*. In contrast to his

work depicting men laboring at sea in the north Atlantic, Homer's subject here, though heroized, is unclothed and submerged in the water. Still, Homer may have found affinity across these disparate bodies—of work, of water, and of human form—when he exhibited similar Bahamas watercolors alongside two major oil paintings of New England fishermen, *The Fog Warning* and *The Herring Net* in Boston in 1886.[22]

In February 1885, Homer left his father in Nassau to spend a month in Cuba. While in the town of Santiago de Cuba, the artist produced an unusual series that focused principally on the old Spanish architecture of the city rather than coastal scenes. Some scholars have read the change in subject matter and the markedly more somber palette of Homer's Cuban watercolors as suffused with the political tensions within Cuba during the late nineteenth century. In *Street Corner, Santiago de Cuba*, two shrouded figures walk up a hill in shadow as sun warms the facade of an old building. Homer experimented with several different techniques to achieve the rusticated facades and gloomy skies in this scene. Some of Homer's Cuba watercolors, including *Street Corner*, did not initially sell. In 1902, Homer sent this watercolor and others from the series to his New York dealers, M. Knoedler & Company, as well as completed his only oil painting inspired by Cuba, *Searchlight on Harbor Entrance, Santiago de Cuba*.[23] Following the Spanish-American War, the United States occupied Cuba between 1898 and 1902, officially ending occupation in May 1902 as the Republic of Cuba gained formal independence. Homer likely saw the opportunity to link his earlier watercolors and new oil painting to current events with the hope that this work would be of renewed interest to collectors.

First traveling to Florida in 1886, Homer returned more frequently during the early 1900s for fishing trips and to escape harsh Maine winters. In 1904, Homer painted *Palm Trees, Florida*, a comparatively late watercolor in his oeuvre, in Homosassa, a coastal town on the Gulf of Mexico, about seventy miles north of Tampa. The work is a landscape, though a small boat with fisherman is seen in the distance to the lower right, and Homer lavished attention on the great and varied palm trees at the center of the composition. A dappled blue sky emerging from passing clouds mirrors the shimmering waters below, and two red birds, painted in opaque watercolor, add a vibrant pop of color to a denser section of trees. Though labeled a "sketch" by the artist (in the lower left corner, next to his initials), the watercolor features a high degree of finish.

Homer also traveled to Bermuda, then as now a British territory, in December 1899 through early 1900. Here, he produced a number of coastal scenes, including *Rocky Shore, Bermuda*, in which two red-coated British soldiers stand apart from the rocky cliffs surrounding the bright blue sea. In 1901, Homer selected twenty-one works from his Bermuda series and previous Bahamas series to send to the Pan-American Exposition in Buffalo, New York, where the group was awarded a Gold Medal. The group likely included some of the Museum's watercolors, though neither Homer nor the Exposition program shared individual titles. This was the last time Homer would select and coordinate the exhibition of his own work.

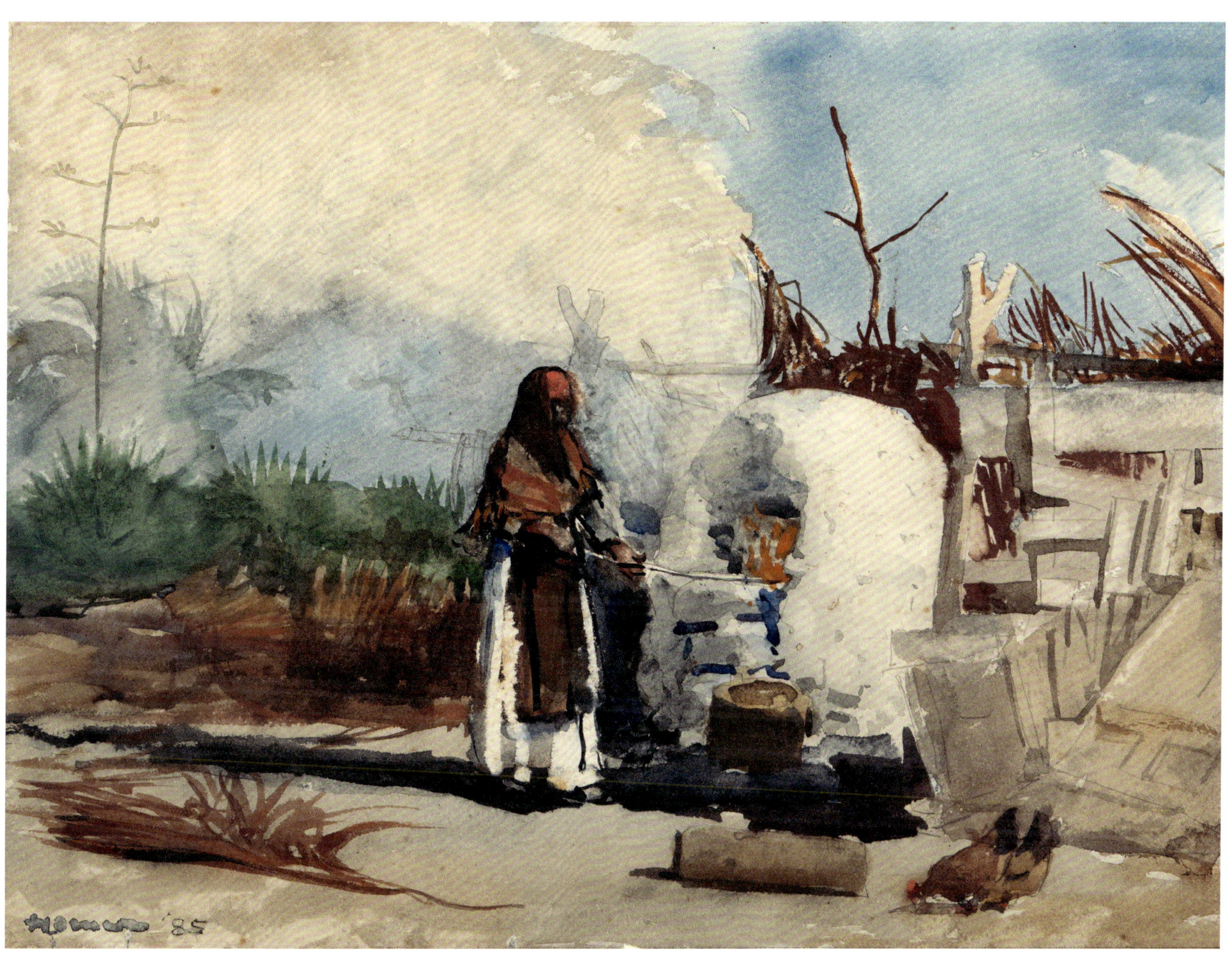

54. *Harbor Island, Bahamas, 1885*

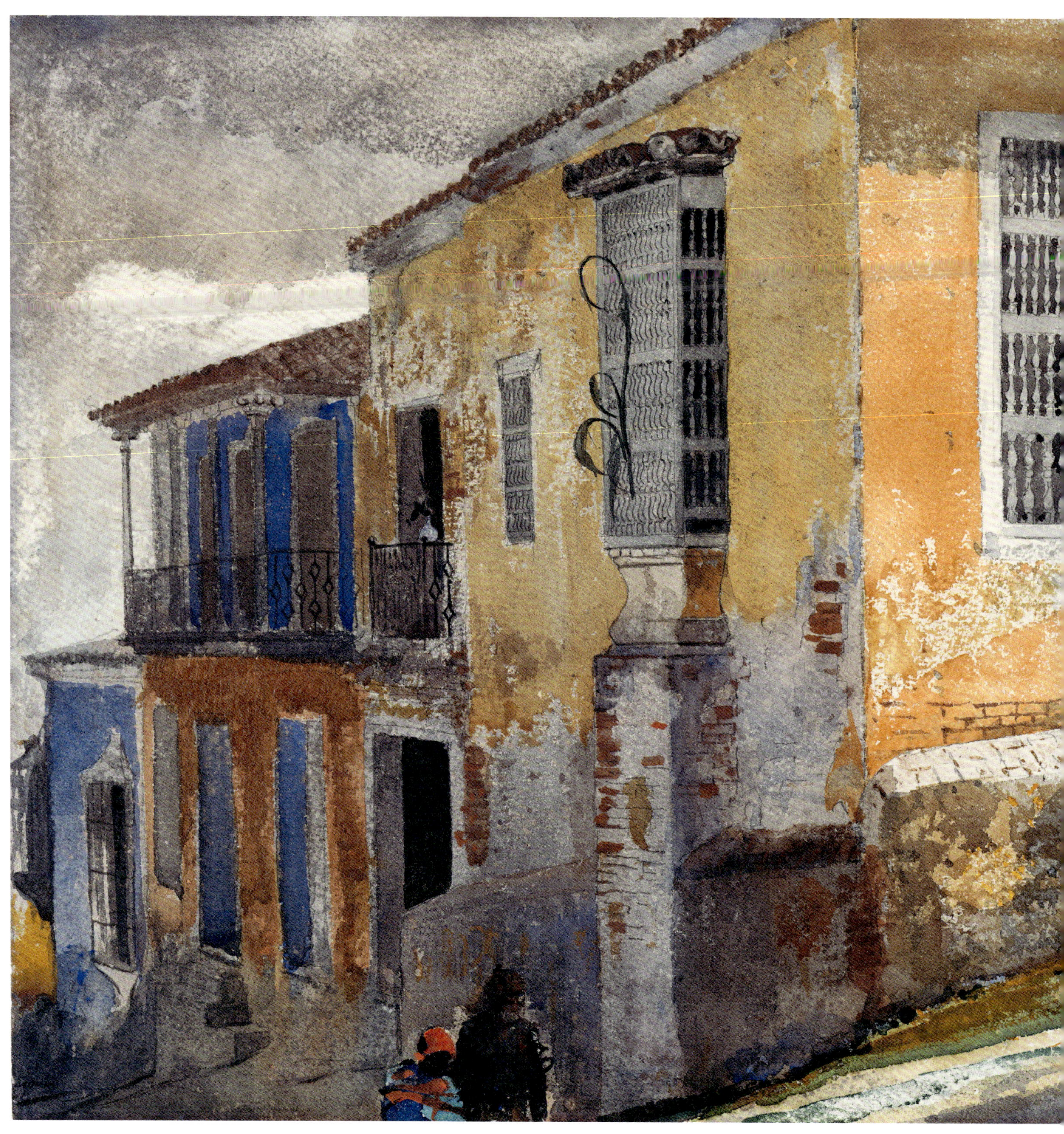

55. *Street Corner, Santiago de Cuba*, 1885

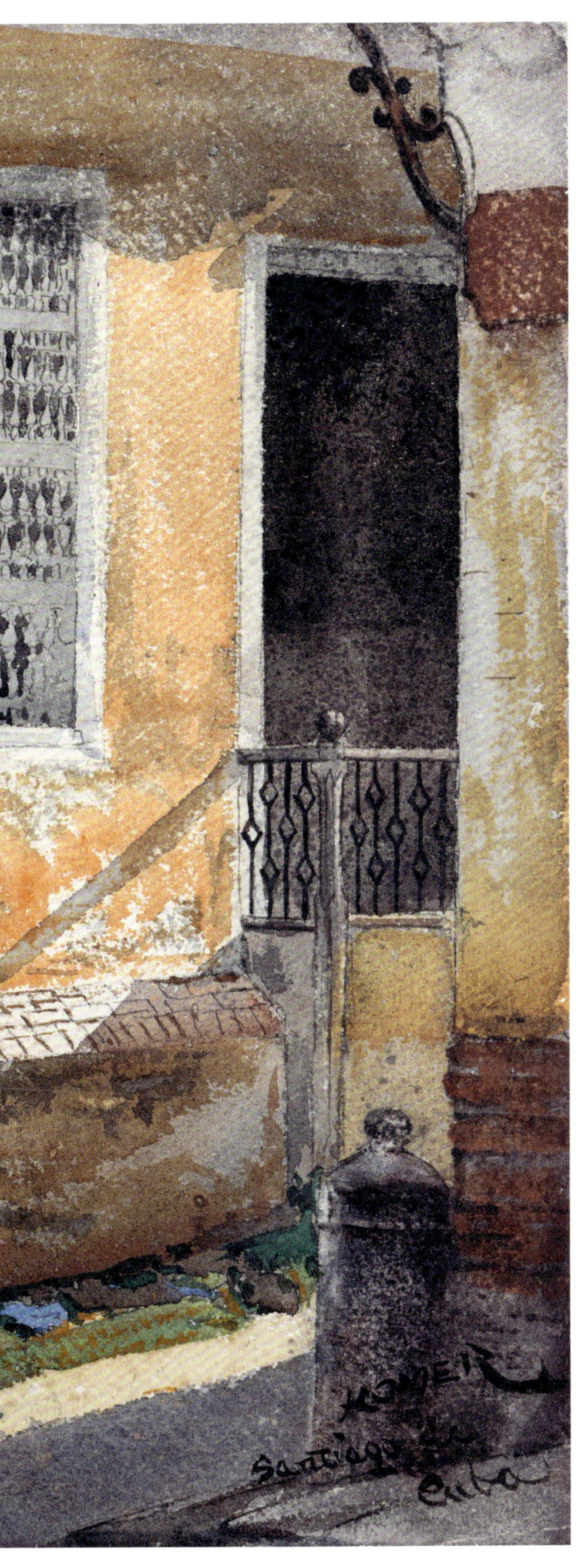
HOMER
Santiago de
Cuba

Watercolor / The main components of watercolor paint are gum (usually gum Arabic), water and color, with glycerin added to produce "moist" colors beginning in the 1830s. Manufacturers and vendors of paints known as colormen, as well as artists, might add other ingredients to modify working properties such as flow, gloss, and penetration.

Watercolor paints in Homer's time, as now, were sold in solid blocks (cake watercolor), in small pans (moist watercolor), or wet in tubes. Cake watercolor is slow to wet up but has the advantage of producing cleaner, less streaky color. Moist color includes glycerin, which makes wetting up easier and is therefore more practical for outdoor painting. Glycerin makes tube watercolor possible by keeping paint fluid in the tube. In practice, glycerin slows paint drying time, offering the artist opportunity to manipulate the wet medium. Glycerin also makes it easier to rewet dried watercolor on paper for further work.

Translucent watercolor (also called transparent watercolor) colors without obscuring the paper below. White paper contributes to the luminosity of translucent watercolor by reflecting light back through paint layers. Lightest colors are typically applied first, with darkest colors painted last. When allowed to dry between applications, partially overlapping paint layers remain discernible but their colors will appear somewhat changed. Note the see-through quality of the green plant fronds. — AM

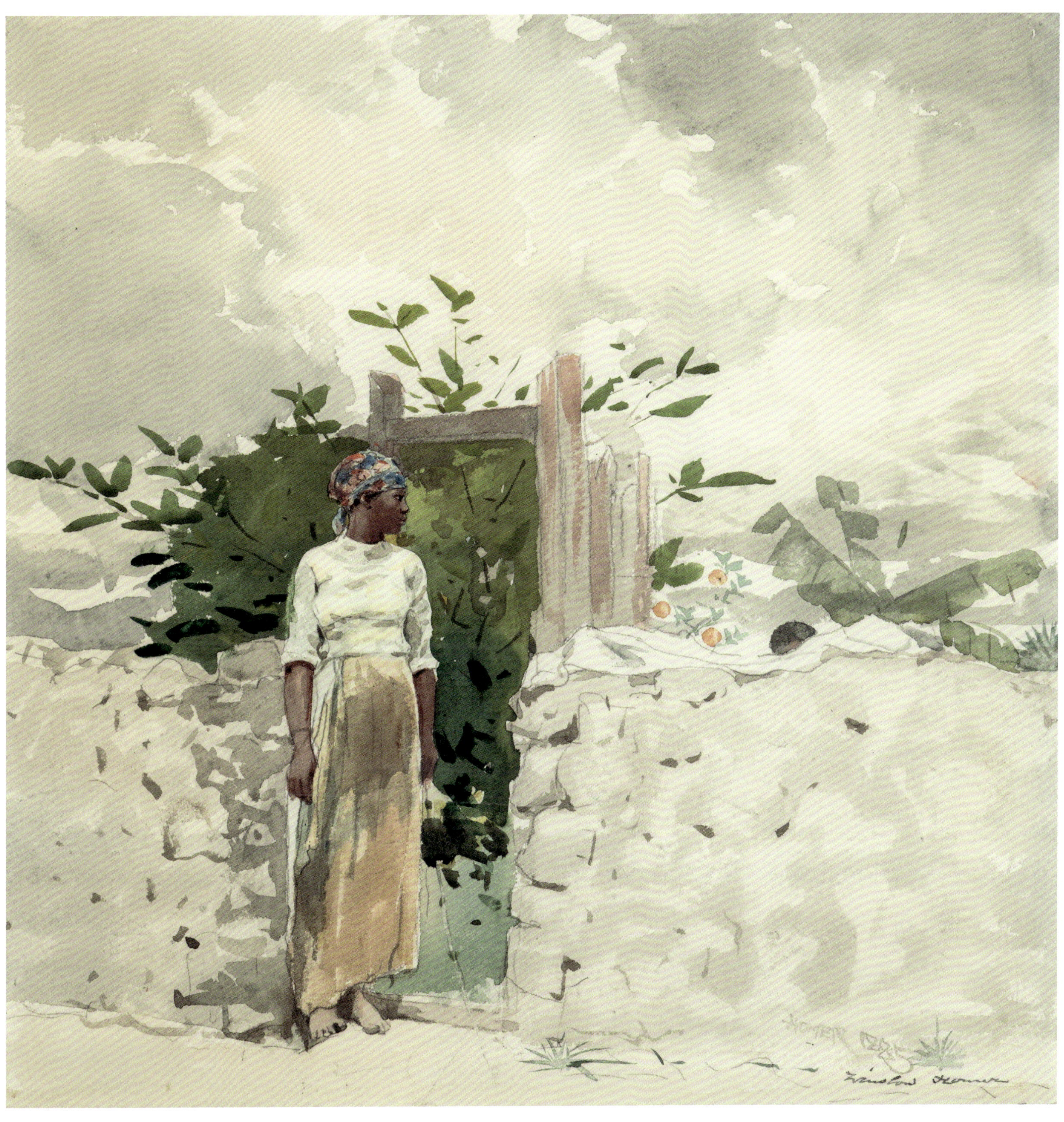

56. *Fox Hill, Bahamas,* 1885

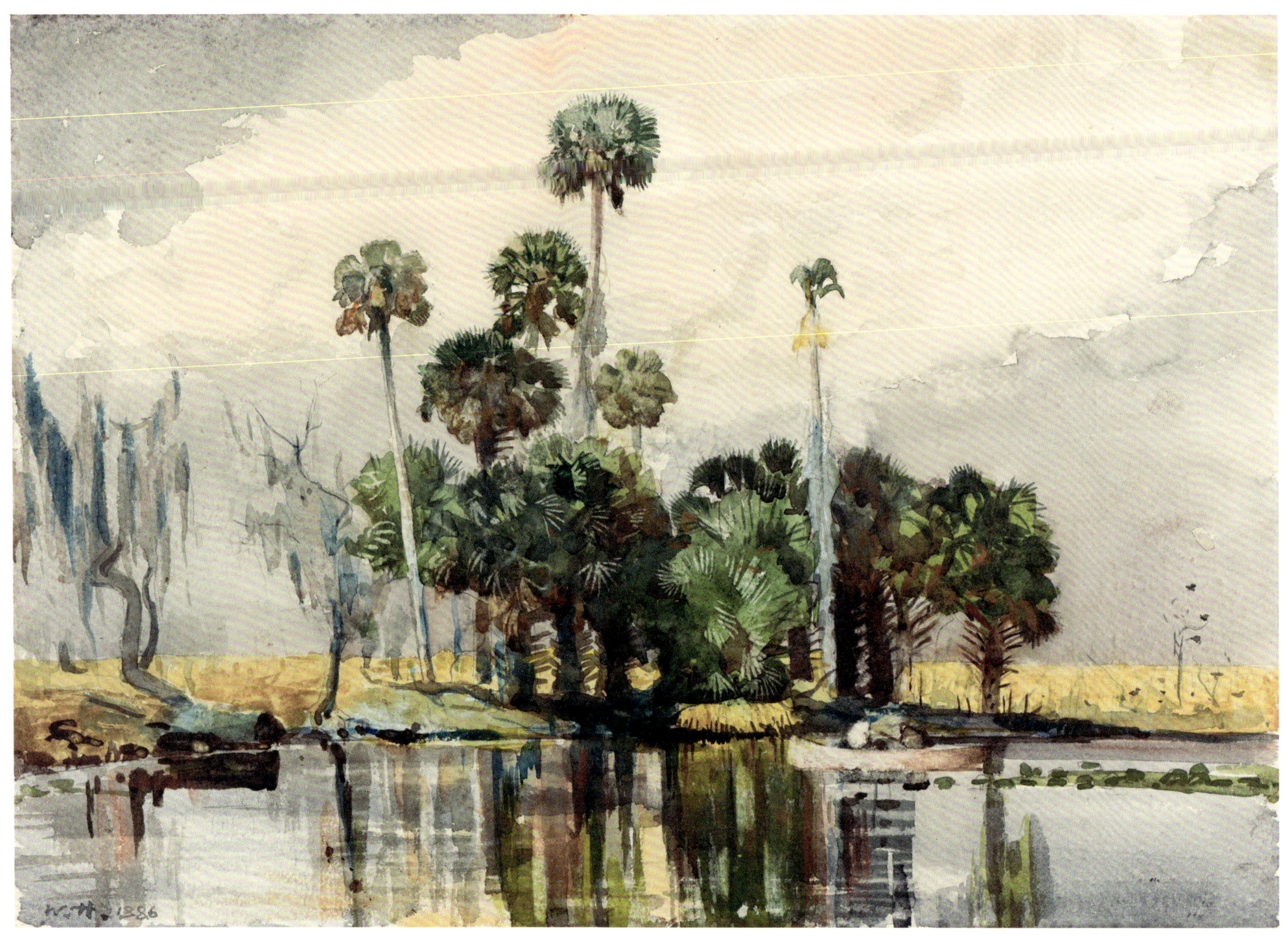

57. *Thornhill Bar (Florida)*, 1886

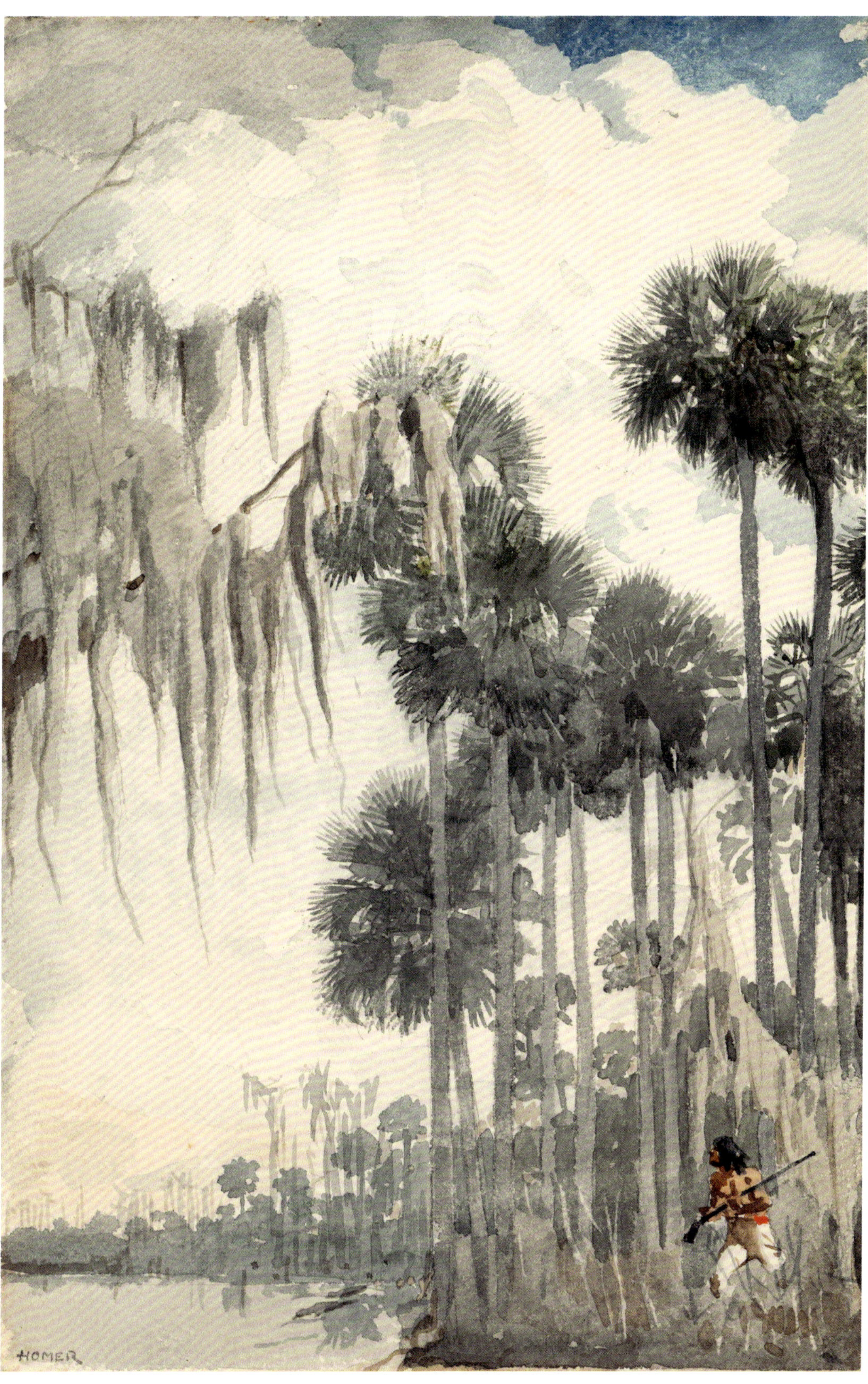

58. *Hunter in the Everglades,* about 1886

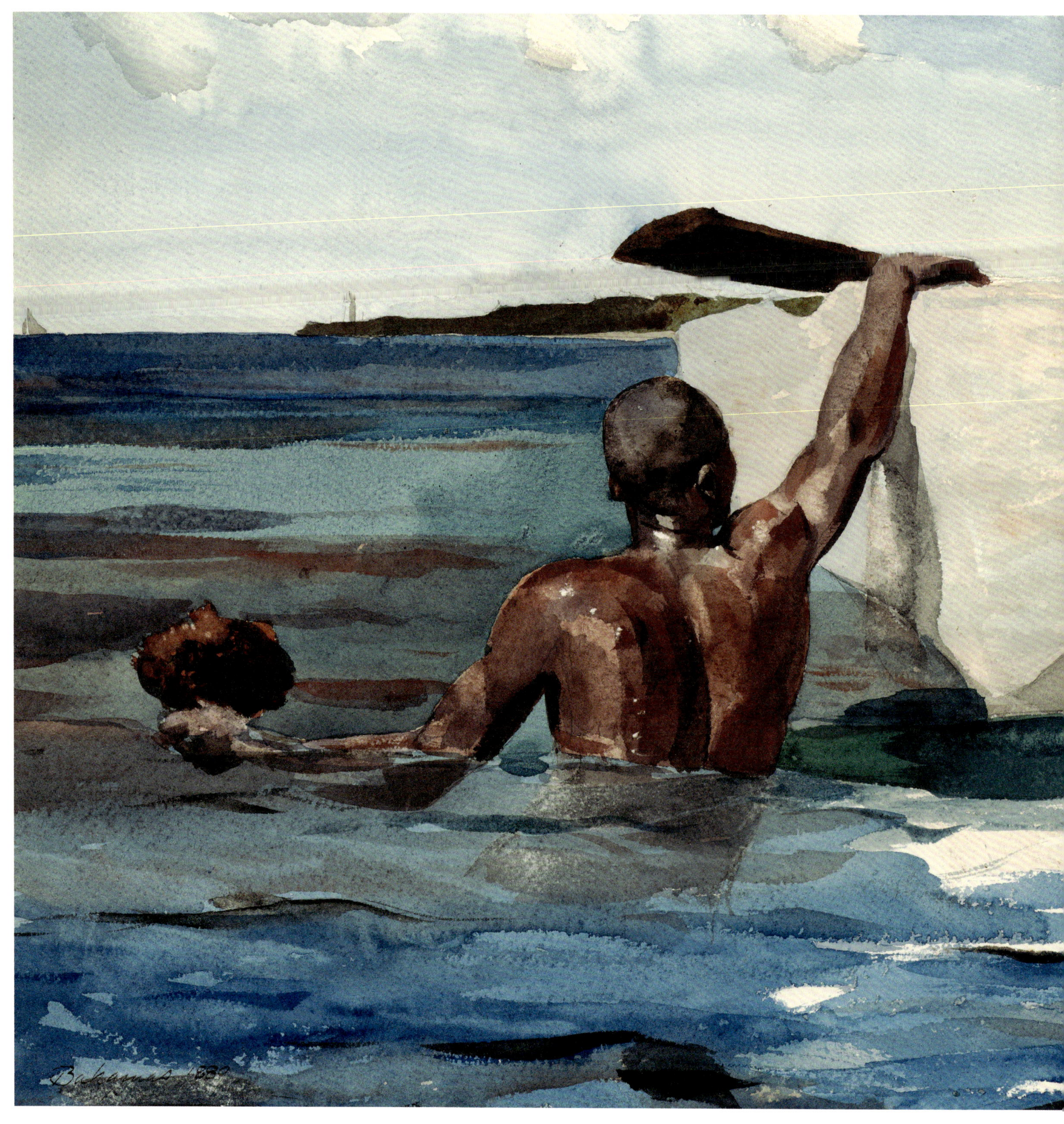

59. *The Sponge Diver*, 1898–99

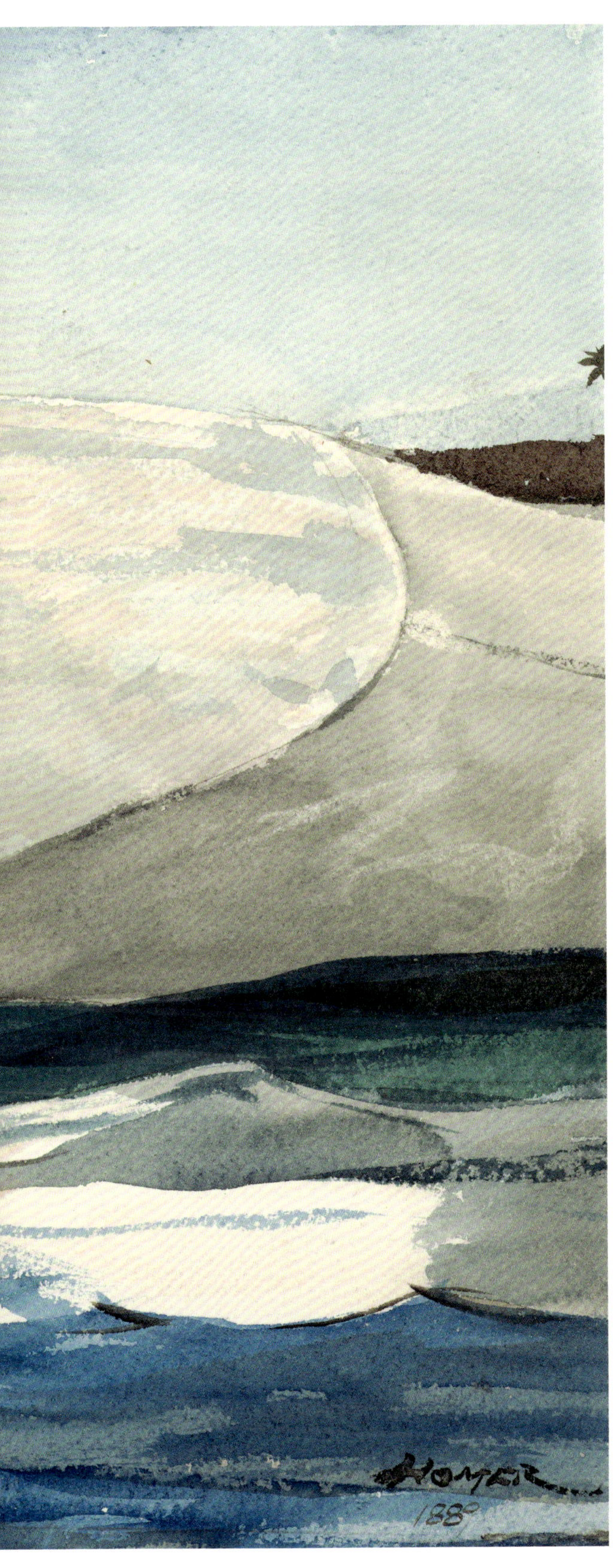

Homer
1889

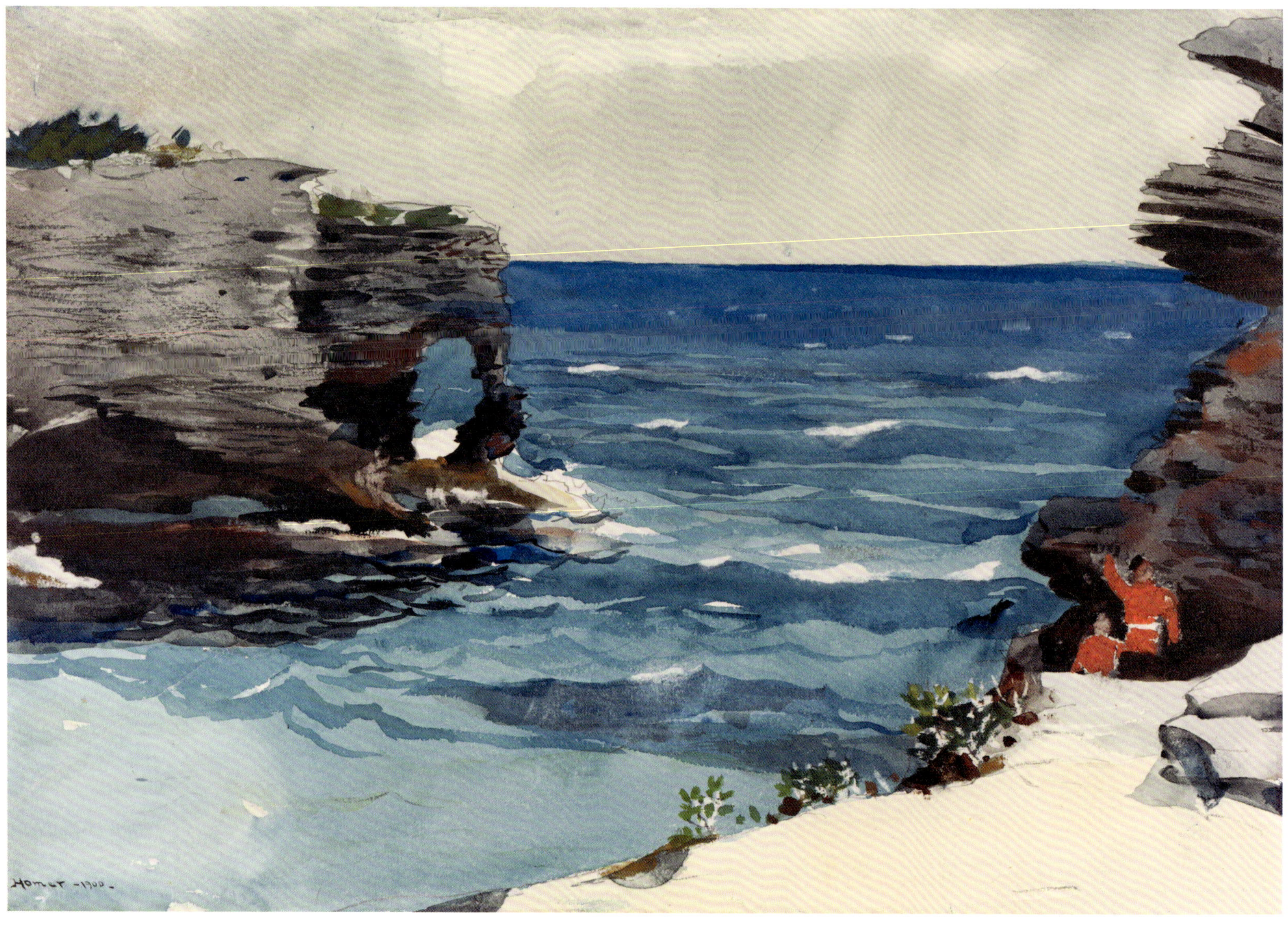

60. *Rocky Shore, Bermuda*, 1900

Paper / The strong paper fibers of typical water-color paper allow for a fairly aggressive working of the paper's surface. Whatman watercolor paper was frequently recommended in nineteenth-century instruction manuals because of its ability to take color and withstand physical manipulation.[24] Here Homer scraped deeply before painting the two figures in red. The roughened surface of the paper is especially visible in raking light. —AM

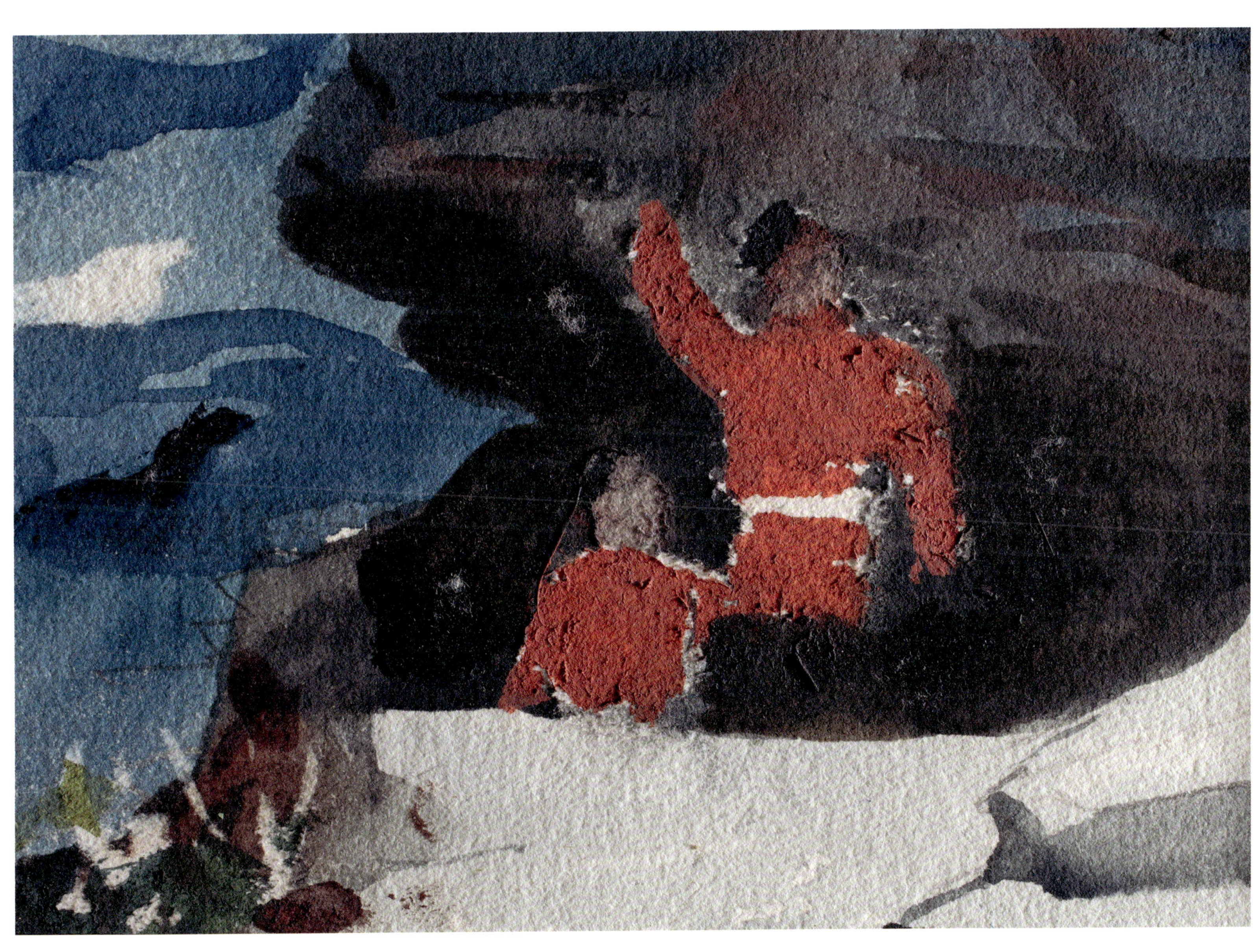

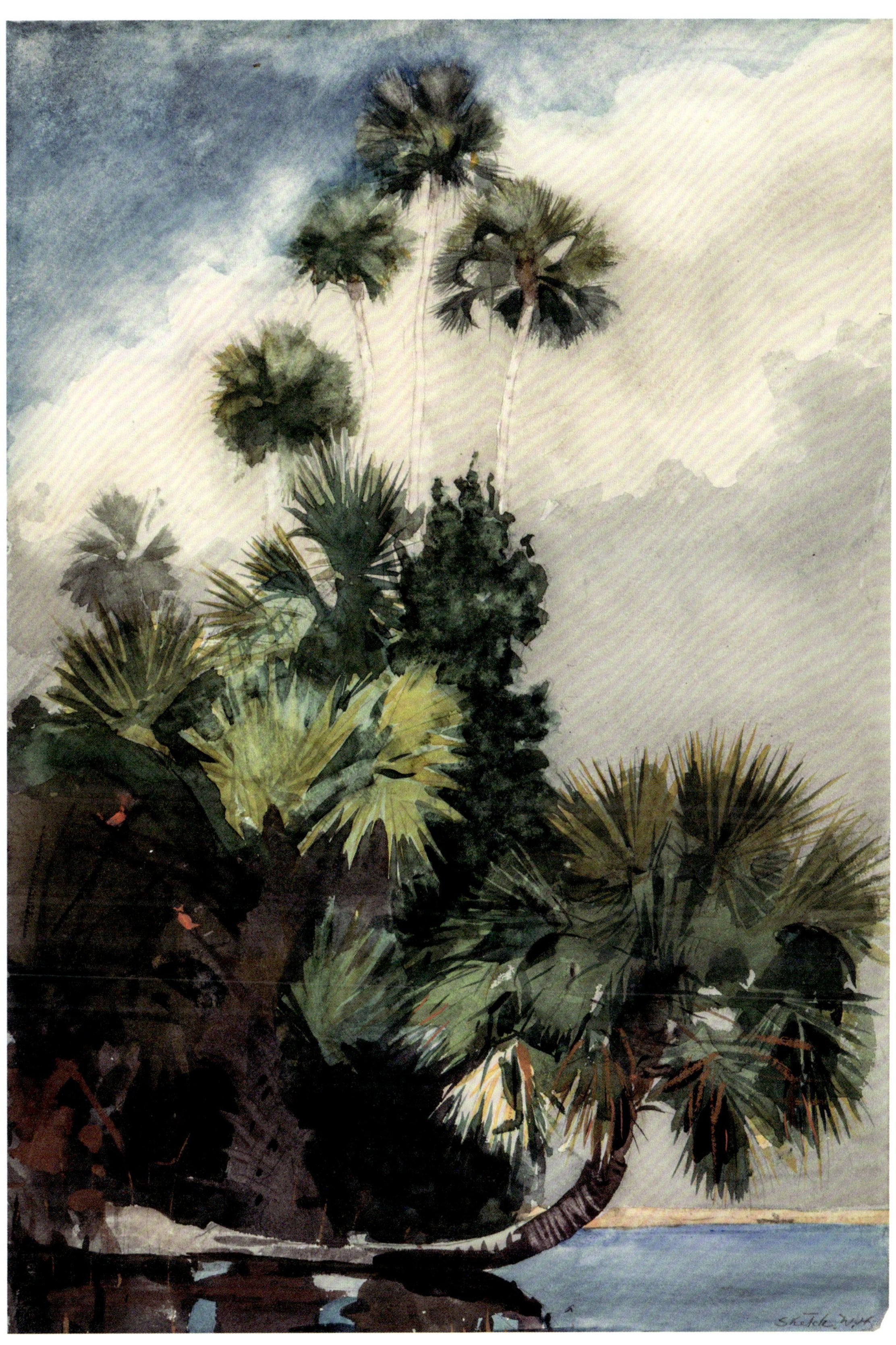

61. *Palm Trees, Florida*, 1904

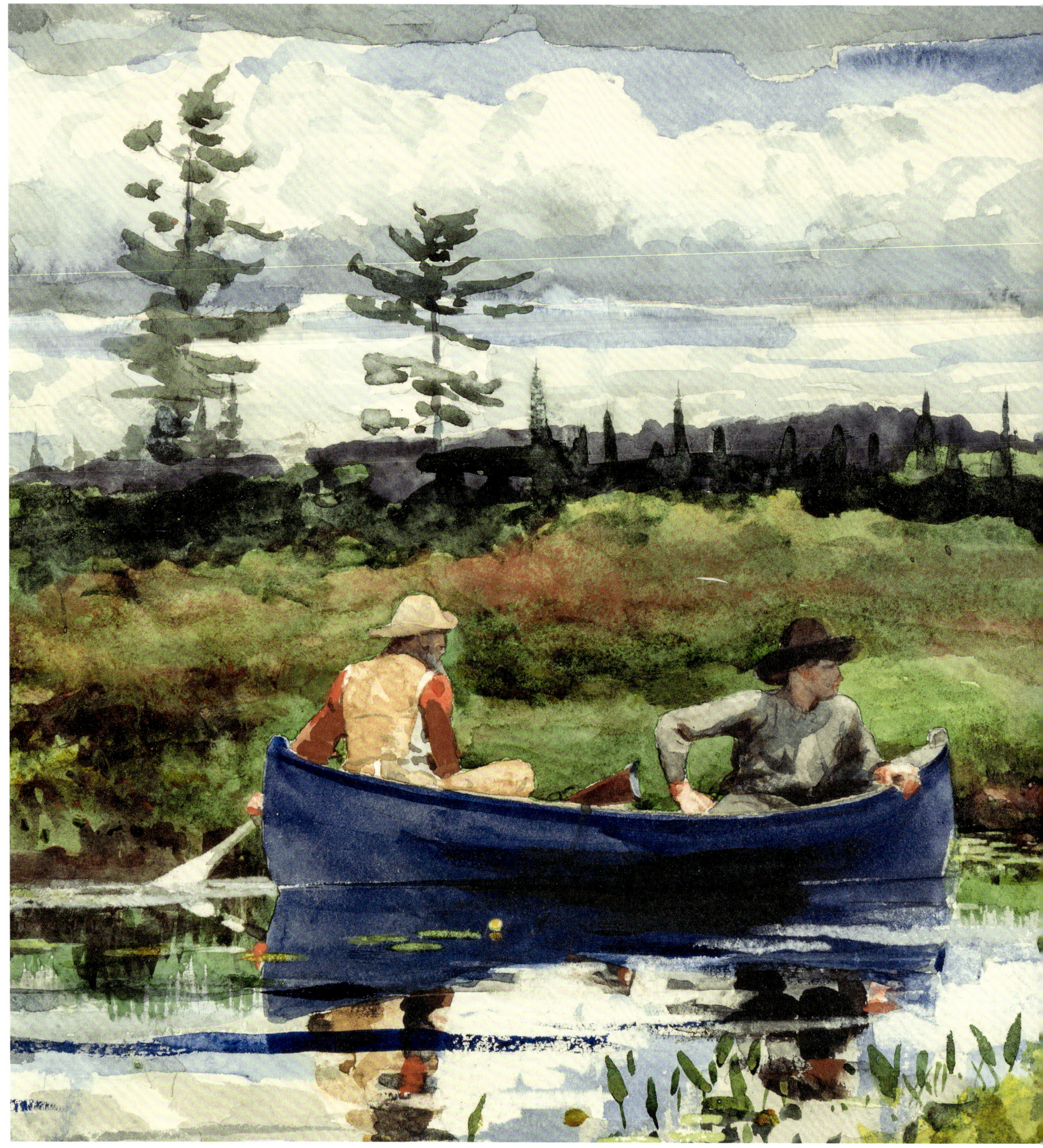

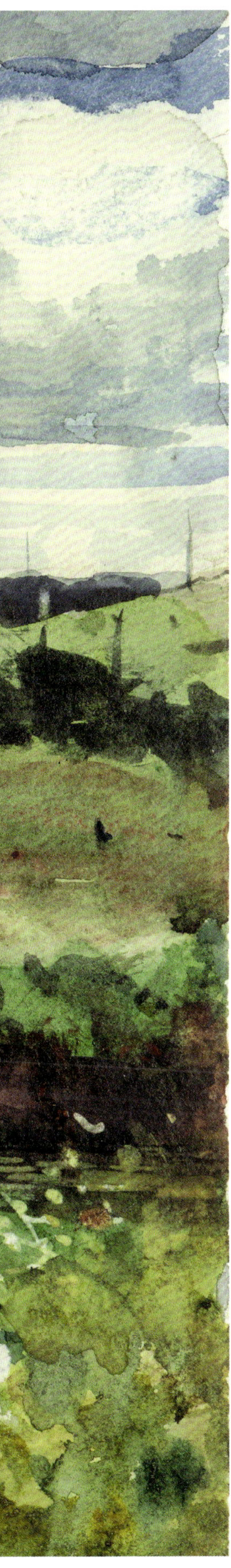

The North Woods

An avid fly fisherman, Winslow Homer first visited the Adirondack Mountains region in the early 1870s. He returned in 1889 as a member of the exclusive North Woods Club and produced some of his most innovative work in watercolor that summer and in years following. Though Homer's fishing scenes usually depict anglers in the act, and often the fish themselves, his hunting scenes instead tend to focus on the lead-up to or the aftermath of the hunt: dogs in the field, men making their way through the wilderness, or a fallen deer.

In *The Blue Boat*, two men — one old, one young — occupy the titular vessel. The pair are venturing out on a hunting trip, as evidenced by the rifle butt resting on the boat's edge between them. Homer often paired an old guide with a younger woodsman, signifying both the passage of life and of generational knowledge about the natural world. Throughout his career, Homer frequently used acquaintances as models but rarely painted portraits, instead evoking types or generalized figures in these scenes. Knowing *The Blue Boat* would have broad and enduring appeal, Homer wrote beneath his signature: "This will do the business." Indeed, *The Blue Boat* and other scenes from the Adirondacks, and later southeastern Canada, would prove to be some of his most popular and salable work. In a similar vein, Homer wrote on the back of *Hunting Dog among Dead Trees*: "This is not bad." Boston collector William Sturgis Bigelow agreed, and acquired *Hunting Dog* and *The Blue Boat*, as well as other Adirondack scenes such as *Hudson River, Woodsman and Fallen Tree*, and the dramatic Maine seascape *Breaking Wave (Prouts Neck)*. Bigelow later gave these watercolors to the Museum, along with his world-class collection of Japanese art.[25]

Though many of Homer's Adirondack scenes suggest a rugged wilderness untouched by industry, some gesture to modern incursions. In *Hudson River*, a man spies two galloping deer from behind a pile of cut logs, an allusion to the emergent logging industry in the region. Tourism to the Adirondacks was increasing at this time as well. Expanding railways and new lodging options made the area more accessible but threatened its vulnerable environments. In the 1890s, Homer sought inspiration (and good fishing) elsewhere and ventured periodically to Quebec. Favoring Lake St. John especially, Homer continued to paint dynamic fishing scenes, albeit with a narrower and more somber palette.

In 1899, the same year that the MFA purchased its first watercolor by Homer (*Leaping Trout*), the Museum purchased three more directly from Homer's Boston gallery Doll & Richards just a few years after they were painted. All three were Canadian scenes. Two were predictably about fishing: *Ouananiche Fishing, Lake St. John, Province of Quebec* and the mysterious grisaille *Trout Fishing, Lake St. John, Quebec*. The third was *Montagnais Indians, Pointe Bleue, Quebec*, depicting the Innu people, known to Homer as the Montagnais. In the foreground, women craft the birchbark canoes used by the fisherman in Homer's other Canadian watercolors. Innu men also served as wilderness guides, appearing in some of Homer's fishing scenes.

Homer exhibited a group of his Canadian watercolors in New York in 1898 to much fanfare. According to one critic, Homer's brushstrokes "all [look] so easy and accidental," belying the skill required to achieve these effervescent effects.[26] The same reviewer described the rabid interest that sportsmen had in these watercolors, lauding both the accuracy and atmosphere of angling that Homer managed to capture on paper.

Manipulation / Used as a glaze or paint additive, gum water and similar materials saturate and deepen color much in the way varnish affects color in oil paintings.[27] By selectively adding gloss, Homer created shadows with complex spatial depth and color nuance in the dense stand of trees and shadowed water at left—a foil to the reclaimed whites. Typically made from gum Arabic, gum water could be purchased or self-made.

In order to capture light breaking through a moisture-laden sky as reflected on the still surface of the lake, Homer scraped and blotted washes of blue watercolor. Areas marked by roughened paper were scraped to clear color and retrieve the pure and tinted whites of the paper. Softer, more diffuse lightening was achieved by blotting wet or rewetted watercolor. — AM

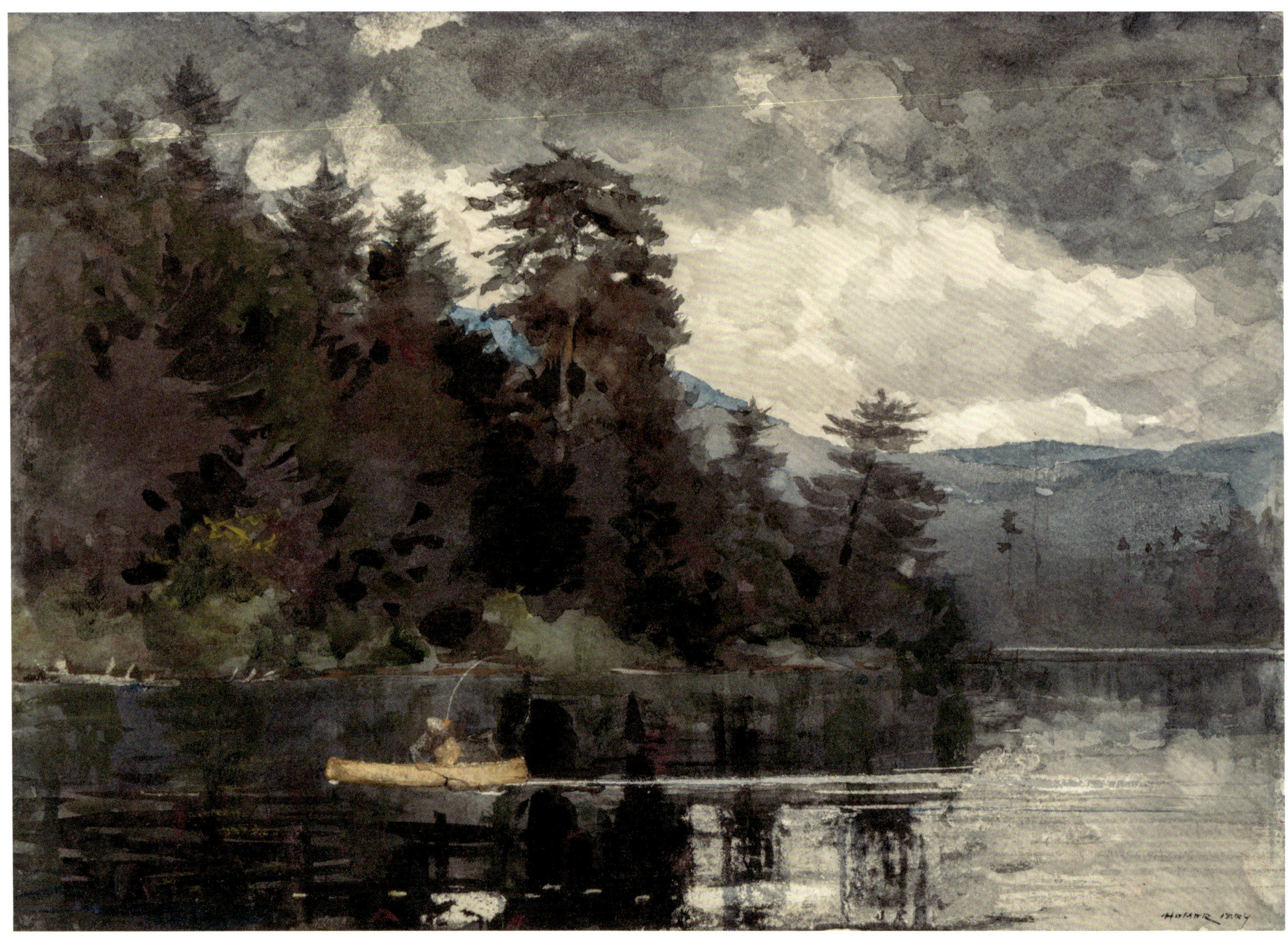

62. *Adirondack Lake*, 1889

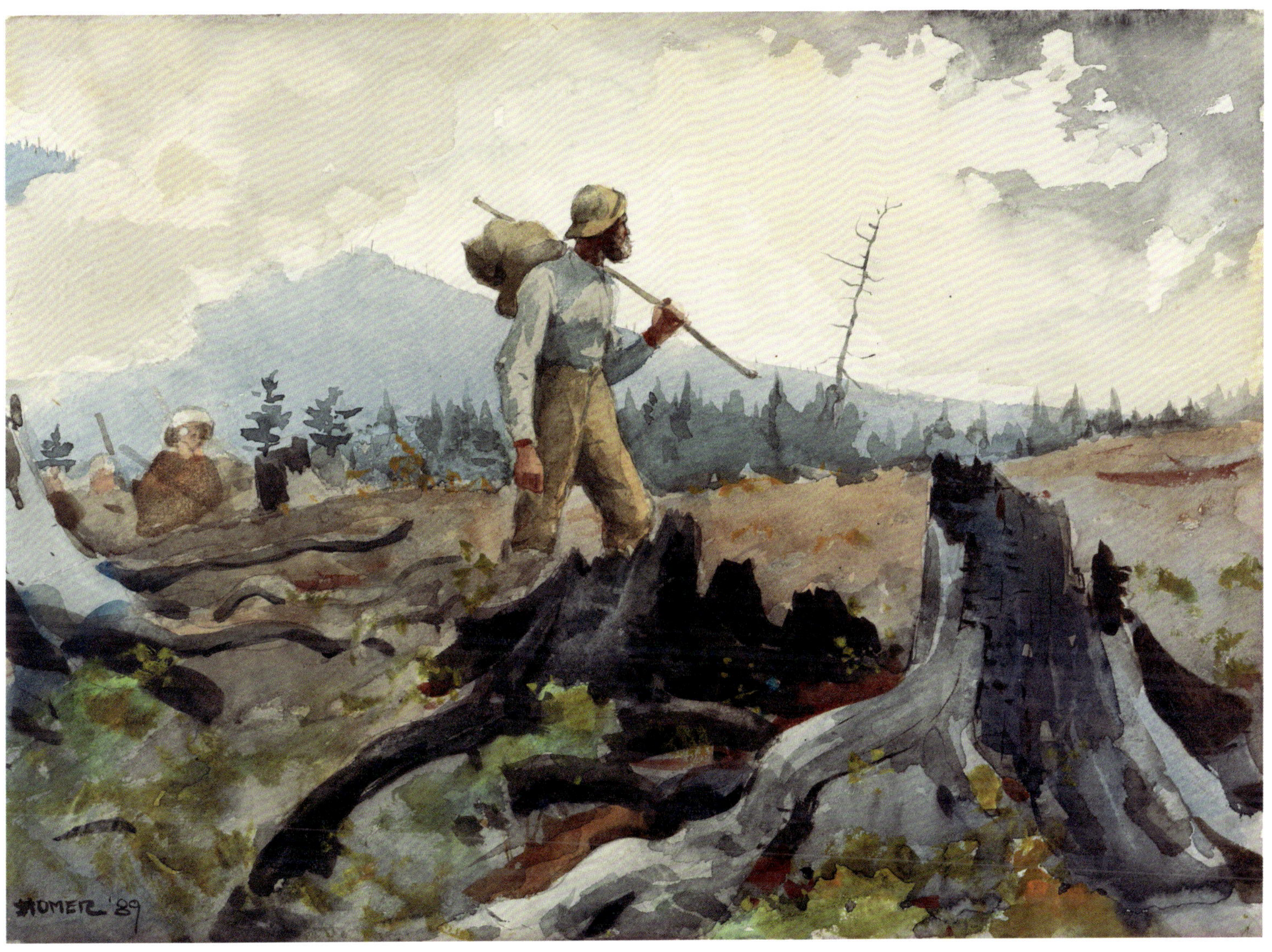

63. *The Guide and Woodsman (Adirondacks)*, 1889

Subject / Homer chronicled his lifelong passion for fishing through his watercolors. His depictions began in childhood and evolved into some of the most extraordinary watercolors in the Museum's collection.

While Homer chose to paint the moment of fish breaking water with some frequency, his approach to the subject changed over time. *Rising to the Fly* and *Trout Breaking* highlight the transition. In *Rising to the Fly*, the earlier watercolor, primal immediacy is front and center. *Trout Breaking* presents a more contemplated and formal study of color, value, and relationships within a space that is both shallow and impenetrably deep.

Although his fishing watercolors are accurate in many respects (multiple flies on a line as seen below), Homer sometimes took license. As noted by Paul Schullery, Homer's leaping fish are typically portrayed "disassociated" from their habitat, unrealistically undripping.[28] —AM

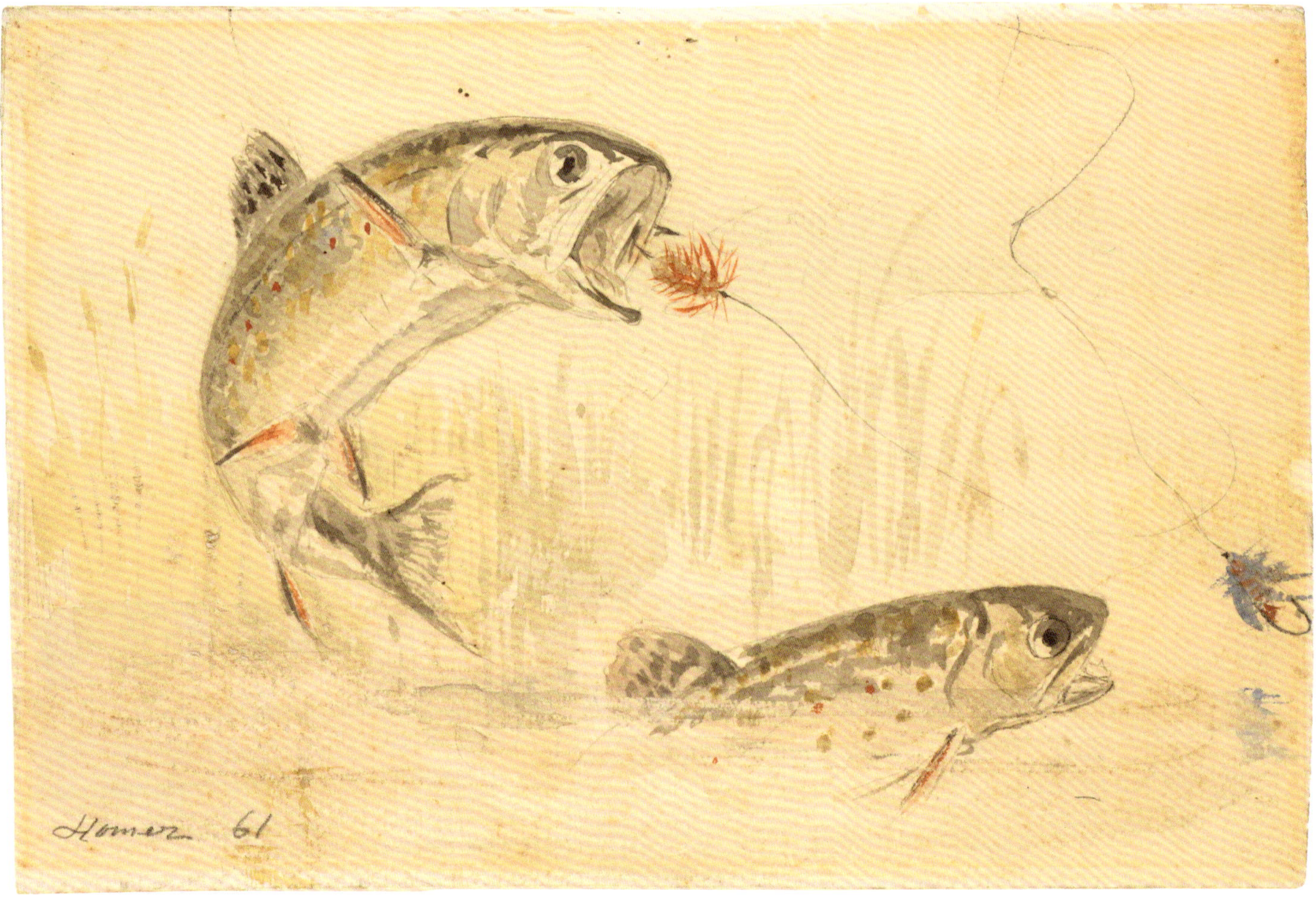

64. *Rising to the Fly*, 1861, RISD Museum

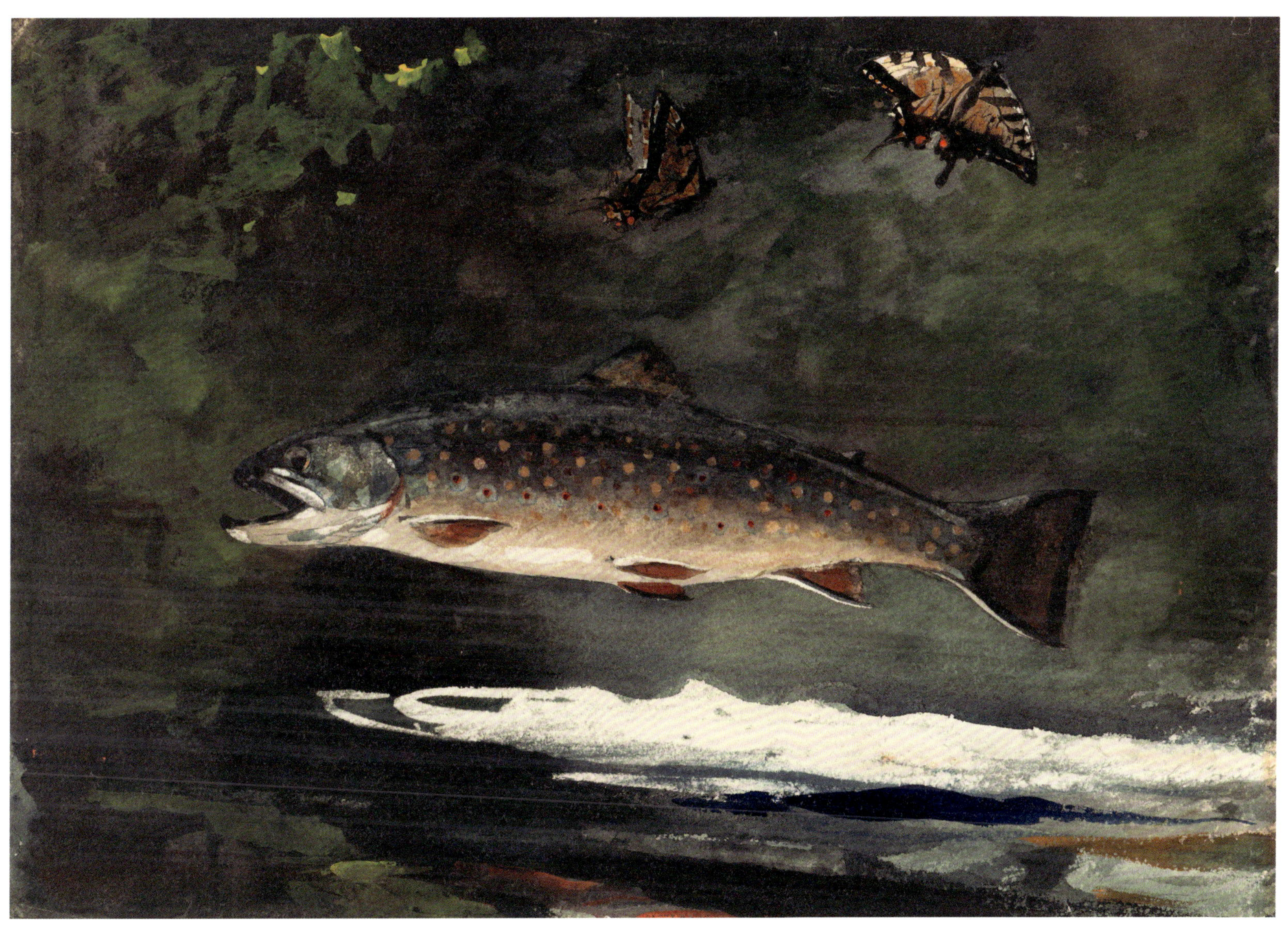

65. *Trout Breaking*, 1889

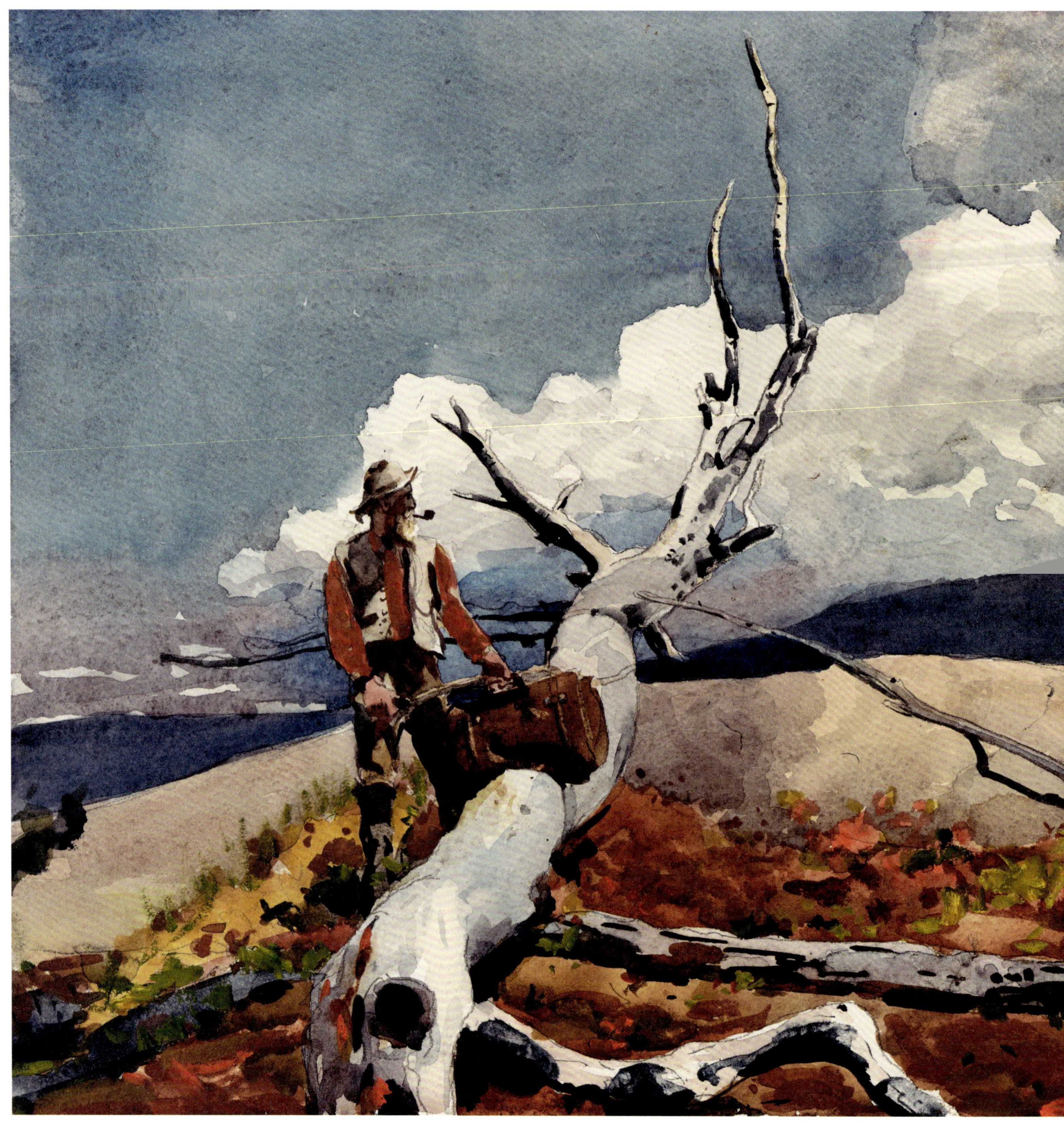

66. *Woodsman and Fallen Tree*, 1891

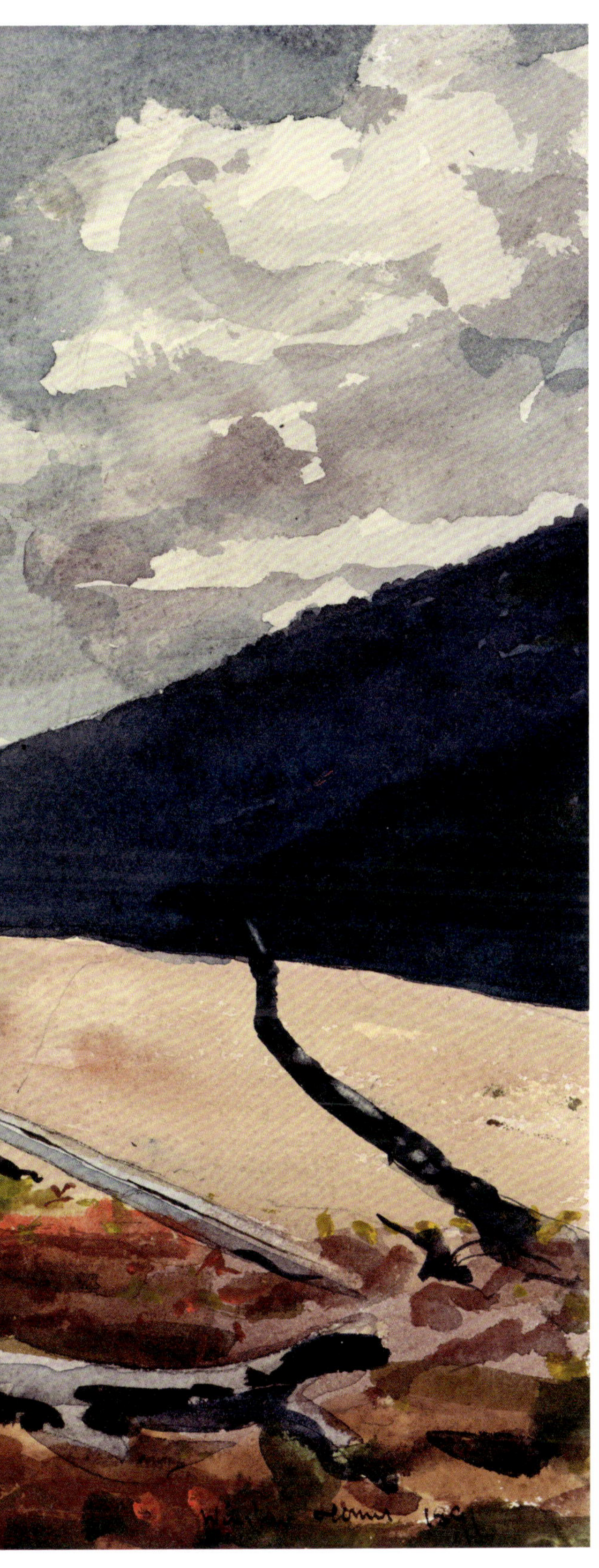

Wet-on-Wet and Dry Brush / Homer's best watercolors set an extraordinary high bar for the medium and give weight to the claim of authors Thomas John Gullick and John Timbs: "Watercolour painting surpasses oil in the purity and clearness of its tones, which arise from the transparency of its medium; it therefore excels in expressing the freshness, vivacity, and brilliancy of nature."[29]

Characterized by feathered edges and/or a diffuse merging of color washes, wet-on-wet technique appears in areas of the sky in this watercolor. When working wet-on-wet, an artist applies a new wash of watercolor to a still wet area. Colors from the two applications move into each other, softening or eliminating distinct boundaries. The technique is not truly controlled but in the right hands offers enormous opportunity to turn "accident" into evocative passage.

To capture different effects of light on water, Homer used a number of techniques, including dry brush, also referred to as dragging.[30] Best carried out on a paper with some texture, dry brush colors only the high points of the paper, creating a skipping effect. Using a lightly loaded brush charged with thicker watercolor, Homer painted several dark blue horizontal lines to establish the water's surface among a myriad of colors and reflections. Paint applied in this way hits only the paper's high points, here, leaving previously laid lighter washes of paint and white paper to flicker through the dark blue.

Located below the boat at center, a single masterful stroke stands apart from the rest. In perfect economy, the blue line conveys three different qualities of light: transitional shade (blotted to lighten at left), deep shadow (left untouched at center) and sparkling reflected sunshine (dry brush dragged across a previously scraped area at right).[31] — AM

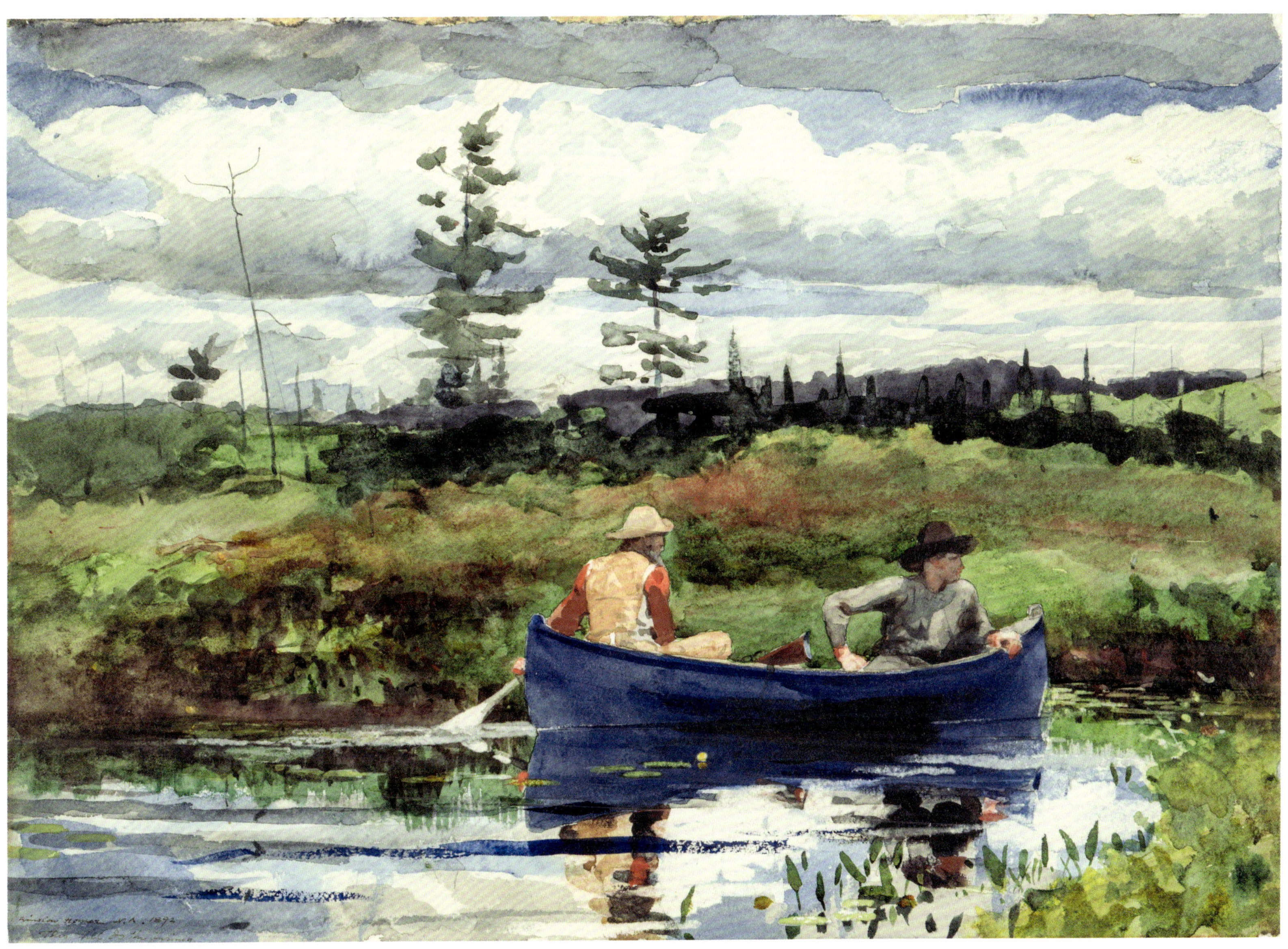

67. *The Blue Boat*, 1892

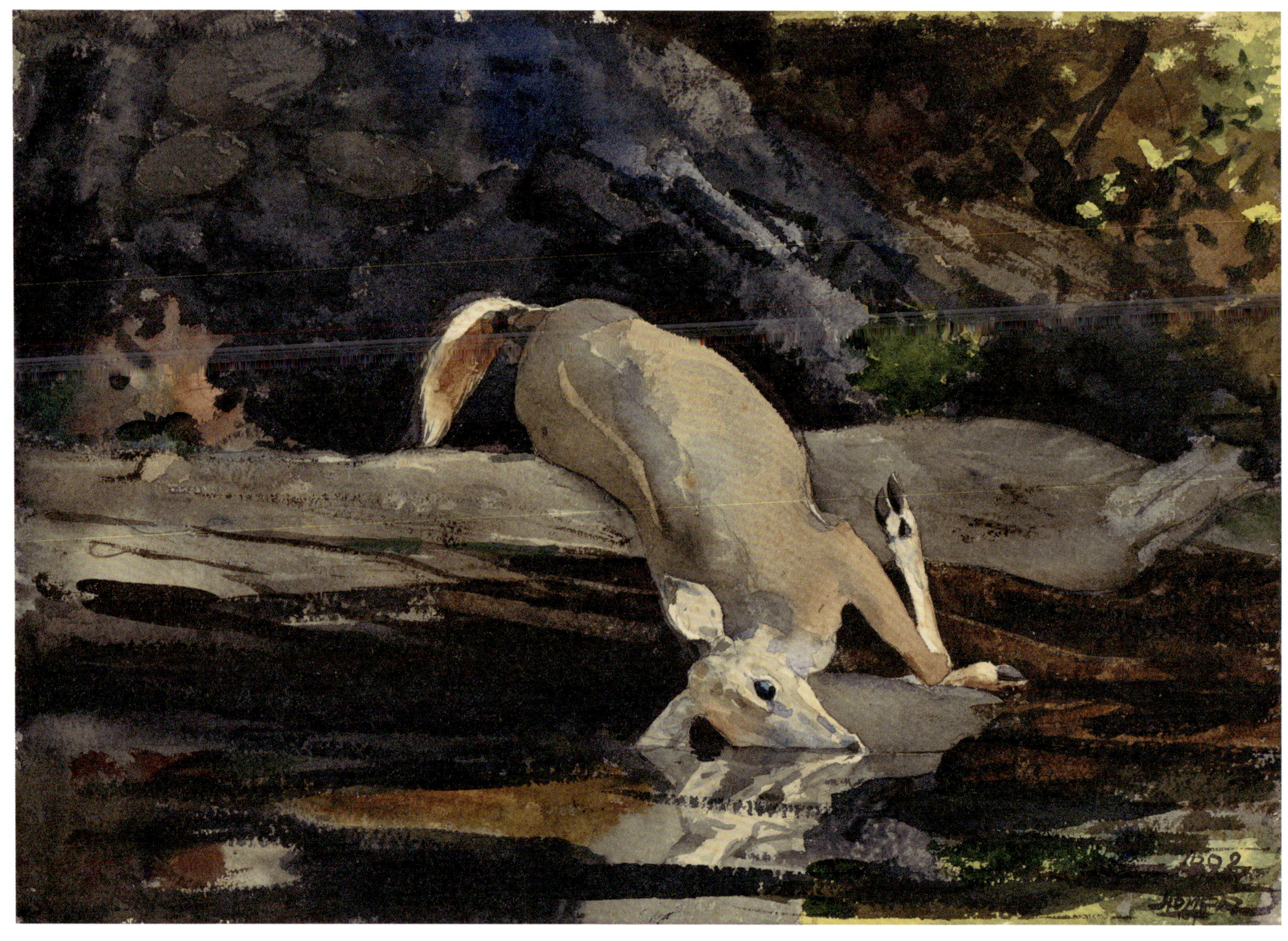

68. *The Fallen Deer*, 1892

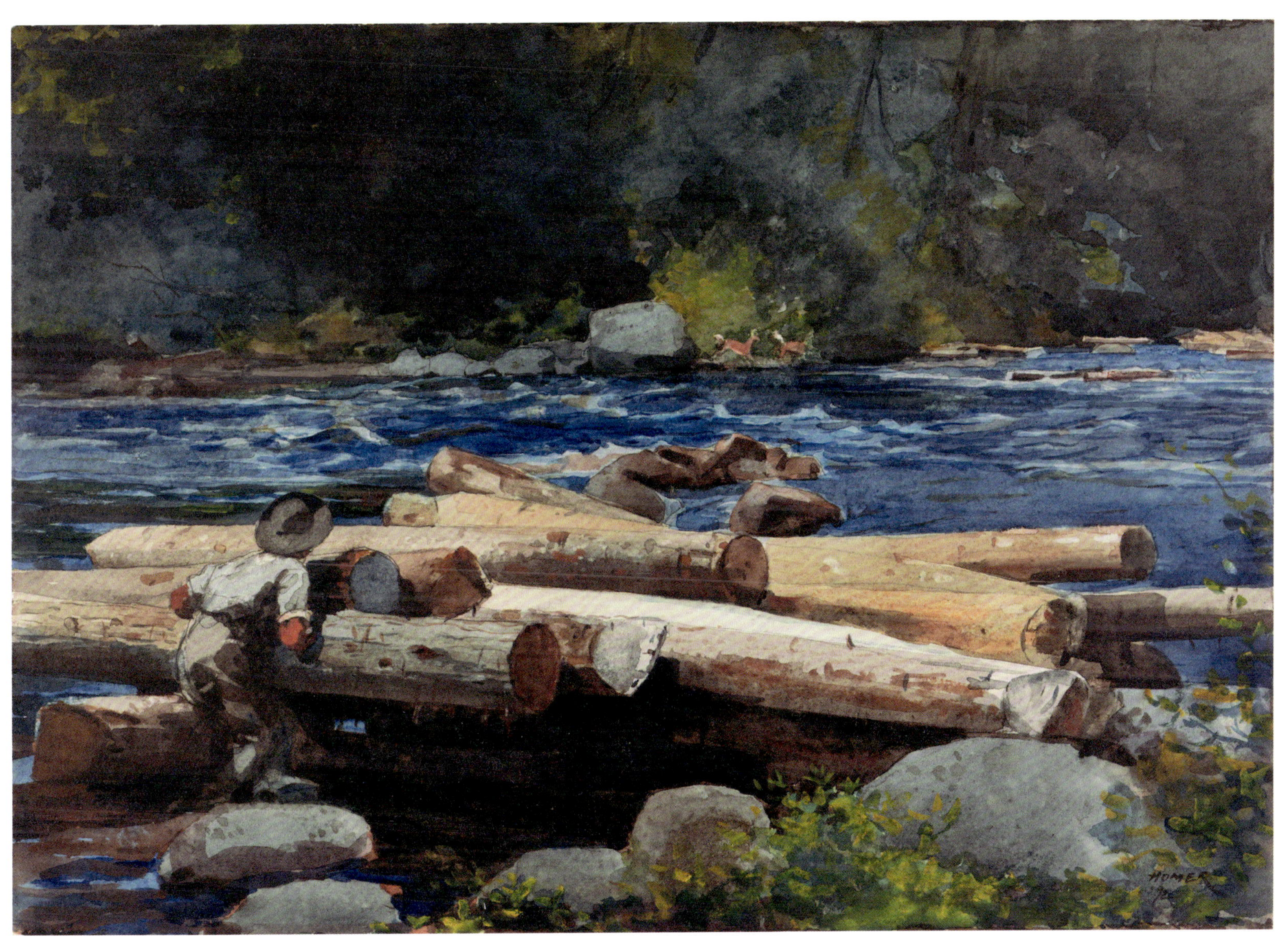

69. *Hudson River*, 1892

Lifting Color / Homer retrieved an extraordinary world of color in this focused view of trout leaping. Simulating deep shadow, Homer cloaked a colorful background with dark washes, sparing the areas reserved for the fish and parts of the water below. Yellows, purples, pinks, greens, and blues emerge by selective removal of the top layer of wet dark paint.

Paper size or sizing, traditionally made from gelatin, makes paper less absorbent. Proper sizing is critical.[32] It allows watercolor to be manipulated, lightened, textured, and nearly completely removed when wet. Lifting can be done with a rag or other absorbent material. Sizing may be added during paper formation or as a final coating or both.

Note the vertical lightening in the detail versus the broader lifting of dark color around the fish at far right. — AM

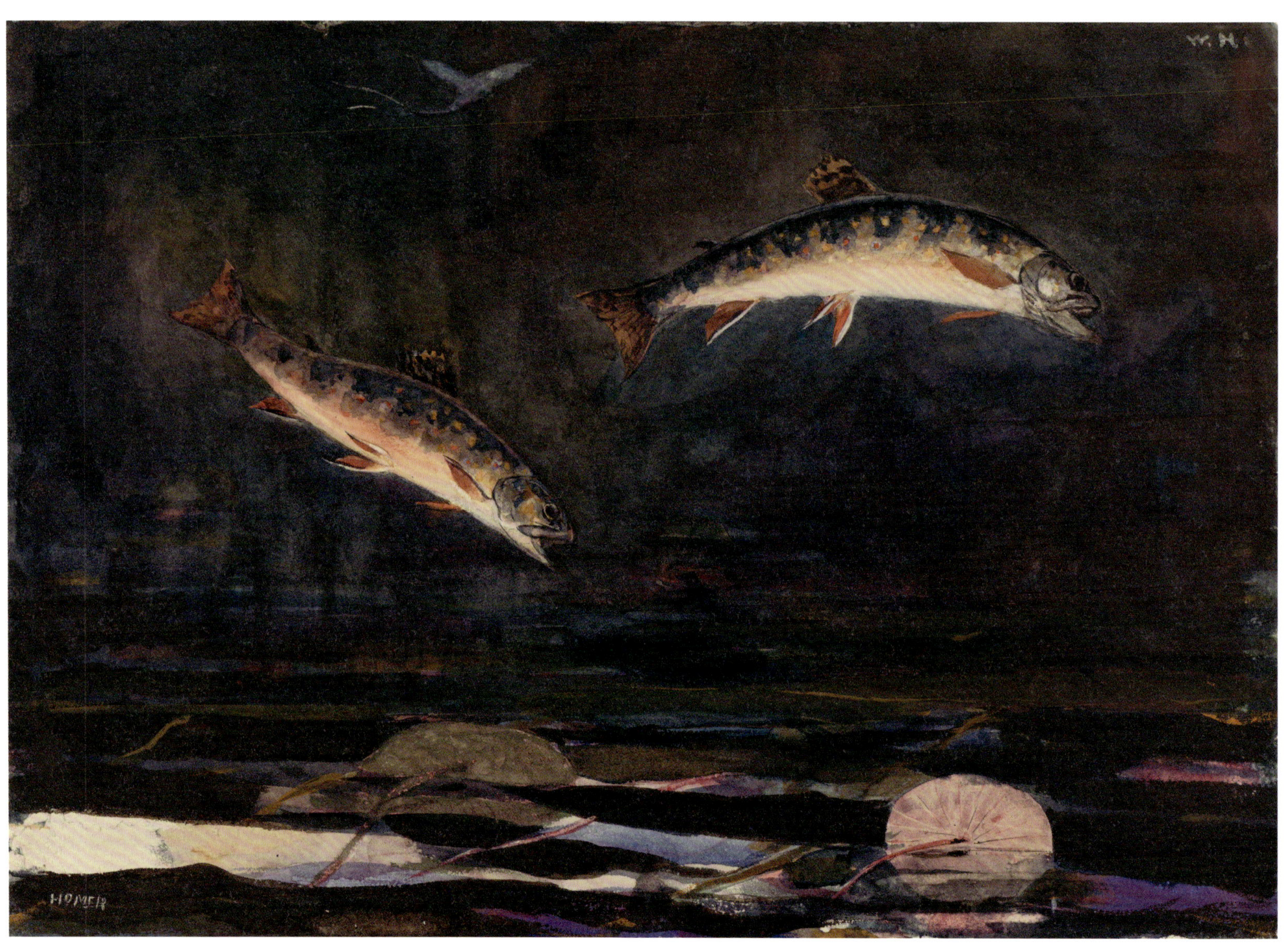

70. *Leaping Trout,* 1892

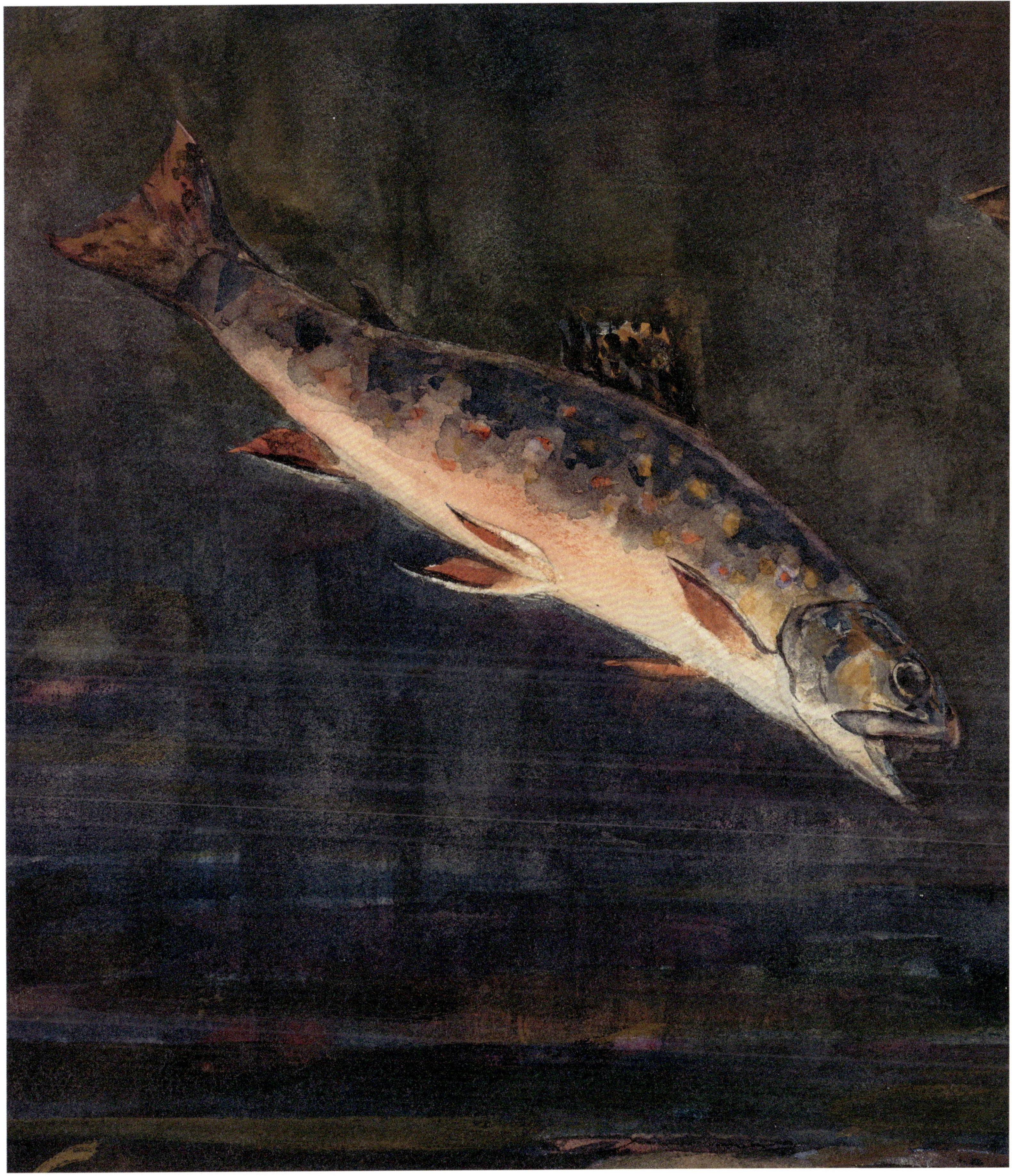

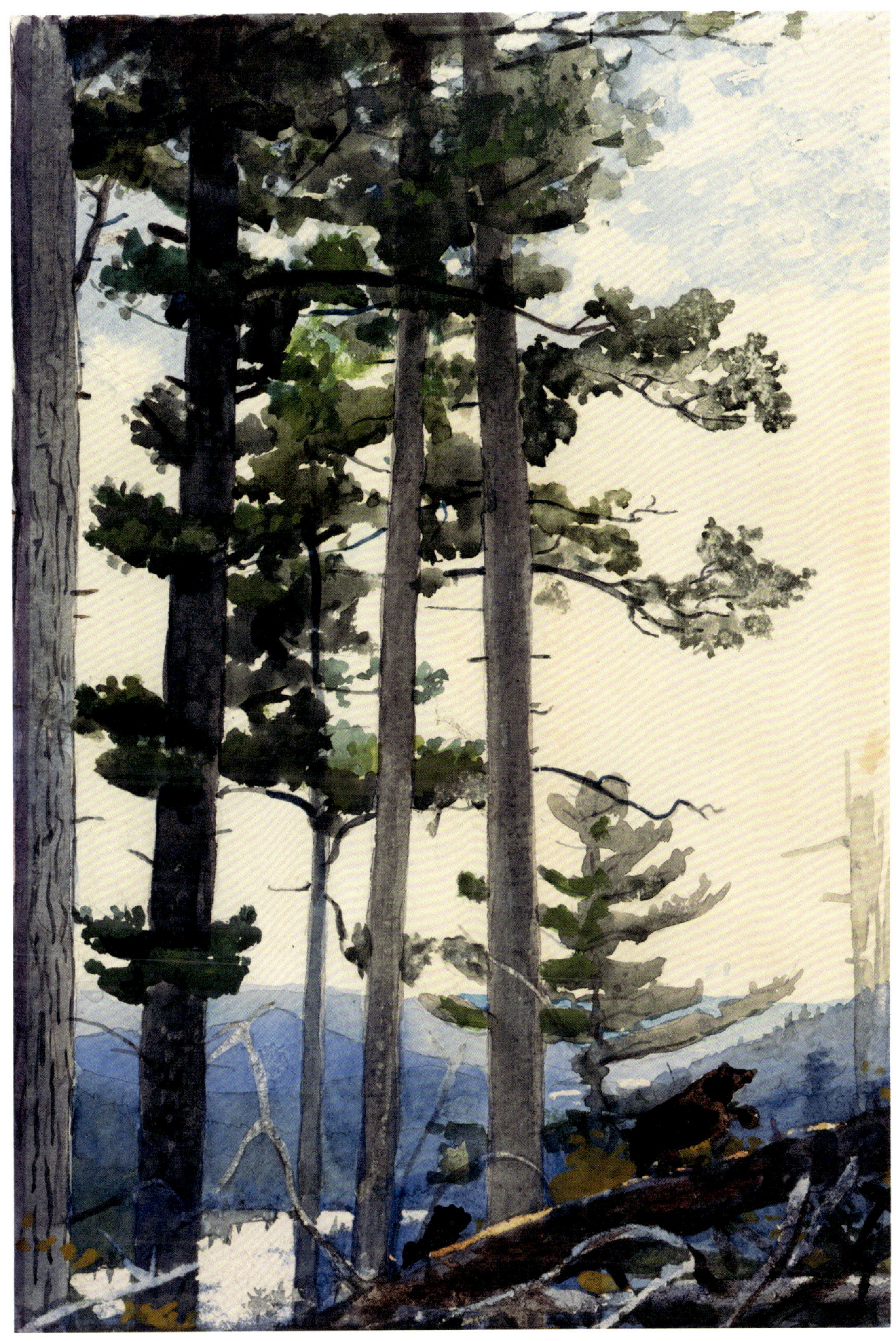

71. *Old Settlers,* 1892

110

Watercolor Block / Artists could purchase watercolor paper as individual sheets, in solid blocks, or in sketchbooks. Because watercolor paper buckles or warps in contact with wet paint, it is typically stretched before use. This involves dampening the paper to expand it and then restraining it as it dries. Restraint can be achieved by gluing the dampened sheet to a drawing board or by putting it in a drawing frame.

A watercolor block, also referred to as a solid block or sketching block, offers artists the convenience of a stack of pre-stretched paper ready for painting. In the nineteenth century, the stack was held together at its edges with glue and gauze. A finished watercolor was and still is separated from a block by inserting a knife below the top sheet and working around the glued edges. A blocked sketchbook had the same construction as the watercolor block except one edge was stitched instead of glued. The stitched edge maintained a book format as top sheets were released from the stack.

Clues to paper block source include sheet dimensions that correspond to advertised block sizes, residual glue, and/or paper remnants from adjacent sheets at paper edges, as well as possible indication of knife insertion. Among the best evidence is a strand of gauze fiber embedded in glue at an edge. It is not always possible to determine watercolor block origin as artists sometimes trimmed sheets, in effect removing physical evidence linking the watercolor to a block source.

This watercolor has traces of glue at its edges and remnants of gauze fiber, indicating it came from a watercolor block. — A M

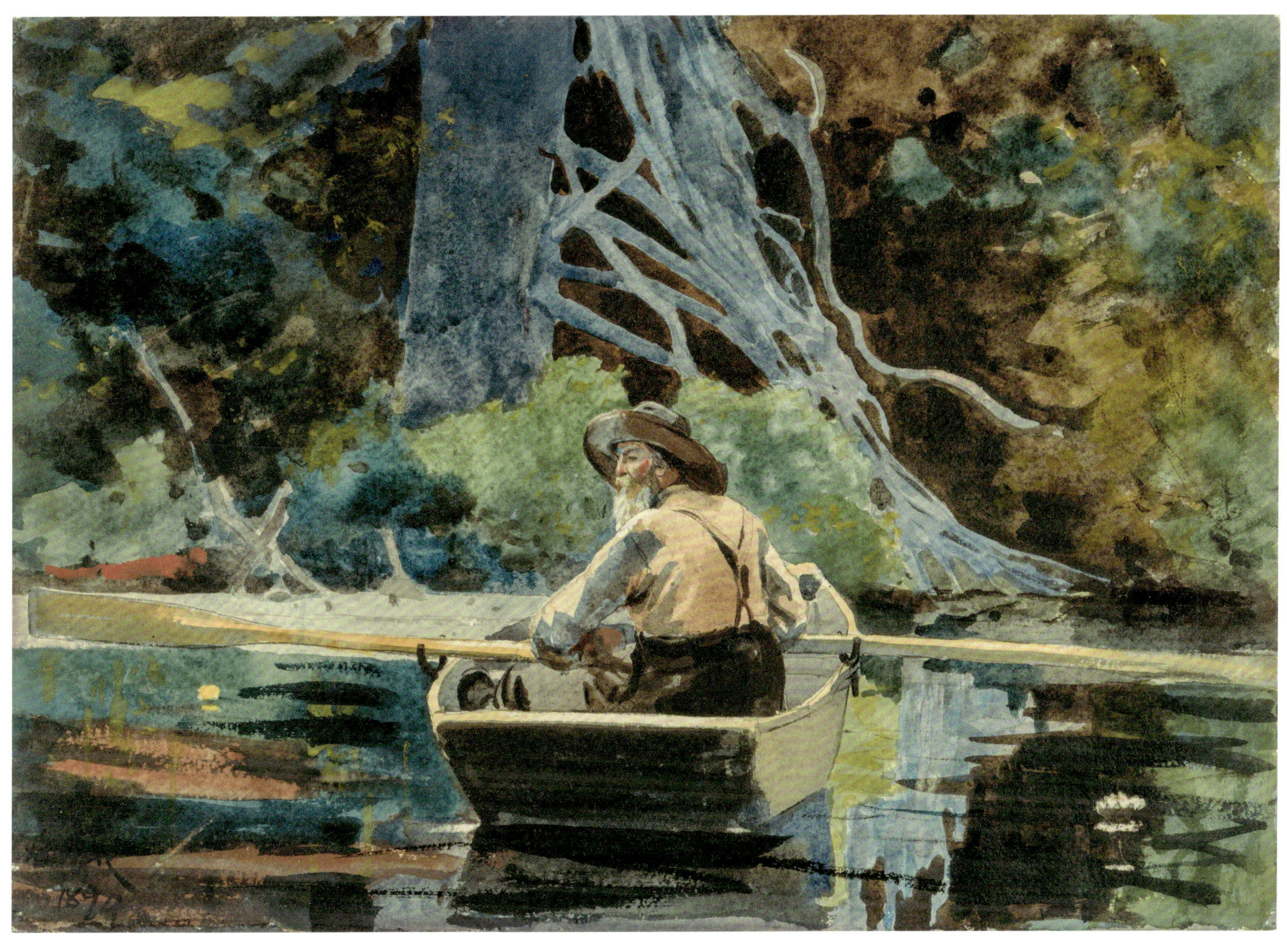

72. *The Adirondack Guide,* 1894

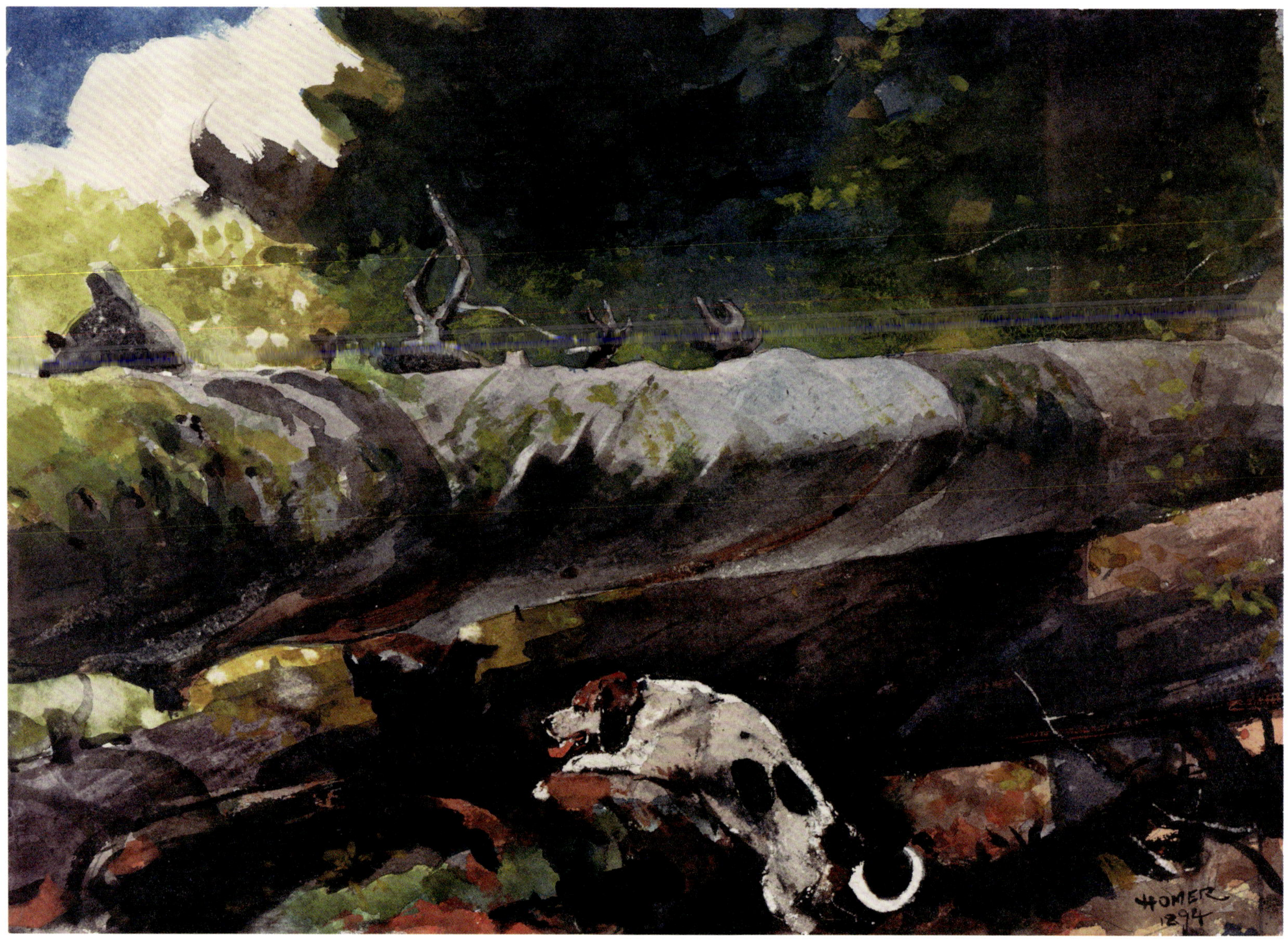

73. *Hunting Dog among Dead Trees*, 1894

Texture / Homer removed watercolor with a sharp tool to return to the white of the paper in fashioning the spotted white hunting dog. The coarseness of Homer's cuts resulted in lifted and rolled paper, left either to stand unpainted or to hold watercolor in shallow relief. The roughened paper convincingly suggests fur and lends a sense of volume, animation, and realism to the scene. As Homer himself concluded in an inscription on the back of the watercolor, "This is not bad." —AM

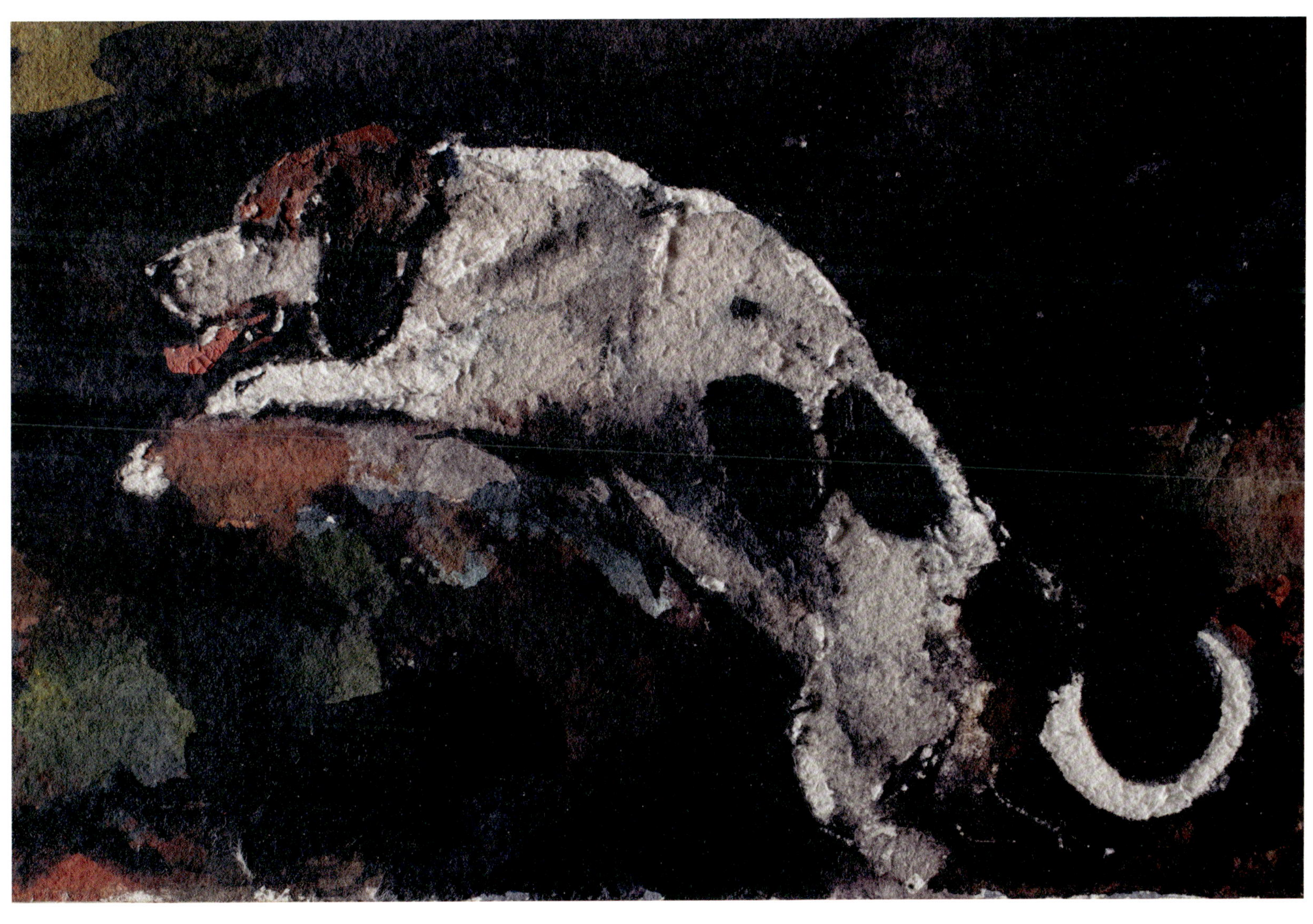

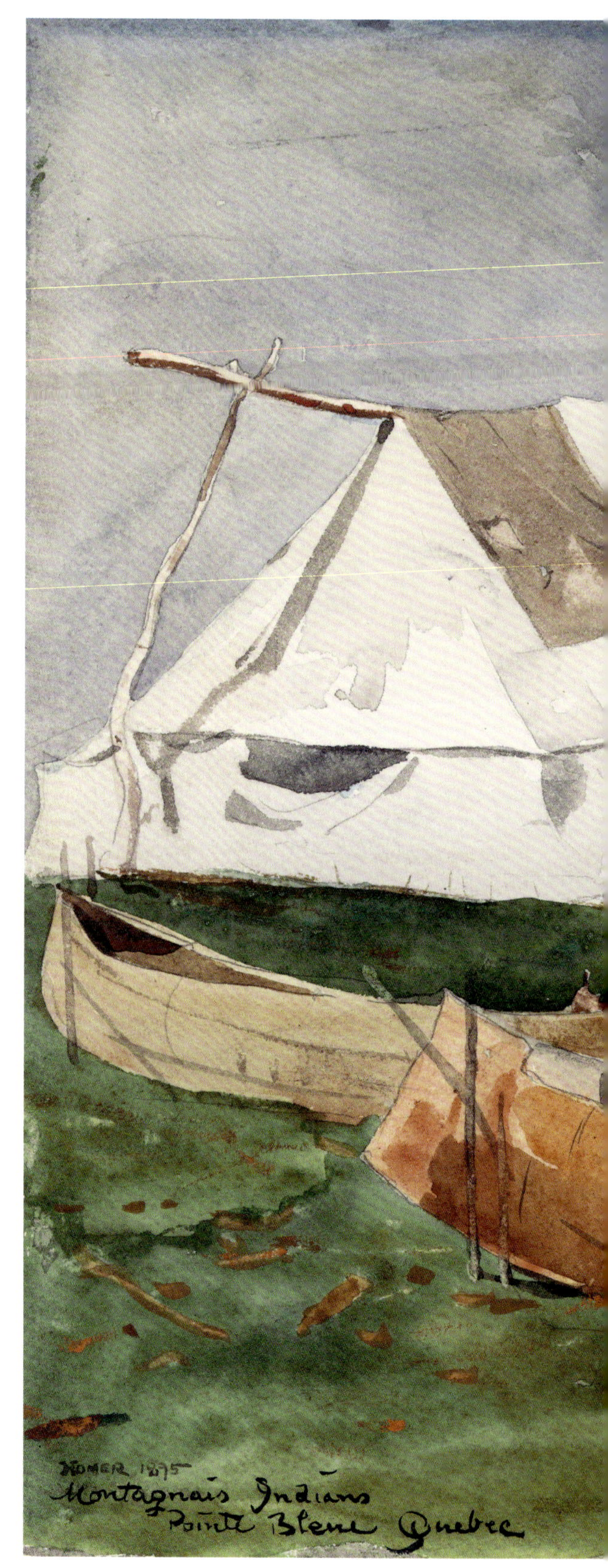
Homer 1895
Montagnais Indians
Pointe Bleue Quebec

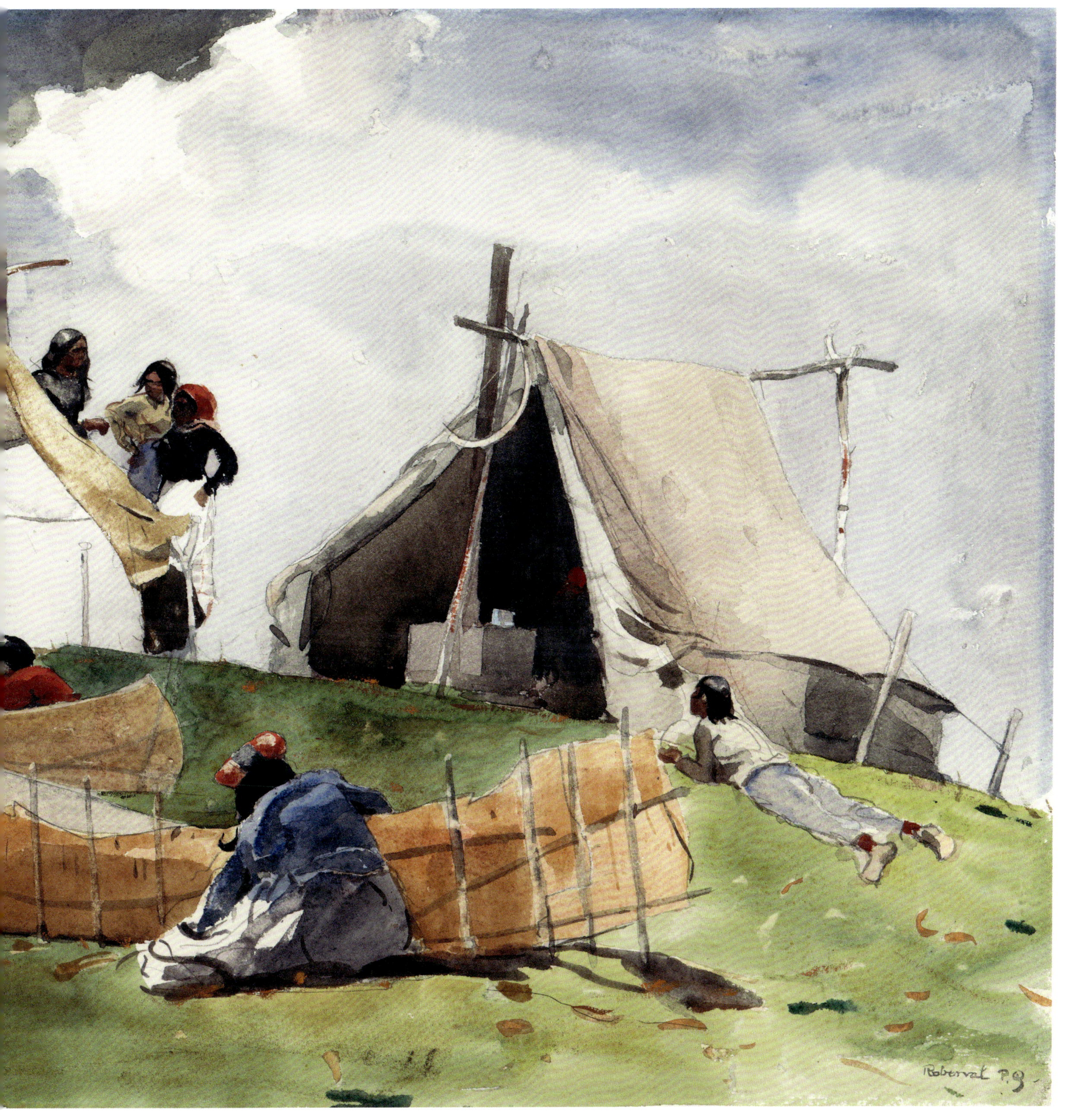

74. *Montagnais Indians, Pointe Bleue, Quebec,* 1895

Trimming and Cropping / Homer sometimes changed the dimensions of his watercolors by trimming or cropping; however, it is unusual for a trimmed piece to survive. The strip at the bottom left belongs to the Cooper Hewitt, Smithsonian Design Museum and is a visual fit for *Trout Fishing, Lake St. John, Quebec*.[33] The fragment is part of a large collection given to the Cooper Hewitt by Homer's brother Charles Savage Homer, Jr.

Although sparingly used, white stands out in this quiet but dramatic scene. Homer typically used Zinc White, but surprisingly did not use it here. Lacking Zinc White's characteristic response to ultraviolet energy, the white was analyzed using x-ray fluorescence (XRF) spectroscopy, which confirmed an absence of zinc and the presence of barium, a component of Constant White.[34] — AM

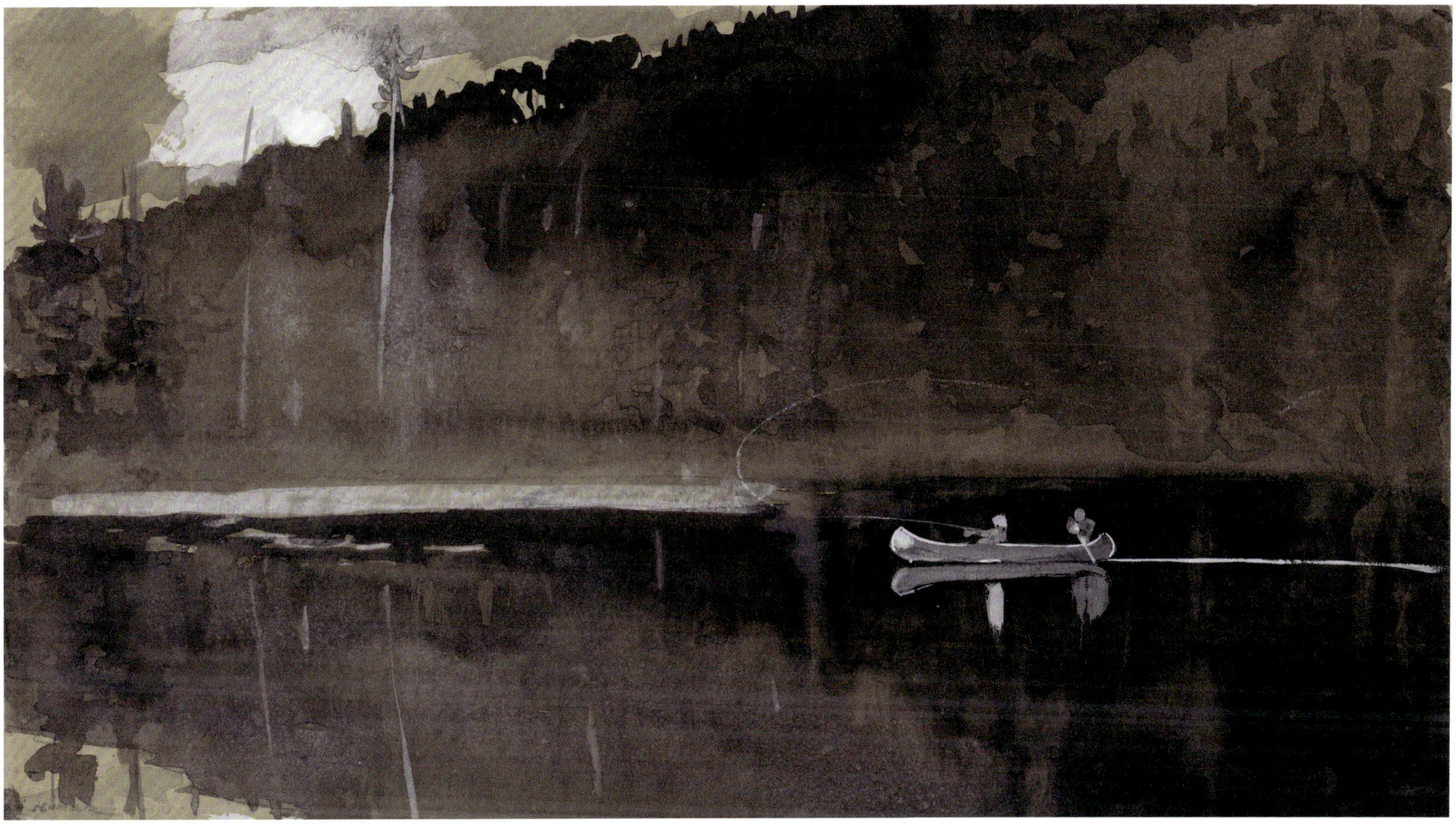

75. *Trout Fishing, Lake St. John, Quebec*, 1895

76. Fragment of *Trout Fishing, Lake St. John, Quebec*, 1895, Cooper Hewitt, Smithsonian Design Museum

M. H. – 1897
Lake S. John

Granulation / Homer favored papers with some texture for his watercolors. Textured papers provide a surface of high and low points, which can be exploited to achieve different effects. A fully charged brush fills both the highs and lows with colored wash. Some pigments disperse evenly, while others settle in the low points of the paper, resulting in variation within the color, or granulation.

Artists can encourage accumulation of pigment in paper hollows by working dry pigment into the paper before painting, adding pigment to the paint or modifying the watercolor with glycerin or a similar material. Such modifiers slow drying and allow aggregation of suspended pigment particles before a wash settles. A softer more subtle variant of the effect can be achieved by lightly blotting watercolor before it dries, lifting color mainly from the high points of the paper.

Some washes appear even naturally. Paints that do not may be improved by adding a wetting agent such as ox gall. Note the uniformity of the pale blue wash in the detail at left, contrasted with the gritty nature of adjacent colors. —AM

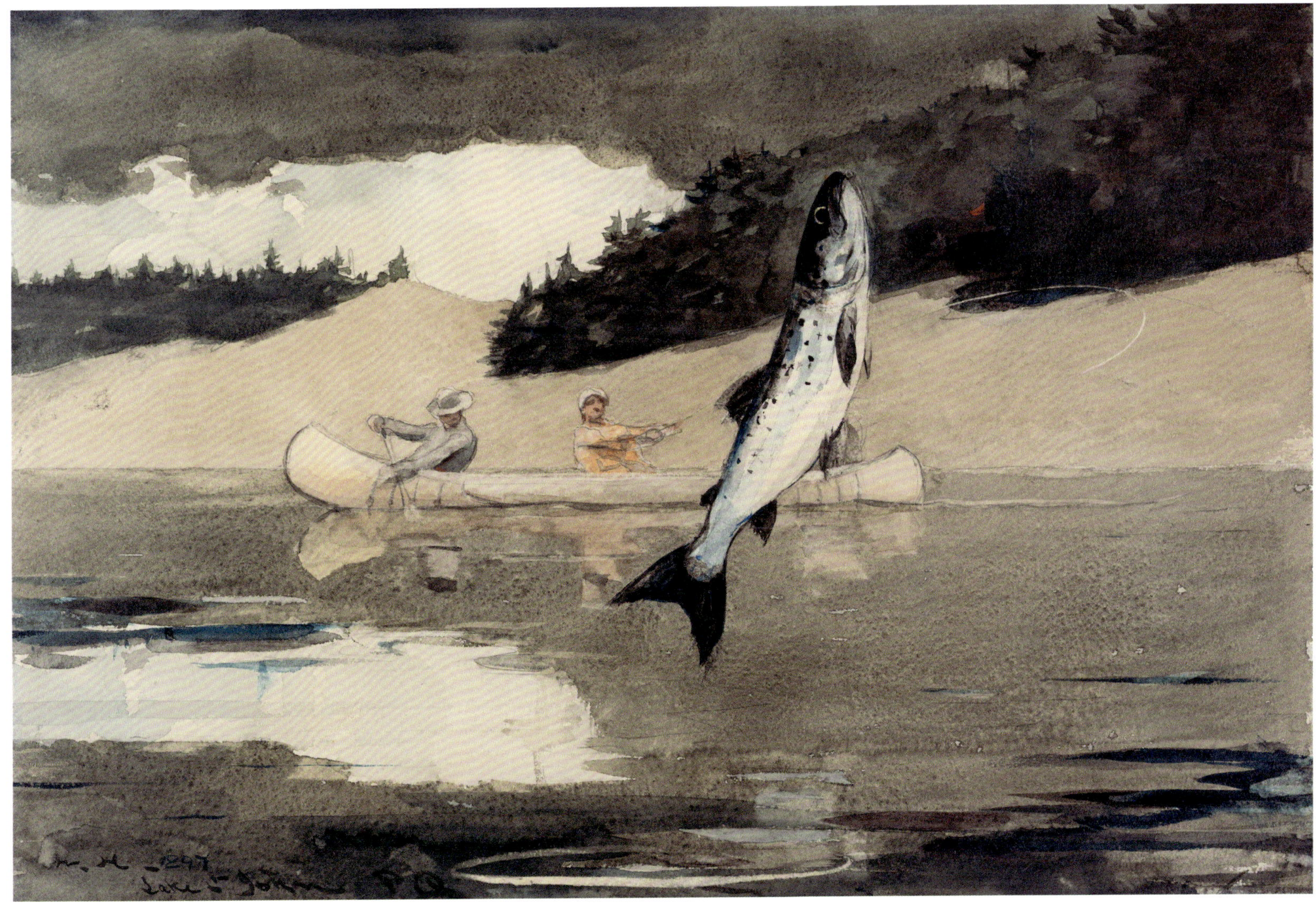

77. Ouananiche Fishing, Lake St. John, Province of Quebec, 1897

Composition / Homer targeted his watercolors of fishing primarily to those who shared his love of this pursuit. Informed anglers of his day appreciated his insider's knowledge and ability to convey sensation and setting without sentiment.

Often only suggestively described in his watercolors, the positions of angler, rod, line, and fly carry distinct narratives that may be lost to all but avid practitioners.[35] Here, the rod appears as a blotted or lightened line that extends back from the angler's hand. The rod transitions to fishing line represented by a black (graphite) arc visible in the sky before changing yet again to a narrow white line cutting downward through the gray hill before disappearing on nearing the water. The line reappears in graphite near the fish at the lower right.

In the detail, note Homer's rejection of the earlier placement of a fish in favor of the final painted pair. — AM

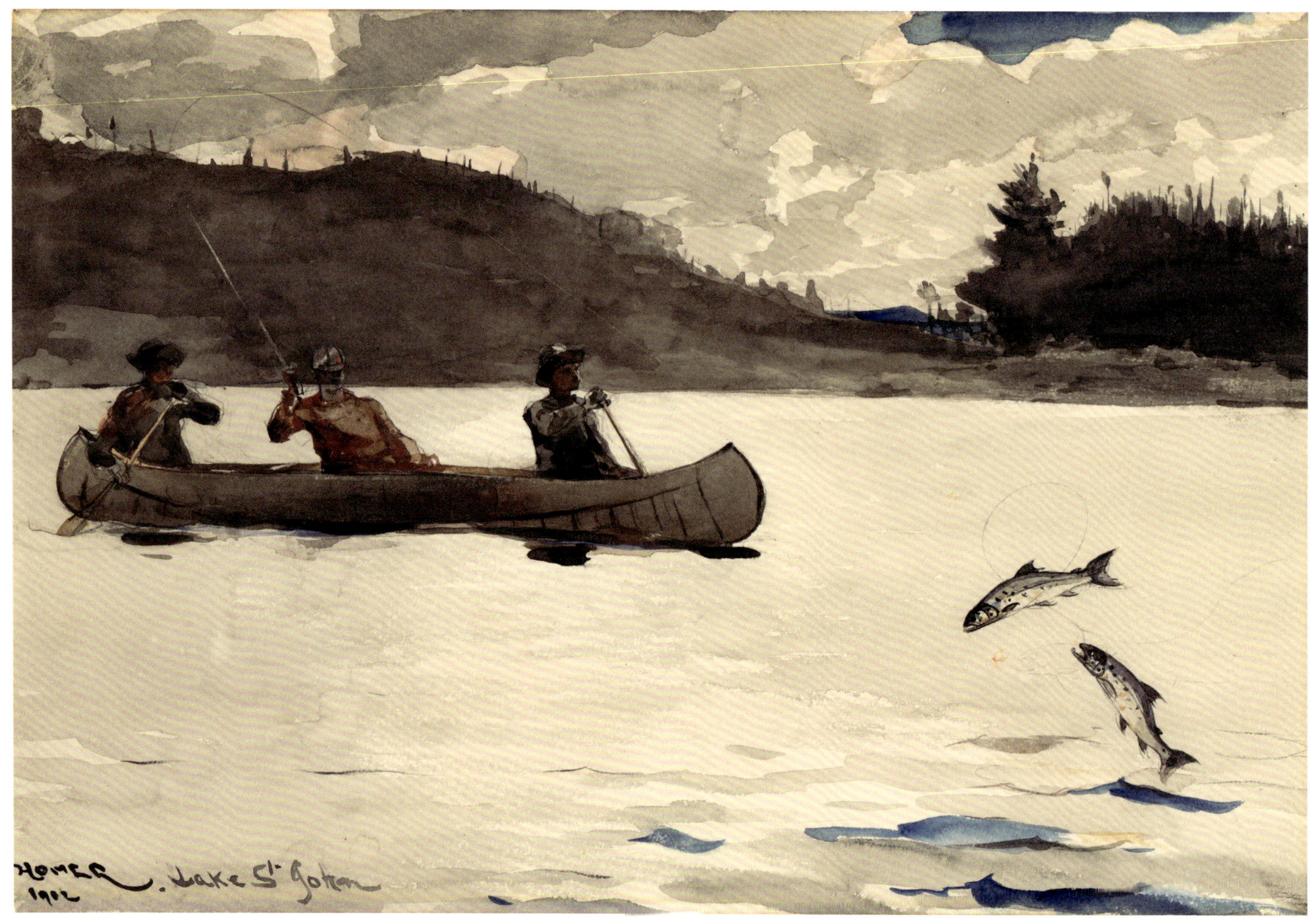

78. *Fishing for Ouananiche, Lake St. John, P.Q. Canada, no. 2,* 1902

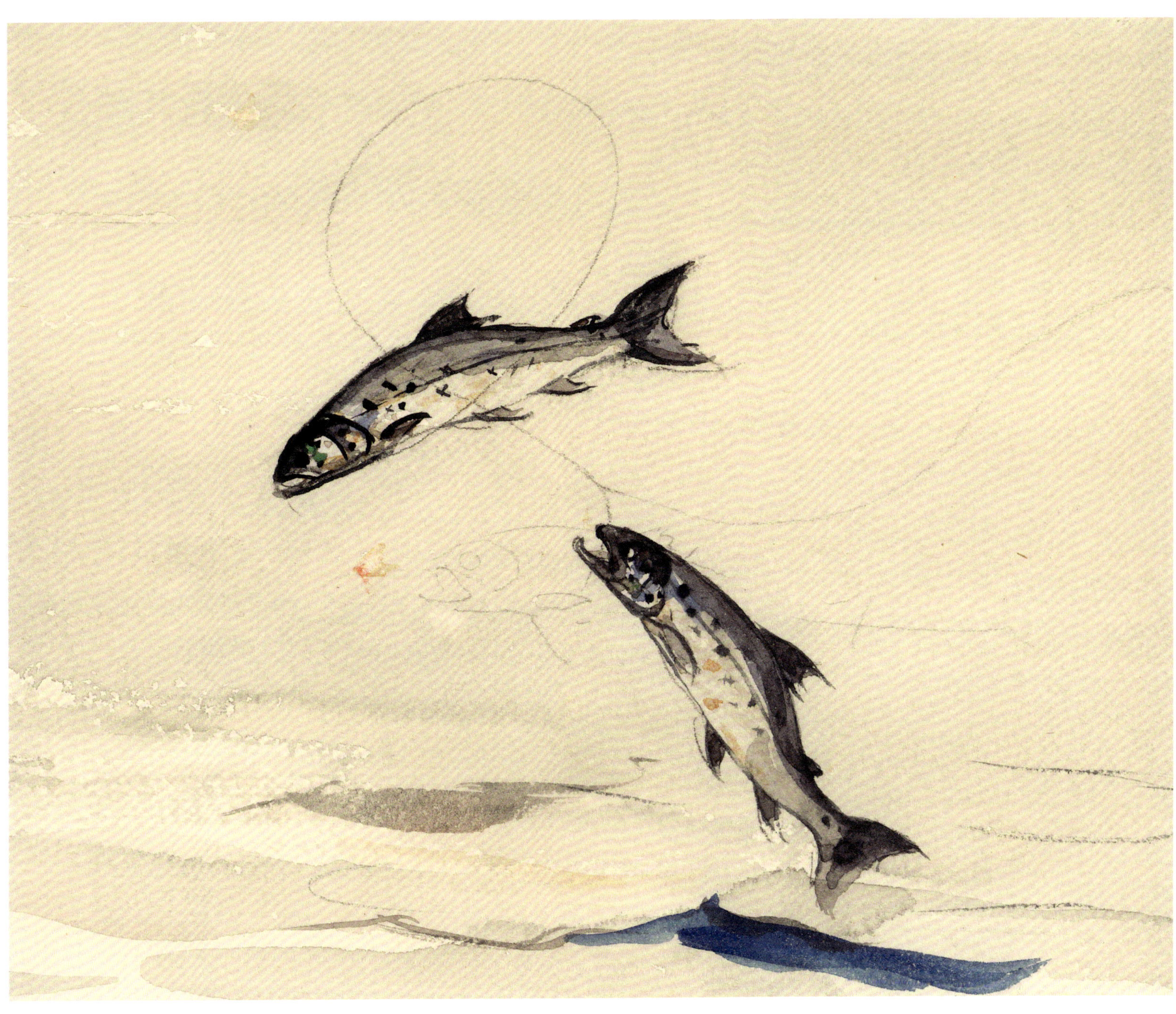

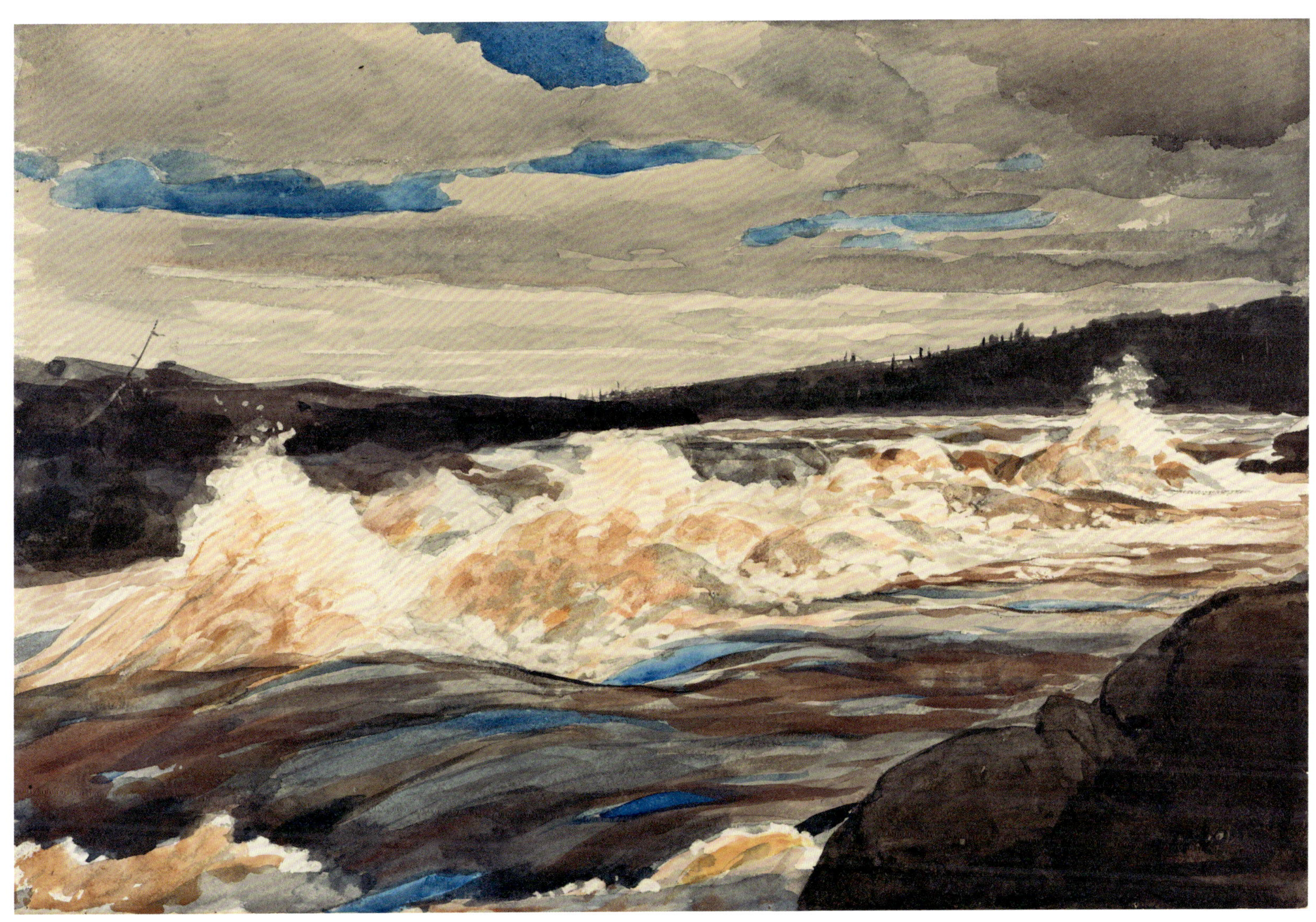

79. *Grand Discharge, Lake St. John, Province of Quebec*, about 1902

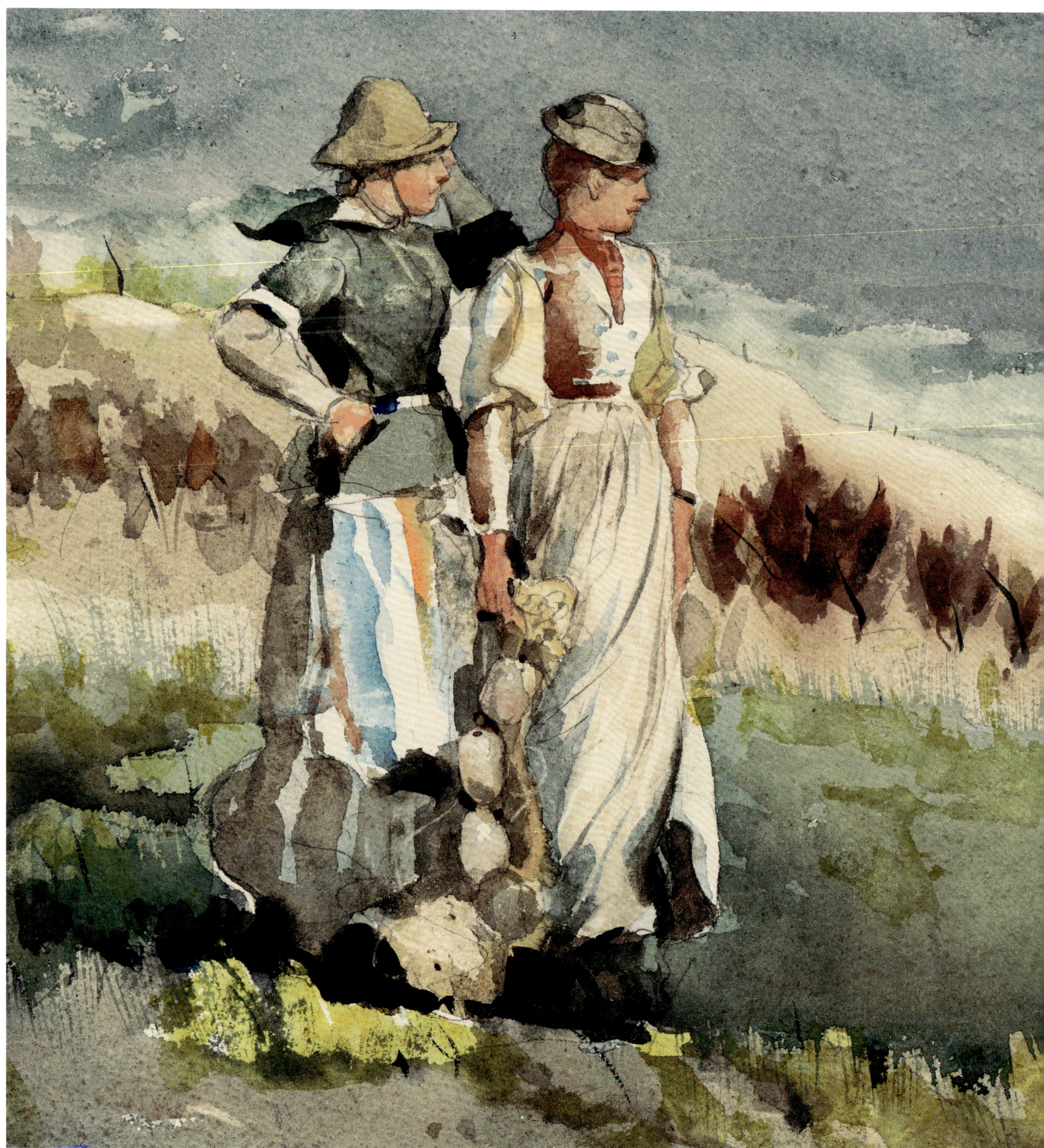

Prouts Neck, Maine

The peninsula of Prouts Neck, Maine, just south of Portland and overlooking Saco Bay, became home not just for Winslow Homer but for his whole family in the mid-1880s. Unfortunately, Homer's mother, Henrietta, who was born in central Maine, passed shortly before they established their coastal compound. The family had summered in Prouts Neck years earlier and saw an opportunity to develop the area.[36] Homer's older brother Charles built a large family home there in 1883, and the following year he converted the carriage house into a studio and living space for Winslow, which became his primary residence between his trips to Boston, New York, and warmer locales.

Homer's Prouts Neck watercolors here span nearly a decade and represent a continuation of themes explored in his earlier work on north Atlantic shorelines, as in Gloucester, Massachusetts, and Cullercoats, England. The labor of fishing, rather than the leisure of his North Woods watercolors, remained the focus of his Prouts Neck pictures in the mid-1880s. *The Dory*, a moody scene of two fishermen hauling in a net from the open ocean, recalls his Gloucester watercolor *Two Boys Rowing* from seven years earlier, with ominous clouds occupying the upper left portion of the sky and a murky green shadow cast on the churning waves by a rocking boat.

A later Maine watercolor, *The Dunes*, recalls his pictures of women on the shores of Cullercoats, gazing out to sea, such as *A Fresh Breeze*. Here, Homer traded the Englishwomen's tartan wraps for smart hats and a desolate marine horizon for the bustling resorts of Old Orchard Beach, just south of Prouts Neck on Saco Bay. Homer suggested a sunny summer's day by using vibrant pigments to articulate the flora of the dunes and paper reserve to create bright white highlights on the women's dresses.

Homer worked in his seaside Prouts Neck studio for over twenty-five years, tirelessly observing the elements and the comings and goings on the water. At one point, Homer wrote "turn, turn, tumble… tumble, tumble, turn…" on the walls of his house, articulating the motion of rolling waves, a phenomenon he frequently strove to capture. In *Breaking Wave (Prouts Neck)*, Homer rendered the swell and spray of the sea against rocks in layers of blue and green, manipulated through blotting to create greater dimensionality. Homer later incorporated a similar crashing wave in his final oil painting, *Driftwood* (see fig. 4).

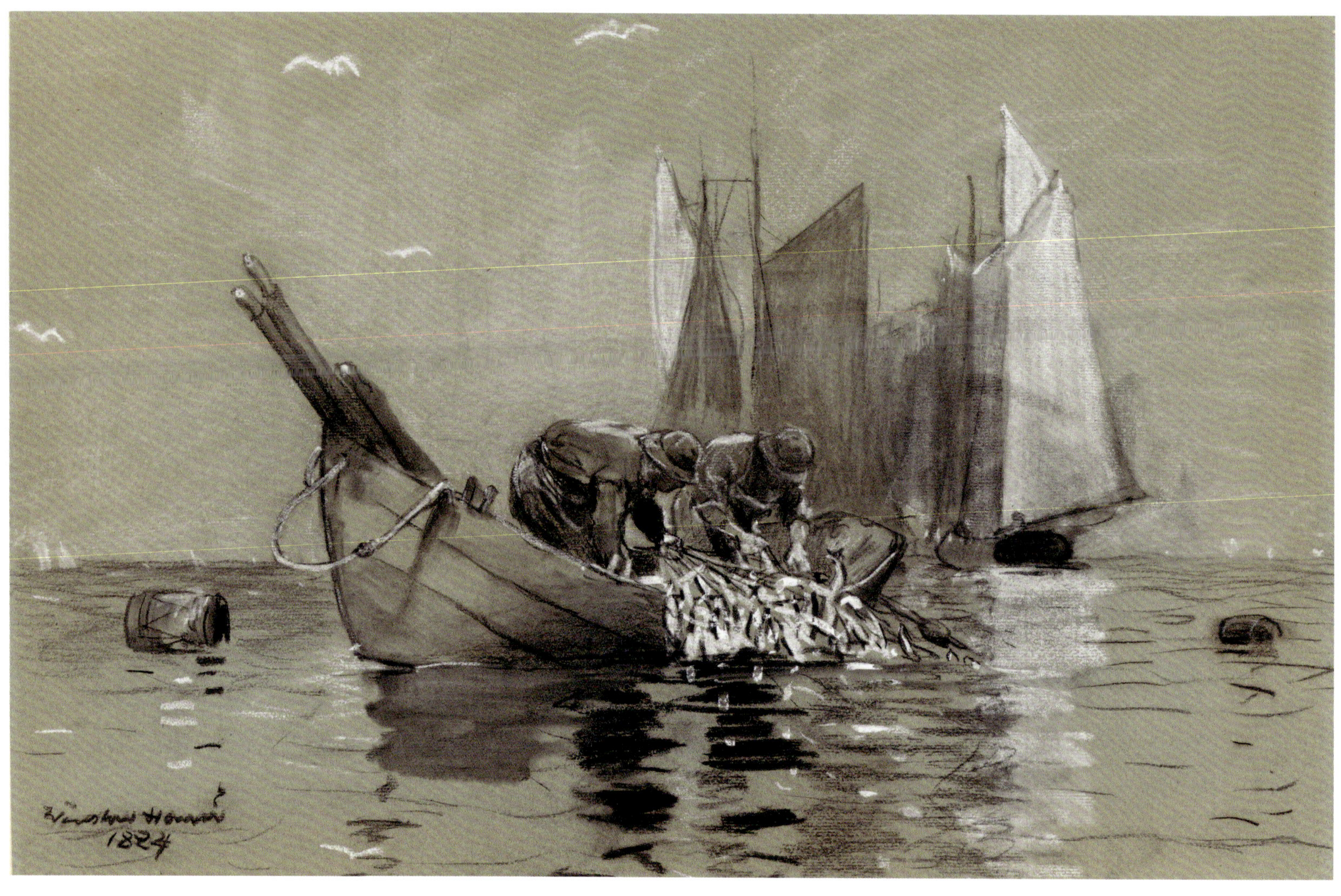

80. *Haul of Herring,* 1884

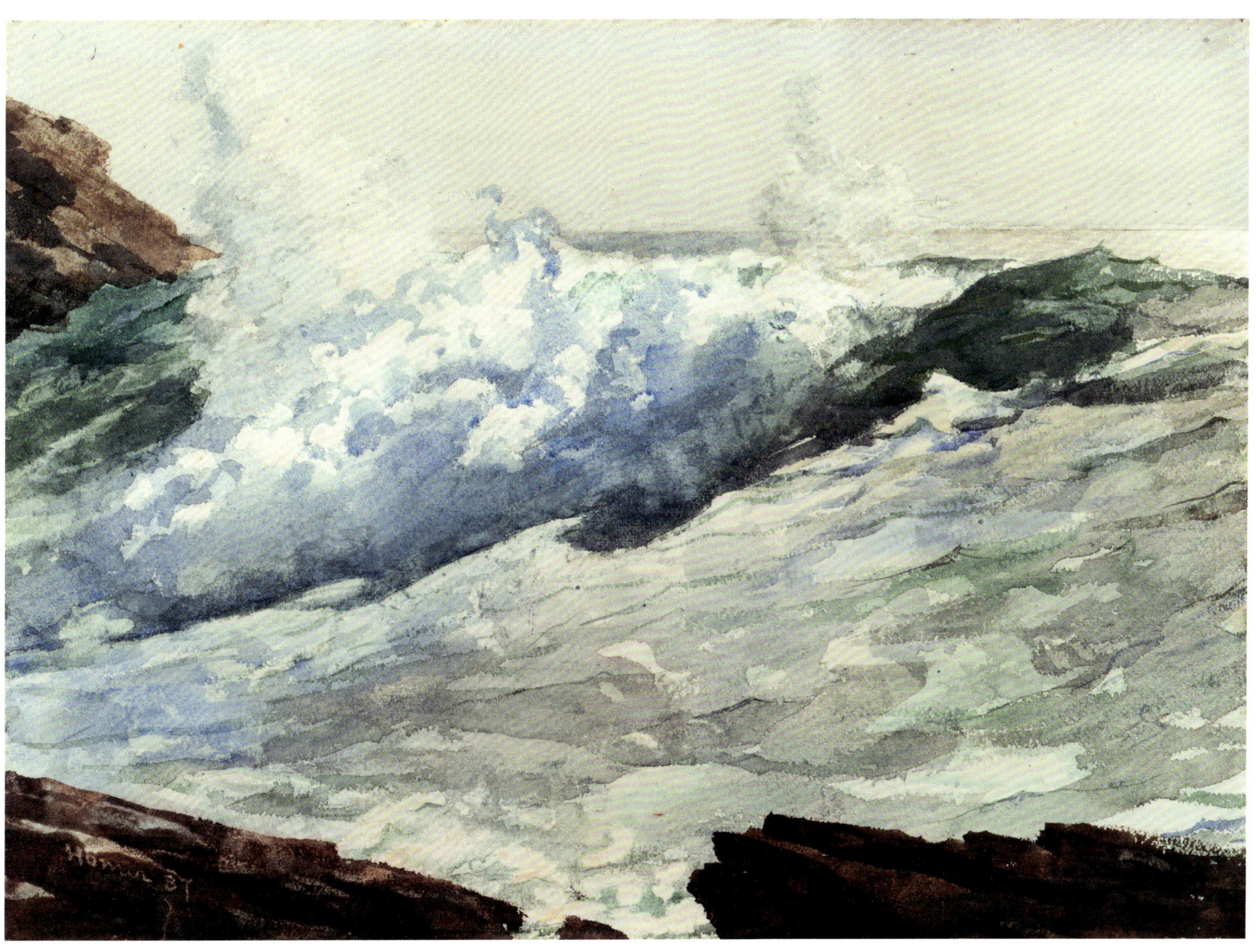

81. *Breaking Wave (Prouts Neck)*, 1887

Light Sensitivity / Homer sometimes edited his watercolors either by trimming the paper or crossing out part of the composition. Crossed-out sections were meant to be covered when the watercolor was matted and framed.

Protected from light by a mat or frame, once covered edges can reveal colors that existed elsewhere in the watercolor but are now diminished or lost. Although here the shift in color is somewhat muted, the reveal can be truly startling. Faded color cannot be restored; however, edge color can provide insight into how a watercolor originally looked.

The issue of watercolor permanence was much debated in the late nineteenth century and led to some heated exchanges. Those who believed watercolors were affected by light pointed to scientific studies and their own experience with the medium. Those who refuted the role of light suggested the scientific investigation was flawed and that the changes that did occur were not due to light.[37]

Studies then and now indicate some colors fade with exposure to light. Some of these colors were in Homer's palette.[38] —AM

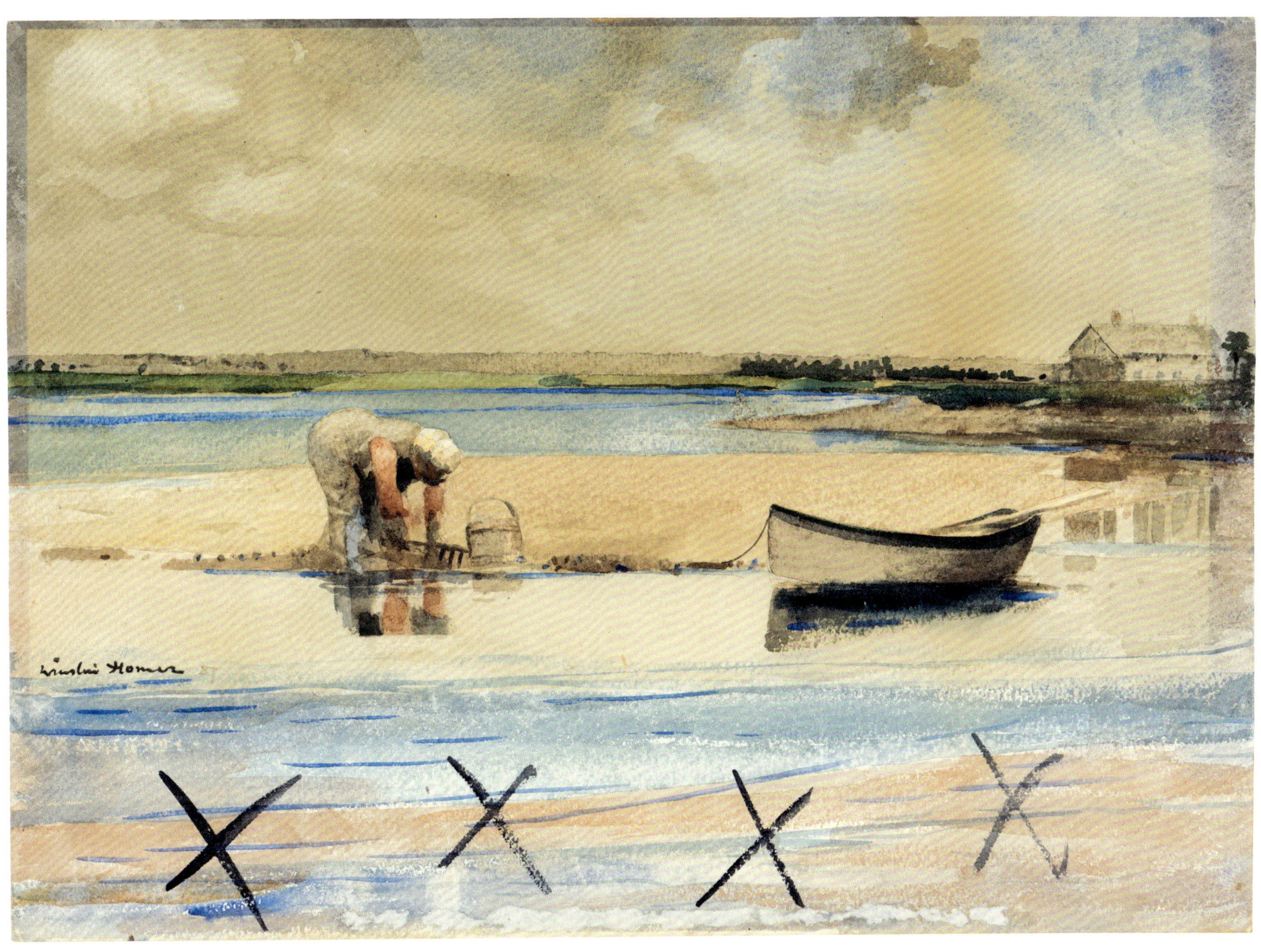

82. *Clamming*, 1887

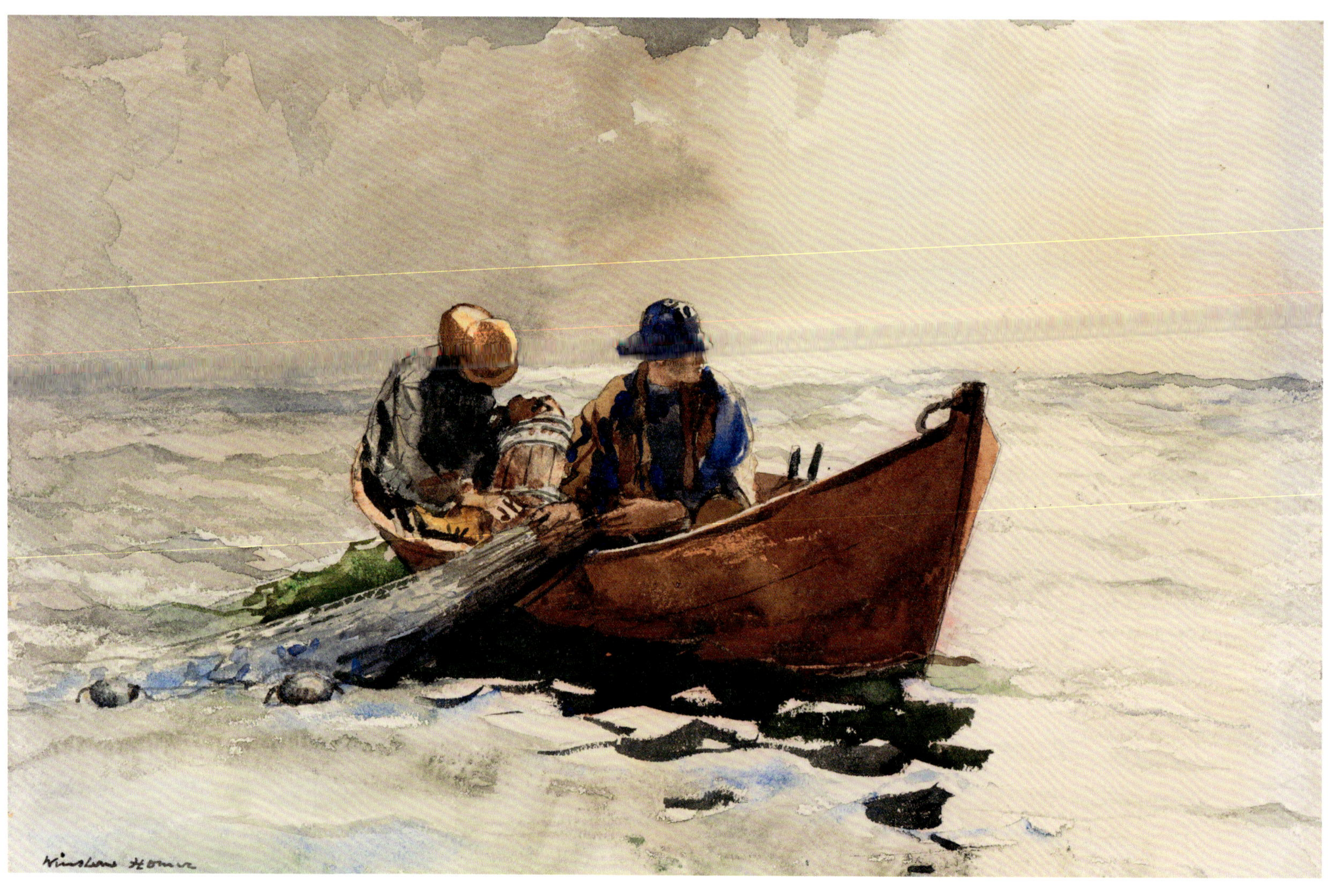

83. *The Dory*, 1887

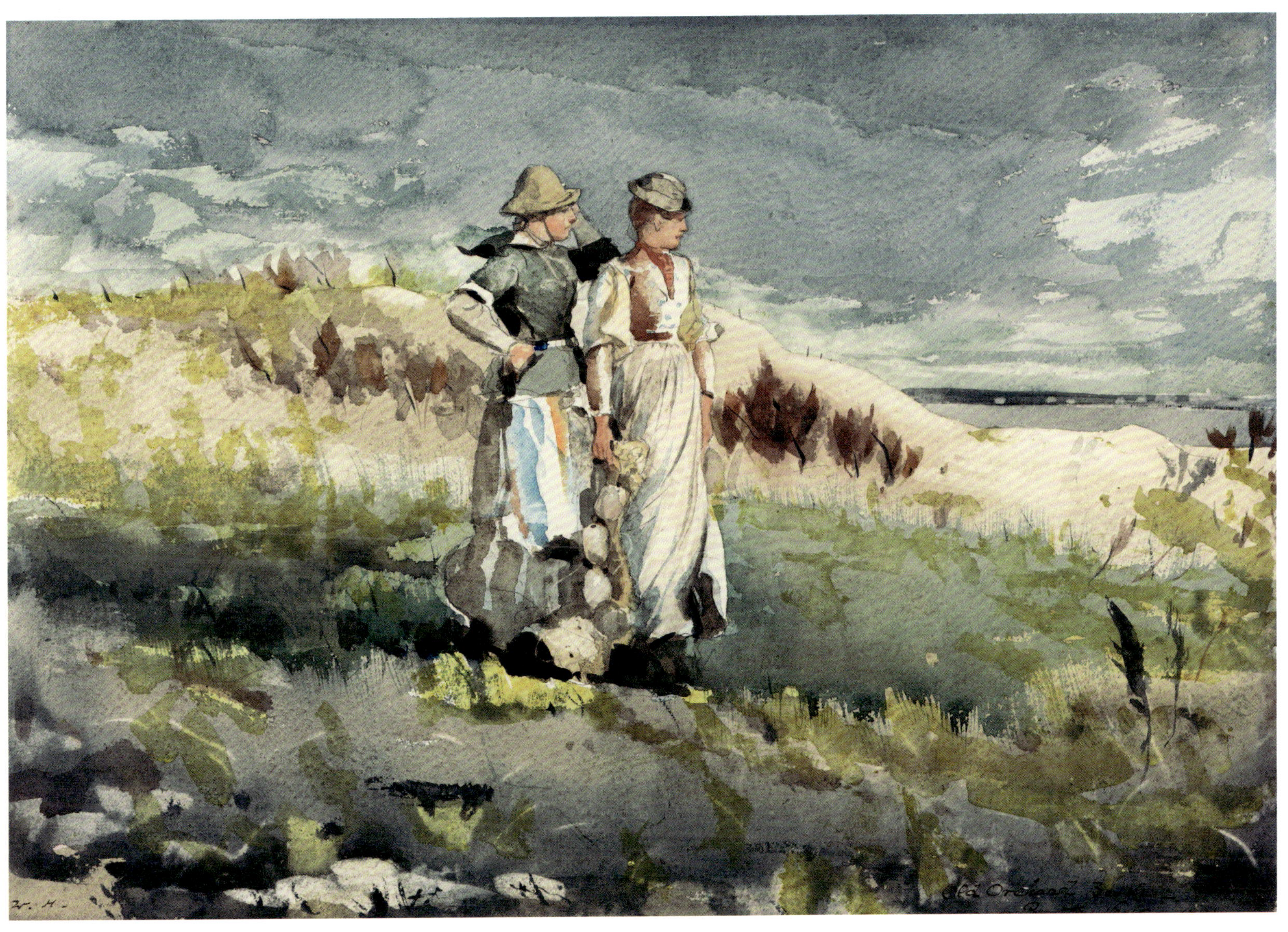

84. *The Dunes*, 1894

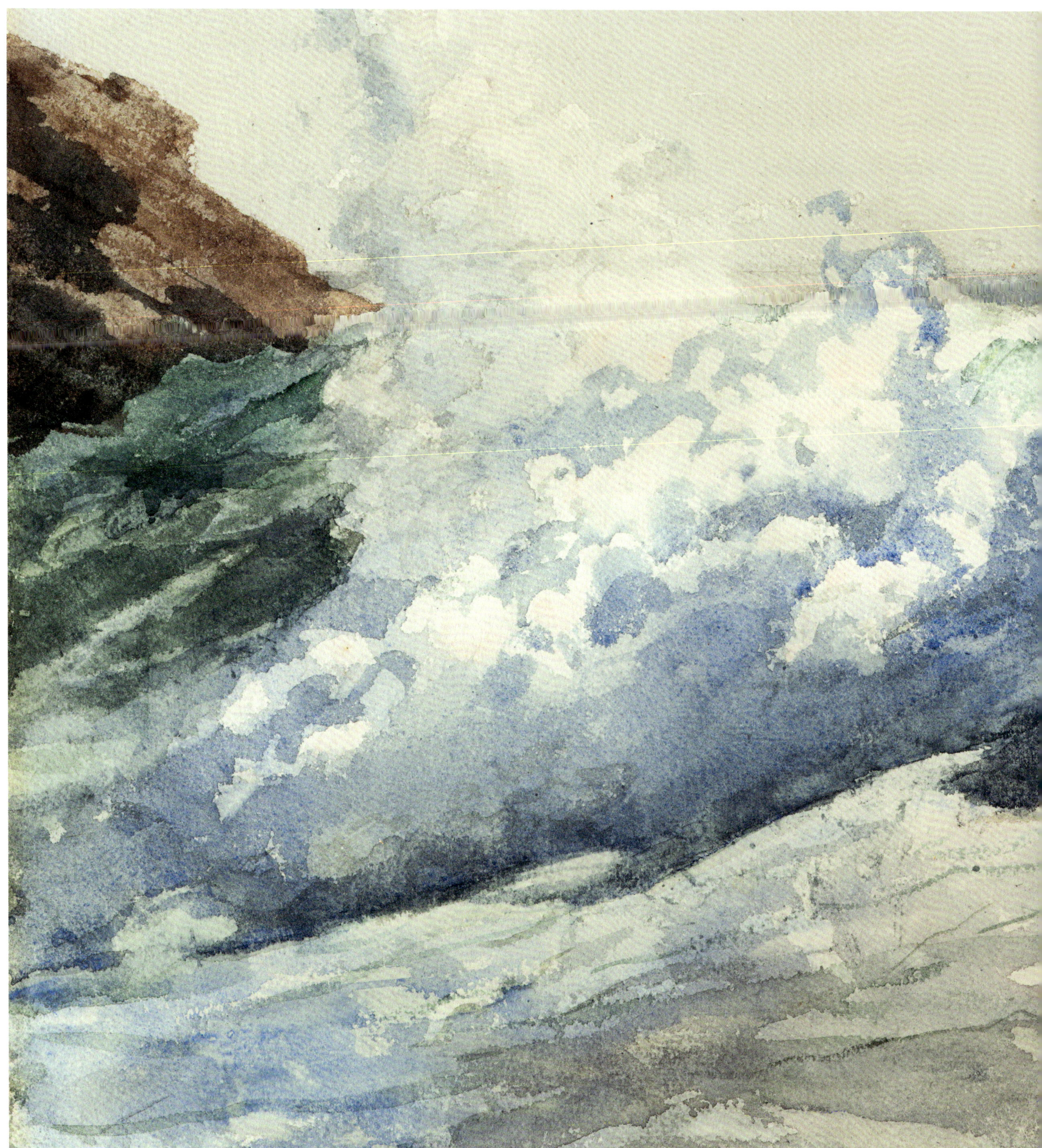

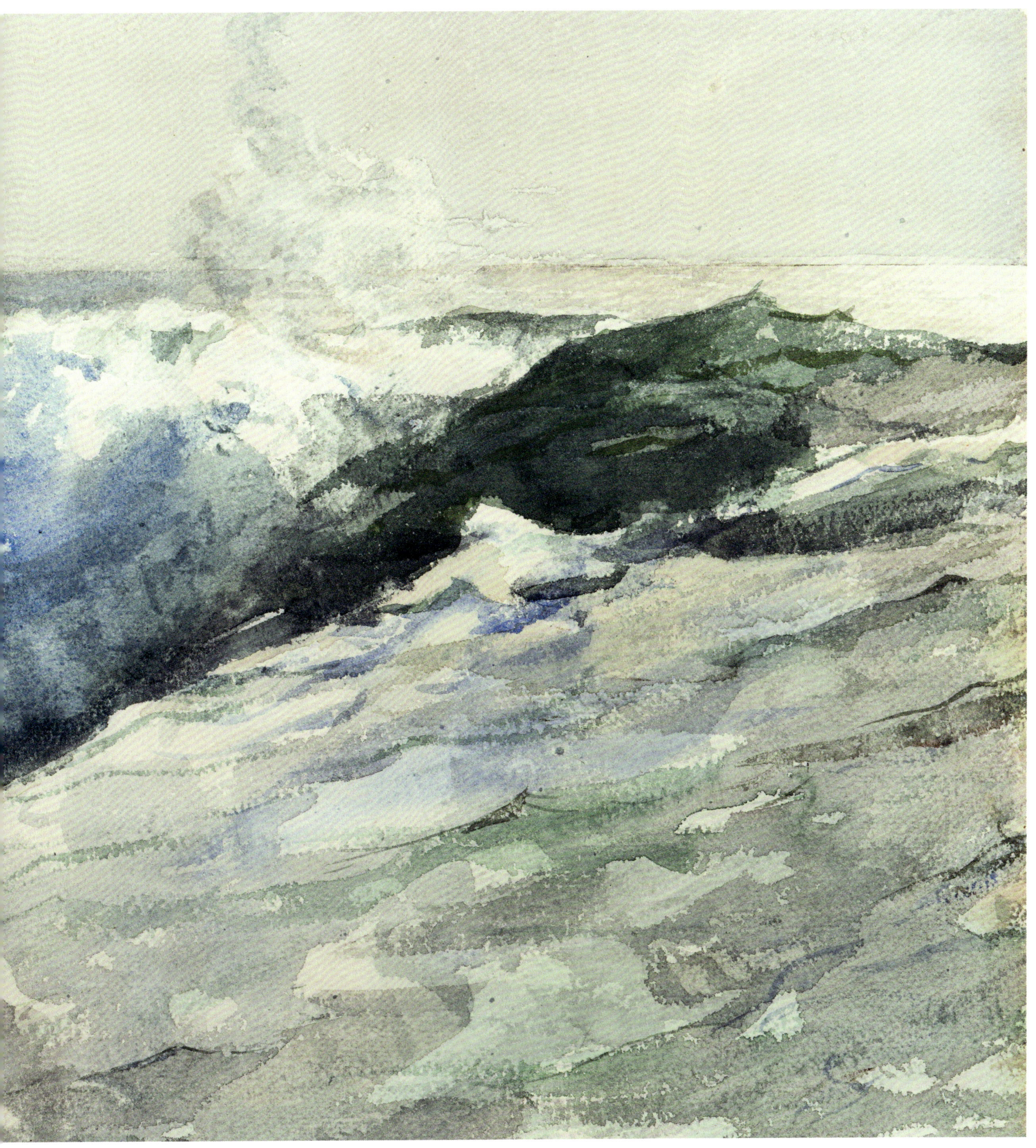

Notes

Of Light and Air

1. Quoted in George W. Sheldon, "Sketches and Studies. II. From the Portfolios of A. H. Thayer, William M. Chase, Winslow Homer, and Peter Moran," *The Art Journal* 6 (1880): 105–109.

2. While many of Homer's watercolors were created outdoors, some began as sketches on site but were finished indoors. Martha Tedeschi and Kristi Dahm, *Watercolors by Winslow Homer: The Color of Light* (New Haven: Yale University Press, 2008), 165.

3. For more on this from an artist's perspective, see James Prosek, "James Prosek on Representation in Art and Nature," *Adirondack Life* (June 2022).

4. *Leaping Trout* was the third watercolor by Winslow Homer to be acquired by a museum in general. *Hunting Dogs in Boat* entered the Rhode Island School of Design's Museum in 1894 as a gift from Rhode Island senator Jesse Houghton Metcalf (1860–1942). In the same year, Bowdoin College acquired *The End of the Hunt*, a gift from Misses Harriet Sarah and Mary Sophia Walker.

5. The Homer family had deep ties to Belmont, with several extended family members living there before Winslow's parents relocated. The opulent house of Homer's uncle, William Flagg Homer, featured in at least one of Homer's wood engravings for *Harper's Weekly*. The historic site is currently managed by the Belmont Woman's Club. For more on Homer's early life in New England, see William R. Cross, *Winslow Homer: American Passage* (New York: Farrar, Straus and Giroux, 2022).

6. Marianna Griswold Van Rensselaer, "An American Artist in England," *The Century Illustrated Monthly Magazine* 27 (November 1883): 14.

7. See Ramey Mize, et al., *Winslow Homer: Painter, Etcher* (New Haven: Yale University Press, 2026; forthcoming).

8. See Museum of Fine Arts, Boston, "Sylvester Koehler: Exploring Print History," 2023, mfa.org/beyond-the-gallery/sylvester-koehler-exploring-print-history.

9. Homer's contemporary Eastman Johnson painted a literal depiction of Whittier's barefoot boy, which in 1868 became a widely distributed chromolithograph by Louis Prang & Company.

10. Kathy Foster, *American Watercolors in the Age of Homer and Sargent* (Philadelphia: Philadelphia Museum of Art, 2017).

11. Joachim Homann, *American Watercolors, 1880–1990: Into the Light* (Cambridge, MA: Harvard Art Museums, 2023), 15. Lloyd Goodrich and Abigail Booth Gerdts, *Record of Works by Winslow Homer* 3 (New York: Spanierman Galleries, 2005), 8.

12. Henry James, "On Some Pictures Lately Exhibited," *The Galaxy* (1875).

Gloucester, Massachusetts

13. Thomas Rowbotham and Thomas L. Rowbotham, *The Art of Landscape Painting in Water Colours*, 36th ed. (London: Winsor and Newton, 1889), 6–7

Central Massachusetts and Upstate New York

14. Mariana Griswold Van Rensselaer, "An American Artist in England," *The Century Illustrated Monthly Magazine* 27 (November 1883): 14.

Cullercoats, England

15. Van Rensselaer, "An American Artist in England," 17.

16. R. P. Noble, *A Guide to Water Colour Painting*, 20th ed. (London: George Rowney & Co., 1850), 12: "The study of black and white is of great importance, since the effect of a picture depends upon its proper management. By a judicious practice of black and white, the masses become disentangled or relieved, and the different distances may be observed at the first glance. The careful study of good engravings will be found of great assistance, the eye not being distracted from these important matters by the charming qualities of colours." Homer's father supplied Homer with prints for study. See Martha Tedeschi "A Bold, Unguided Effort: The Self-Education of America's Master in Watercolor" in Tedeschi and Dahm, *Watercolors by Winslow Homer: The Color of Light*, 22.

17. First noted by Roy Perkinson in "Observations on the Drawings of Winslow Homer," *The Book and Paper Group Annual* 5 (1986): 1–9.

18. Rowbotham and Rowbotham, *The Art of Landscape Painting in Water Colours*, 30–31: "The variety of effects of light, and often some of the best in the drawing, are frequently the result of accident. The colours may run, or may combine with each other, in a manner altogether unexpected by the operator; and with an effect which perhaps no effort on his part could have produced. It requires, however, imagination, as well as a certain amount of skill and practice, to take advantage of these accidental circumstances, which, in colouring from nature, are of frequent occurrence, in consequence of the rapidity with which the work is generally and necessarily carried on."

19. Rowbotham and Rowbotham, *The Art of Landscape Painting in Water Colours*, 28–29.

Florida and the Caribbean

20. See Dana Byrd, "Trouble in Paradise? Winslow Homer in the Bahamas, Cuba, and Florida, 1884–1886," in Frank H. Goodyear III and Dana Byrd, *Winslow Homer and the Camera: Photography and the Art of Painting* (New Haven: Yale University Press, 2018), 103–40; Maggie Cao, *Painting US Empire: Nineteenth-Century Art and Its Legacies* (Chicago: University of Chicago Press, 2025), 197–228; and Stephanie L. Herdrich, et al., *Crosscurrents* (New York: The Metropolitan Museum of Art, 2022).

21. Homer was likely on assignment from *The Century Magazine* to illustrate the feature article "A Midwinter Resort: With Engravings of Winslow Homer's Water-Color Studies in Nassau," which later appeared in the February 1887 issue. *Fox Hill, Bahamas* is photomechanically reproduced in the article as *A Nassau Gateway* with the note that the watercolor was then in the collection of Bostonian E. W. Hooper.

22. *The Herring Net*, 1885, oil on canvas, 76.5 × 122.9 cm (30 ⅛ × 48 ⅜ in.), Art Institute of Chicago, Mr. and Mrs. Martin A. Ryerson Collection, 1937.1039.

23. Homer's daybook from 1901–1902 includes a thumbnail sketch of *Street Corner, Santiago de Cuba* and a notation about sending that work and others to Knoedler in an entry dated July 5, 1902. See *Memorandum and Sketchbook (Daybook)*, ink on paper, 22.86 × 14.6 cm (9 × 5 ¾ in.), Bowdoin College Museum of Art, Gift of the Homer Family, 1964.69.2. *Searchlight on Harbor Entrance, Santiago de Cuba*, 1902, oil on canvas, 77.5 × 128.3 cm (30 ½ × 50 ½ in.), The Metropolitan Museum of Art, Gift of George A. Hearn, 1906, 06.1282.

24. Rowbotham and Rowbotham, *The Art of Landscape Painting in Water Colours*, 13.

The North Woods

25. Numerous scholars have referenced the influence of Japanese art on Homer's work, and his watercolors in particular. See Judith Walsh, "Innovation in Homer's Late Watercolors," in Nicolai Cikovsky, et al., *Winslow Homer* (Washington, DC: National Gallery of Art, 1995). Scholars in Homer's time made the connection between American watercolor painting and Japanese art as well; eleven of Homer's watercolors, along with over a hundred by other artists, were featured alongside Japanese painting in an 1890 exhibition at the MFA. Walsh also posits that Homer may have seen or studied Japanese art in Boston, given his connection to major collectors like Bigelow, or while it was on display at the MFA.

26. Orson Lowell, "New York Letter," *Brush and Pencil* 2, no. 3 (June 1898): 132.

27. Aaron Penley, *A System of Water-Colour Painting*, 40th ed. (London: Winsor and Newton, 1867), 57: "If great power and transparency be required, the effect will be greatly heightened by passing a little gum-water, or other vehicle, over the strongest parts; this will cause the colours to shine out with much force, and bring them completely in advance." The gloss here is in keeping with a gum additive; however, analysis was not undertaken.

28. Paul Schullery, "The Fly-fishing Stories in Winslow Homer's Art," in Patricia Junker and Sarah Burns, *Winslow Homer: Artist and Angler* (New York: Thames and Hudson. 2005), 85–86.

29. Thomas John Gullick with John Timbs, *Painting Popularly Explained*, 4th ed. (London: Crosby Lockwood and Co. 1876), 281.

30. H. W. Herrick, *Water Colour Painting: Description of Materials with Directions for their Use in Elementary Practice. Sketching from Nature in Water Color* (New York: F. W. Devoe & Co., 1882), 92.

31. With appreciation to Roy Perkinson for sharing this observation.

32. Gullick, *Painting Popularly Explained*, 283: "That the paper should be properly sized is of great importance. If sized too strongly, colour will not float or work well upon it, but will look hard and streaky. If sized too little, the colour will be absorbed into the fabric, and appear poor and dead."

33. Suggested by Sue W. Reed and published in Goodrich and Gerdts, *Record of Works by Winslow Homer*, 204–205.

34. XRF analysis done at the Museum of Fine Arts, Boston, by Marcie Wiggins, April 3, 2025.

35. Paul Schullery, "The Fly-fishing Stories in Winslow Homer's Art," in *Winslow Homer: Artist and Angler*.

Prouts Neck, Maine

36. Ross Barrett, *Speculative Landscapes: American Art and Real Estate in the Nineteenth Century* (Oakland: University of California Press, 2022), 135–70.

37. See the introductory essay in John Scott Taylor, *A Descriptive Handbook of Modern Water Colour Pigments* (London: Winsor and Newton, 1887).

38. See Kristi Dahm, "Intention and Alteration in Winslow Homer's Watercolor Palette," in Tedeschi and Dahm, *Watercolors by Winslow Homer: The Color of Light*, 206–15.

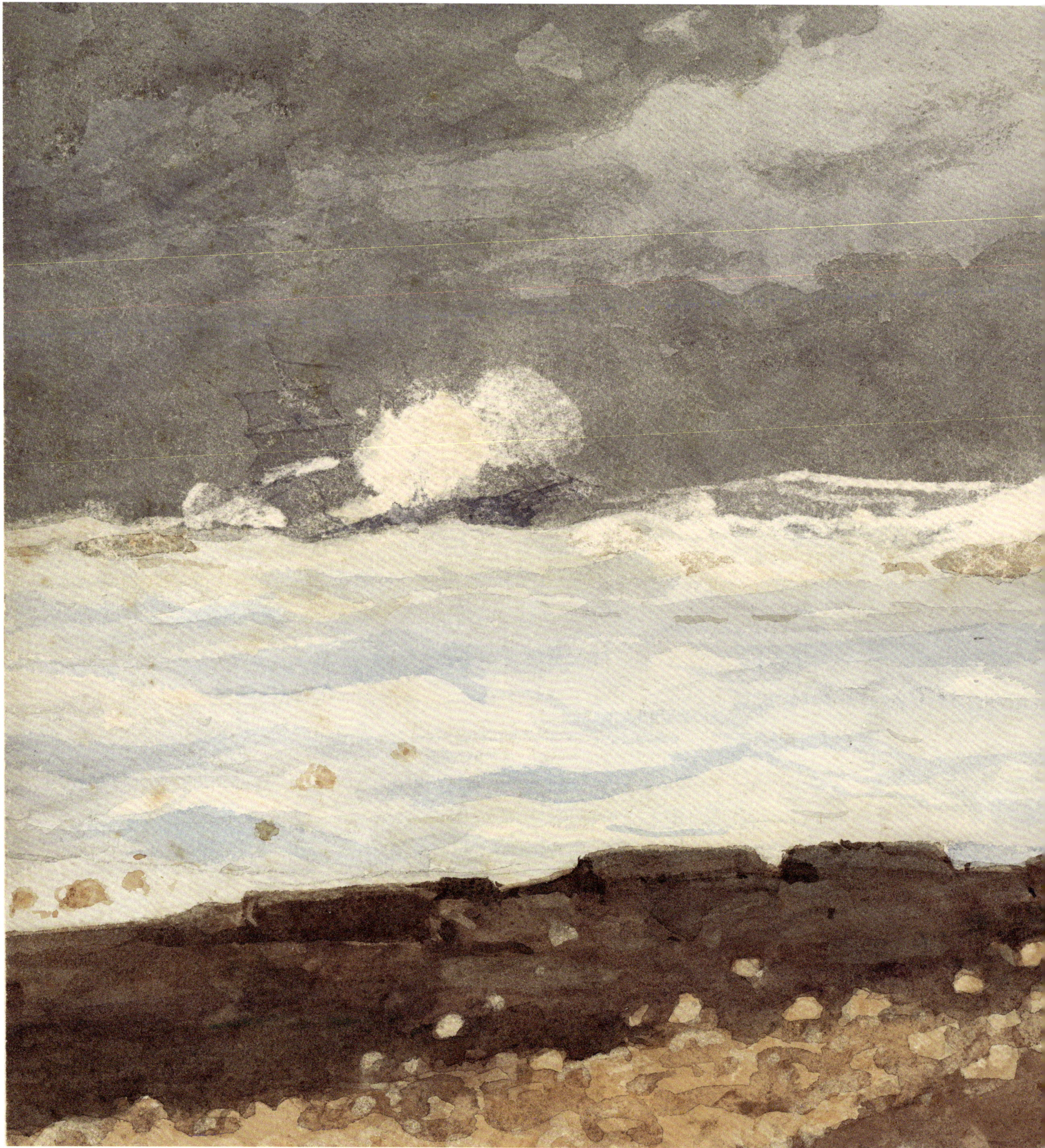

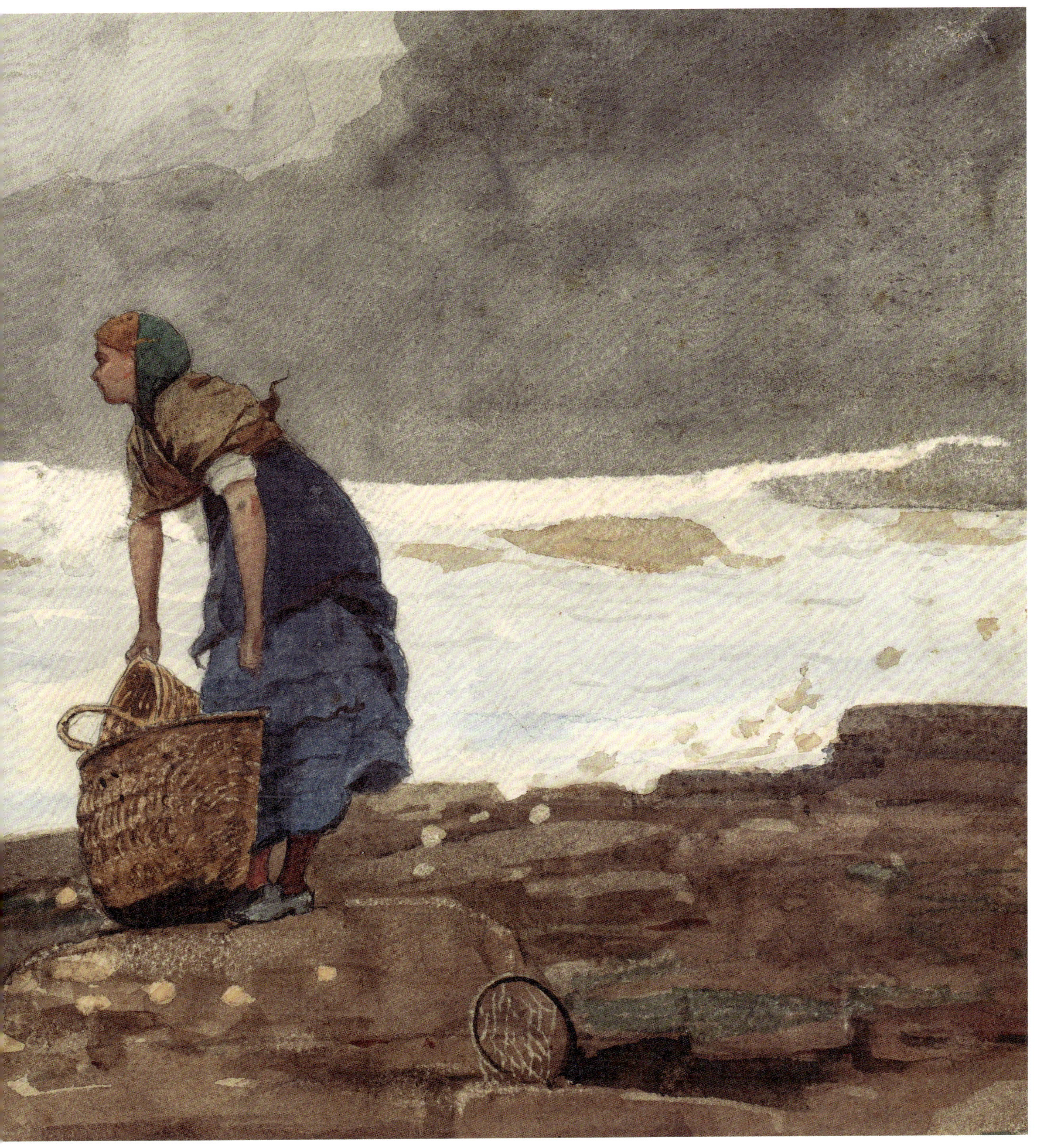

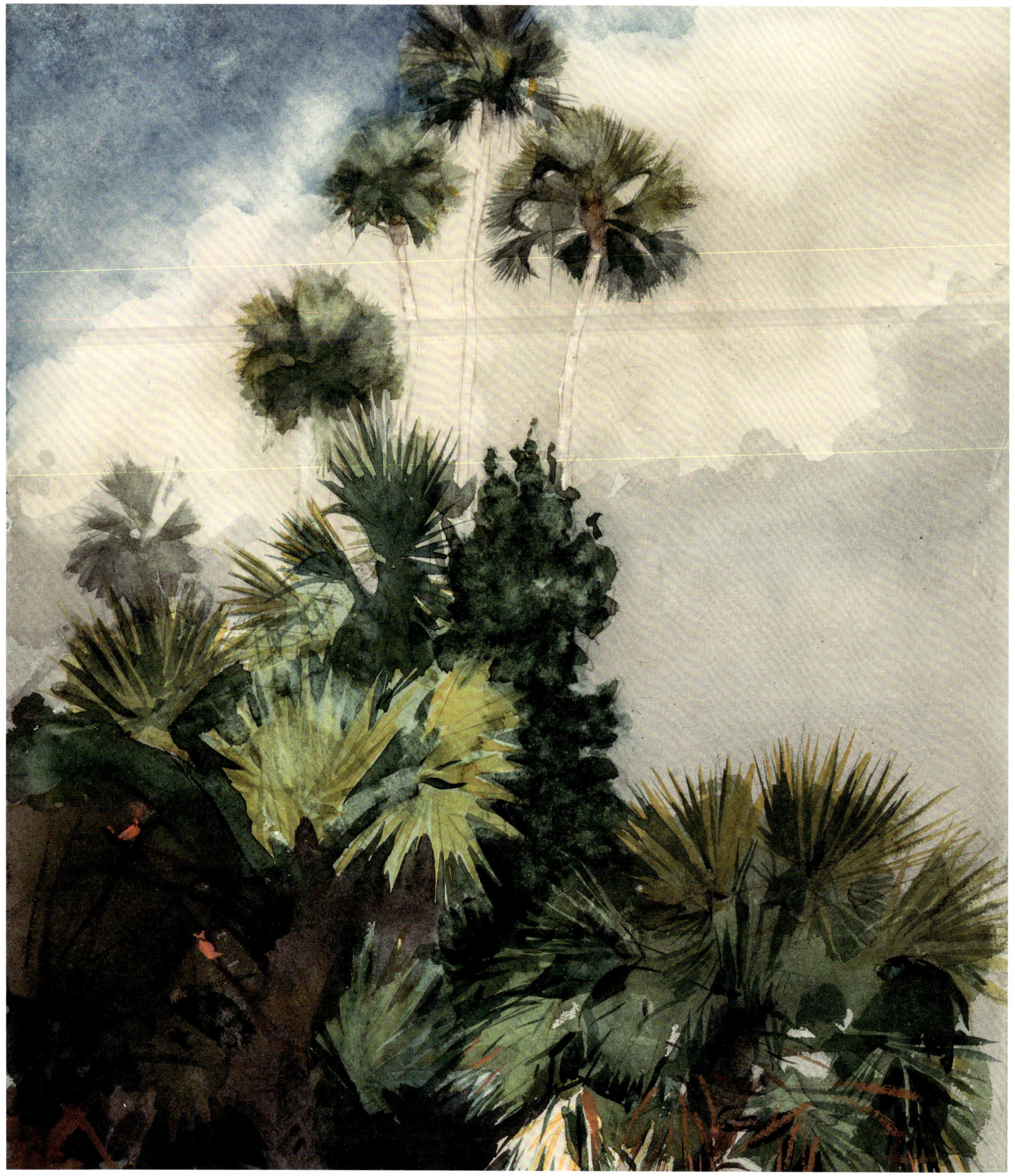

List of Illustrations

Unless otherwise noted, all works are by Winslow Homer (American, 1836–1910).

1. *Right and Left*, 1909
   Oil on canvas
   71.8 × 122.9 cm (28 ¼ × 48 ⅜ in.)
   National Gallery of Art
   Gift of the Avalon Foundation, 1951.8.1
   Courtesy National Gallery of Art, Washington

2. *The Lookout—"All's Well,"* 1896
   Oil on canvas
   101.3 × 76.5 cm (39 ⅞ × 30 ⅛ in.)
   Museum of Fine Arts, Boston
   Warren Collection—William Wilkins Warren
   Fund, 99.23

3. *The Fog Warning*, 1885
   Oil on canvas
   76.8 × 123.2 cm (30 ¼ × 48 ½ in.)
   Museum of Fine Arts, Boston
   Anonymous gift with credit to the Otis Norcross
   Fund, 94.72

4. *Driftwood*, 1909
   Oil on canvas
   62.2 × 72.3 cm (24 ½ × 28 ½ in.)
   Museum of Fine Arts, Boston
   Henry H. and Zoe Oliver Sherman Fund
   and other funds, 1993.564

5. Unidentified photographer
   Home of John Taylor Spaulding,
   between 1923 and 1948
   Photograph
   35 × 26.8 cm. (13 ¾ × 10 ⁹⁄₁₆ in.)
   Museum of Fine Arts, Boston

6. *Rocket Ship*, 1849–50
   Graphite
   9.5 × 38.4 cm (3 ¾ × 15 ⅛ in.)
   Museum of Fine Arts, Boston
   Gift of Edwin A. Wyeth, 13.4499

7. *Farm Scene*, 1847
   Watercolor and black ink
   9 × 12.5 cm (3 ½ × 4 ⅞ in.)
   Bowdoin College Museum of Art
   Gift of the Homer Family, 1964.69.173

8. Unidentified artist
   Henrietta Benson Homer, 19th century
   Photograph
   9 × 6.2 cm. (3 ⁹⁄₁₆ × 2 ⁷⁄₁₆ in.)
   Bowdoin College Museum of Art
   Gift of the Homer Family, HomerMemorabilia12

9. Henrietta Benson Homer (American, 1808–1884)
   Untitled (study of two butterflies), 19th century
   Watercolor and gouache, with traces of graphite
   22.1 × 21.1 cm (8 ¾ × 8 ¼ in.)
   Bowdoin College Museum of Art
   Gift of the Homer Family, 1964.69.186.2

10. *Miss Florence Tryon*, 1868
    Black and white chalk
    21.9 × 17.1 cm (8 ⅝ × 6 ¾ in.)
    Museum of Fine Arts, Boston
    Bequest of Grenville H. Norcross, 37.497

11. *Annie Lawrie*, 1856
    Printed by J. H. Bufford & Company
    (American, 19th century)
    Lithograph
    33.1 × 19.7 cm (13 ¹⁄₁₆ × 7 ¾ in.)
    Museum of Fine Arts, Boston
    Gift of J. Francis Driscoll, 51.61

12. *The North Woods (Playing Him)*, 1894
    Watercolor on paper
    38.4 × 54.6 cm (15 ⅛ × 21 ½ in.)
    Currier Museum of Art
    Gift of Mr. and Mrs. Frederic H. Curtiss, 1960.13

13. *Fly Fishing from a Canoe, North Woods*, 1895
    Printed by Louis Prang & Company
    (American, active 1860–1897)
    Chromolithograph
    38 × 53.8 cm (15 × 21 ⅛ in.)
    Museum of Fine Arts, Boston
    Bequest of W. G. Russell Allen, 63.335

14. *Sea and Rocks During a Storm*, 1896
    Printed by Louis Prang & Company
    Lithograph
    15.8 × 22.8 cm (6 ¼ × 9 in.)
    The Art Students League
    Donated by William D. Forest, 101039

15. James David Smillie (American, 1833–1909)
    A Voice from the Cliffs
    After Winslow Homer
    Etching
    28.2 × 36.9 cm. (11 ⅛ × 14 ½ in.)
    Museum of Fine Arts, Boston
    Gift of the artist, 87.861

16. *Rebel Works Seen from General Porter's Division,
    Yorktown*, 1862
    Graphite and wash
    20.7 × 33.9 cm (8 ⅛ × 13 ⅜ in.)
    Museum of Fine Arts, Boston
    Gift of Maxim Karolik for the M. and M. Karolik
    Collection of American Watercolors and Drawings,
    1800–1875, 50.3916

17. Unidentified artist
    Our Army Before Yorktown, Virginia, 1862
    After Winslow Homer
    For *Harper's Weekly*, May 3, 1862, pp. 280–281
    Wood engraving
    35 × 52.8 cm (13 ¾ × 20 ¾ in.)
    Museum of Fine Arts, Boston
    Bequest of Grenville H. Norcross, 38.151

18. Preparatory drawing for *On Guard*, about 1864
    Graphite and white chalk
    19.7 × 10.5 cm (7 ¾ × 4 ⅛ in.)
    Museum of Fine Arts, Boston
    Source unidentified, 97.886

19. *Watching the Crows*, 1868
    Engraved by John Parker Davis (American, 1832–1910)
    Wood engraving
    15 × 9.3 cm (5 ⅞ × 3 ⅝ in.)
    Museum of Fine Arts, Boston
    Gift of W. G. Russell Allen, 38.843

20. *On Guard*, 1864
    Oil on canvas
    31.1 × 23.5 cm (12 ¼ × 9 ¼ in.)
    Terra Foundation for American Art
    Daniel J. Terra Collection, 1994.11

21. *Boys in a Pasture*, 1874
    Oil on canvas
    40.32 × 58.1 cm (15 ⅞ × 22 ⅞ in.)
    Museum of Fine Arts, Boston
    The Hayden Collection — Charles Henry Hayden
    Fund, 53.2552

22. *Rocky Coast and Gulls*, 1869
    Oil on canvas
    41.27 × 71.44 cm (16 ¼ × 28 ⅛ in.)
    Museum of Fine Arts, Boston
    Bequest of Grenville H. Norcross, 37.486

23. *Long Branch, New Jersey*, 1869
    Oil on canvas
    40.6 × 55.2 cm (16 × 21 ¾ in.)
    Museum of Fine Arts, Boston
    The Hayden Collection — Charles Henry Hayden
    Fund, 41.631

24. *Women and Children on Beach at Long
    Branch, New Jersey*, 1869
    Black chalk and blue wash
    14.6 × 30.5 cm (5 ¾ × 12 in.)
    Yale University Art Gallery
    Gift of Allen Evarts Foster, B.A. 1906, 1965.33.10
    Image from Yale University

25. Winsor & Newton (English, founded 1832)
    Homer's watercolor box, 1900–10
    Watercolor pigments and metal
    20.6 × 20.9 cm (8 ⅛ × 8 ¼ in.)
    Bowdoin College Museum of Art
    Gift of the Homer Family, 1964.69.191

26. Lillian Baynes Griffin (American, 1871–1916)
    Winslow Homer at the door of his studio,
    Prouts Neck, Me., about 1907
    Photographic print
    16.4 × 11.6 cm (6 ½ × 4 ⅝ in.)
    Boston Athenaeum
    Gift of Alfred B. Downes, 1976.151

Gloucester, Massachusetts

27. *Three Boys on a Beached Dory*, 1873
    Black crayon and white watercolor
    18 × 39.5 cm (7 1/16 × 15 9/16 in.)
    Bequest of Katharine Dexter McCormick, 68.575

28. *Children Playing under a Gloucester Wharf*, 1880
    Watercolor over graphite
    20.5 × 34.2 cm (8 1/16 × 13 ½ in.)
    The Hayden Collection — Charles Henry Hayden
    Fund, 21.2554

29. *Gloucester Harbor*, 1880
    Watercolor over graphite
    34.5 × 49.2cm (13 9/16 × 19 ⅜ in.)
    Gift in memory of Edward William Hooper,
    Trustee of the Museum 1879-1901, from a grandson,
    1996.458

30. *The Green Dory*, 1880
    Watercolor over graphite
    34.9 × 49.9 cm (13 ¾ × 19 ⅝ in.)
    Bequest of Dr. Arthur Tracy Cabot, 42.538

31. *Two Boys Rowing*, 1880
    Watercolor over blue carbon paper transfer
    and graphite
    25 × 35.6 cm (9 ⅞ × 14 in.)
    Gift of James J. Minot, 1974.588

Central Massachusetts and Upstate New York

32. *On the Edge of the Farm*, 1875
Graphite and white watercolor
25.4 × 35.4 cm (10 × 13 ¹⁵⁄₁₆ in.)
Gift of Maxim Karolik for the M. and M. Karolik
Collection of American Watercolors and Drawings,
1800–1875, 55.756

33. *Spring (Women and Men at Well)*, about 1875
Graphite, wash, and white watercolor
23.2 × 22.7 cm (9 ⅛ × 8 ¹⁵⁄₁₆ in.)
Bequest of Grenville H. Norcross, 37.496

34. *Two Girls Looking at a Book*, about 1877
Watercolor over charcoal
13.6 × 22 cm (5 ⅜ × 8 ¹¹⁄₁₆ in.)
Bequest of Katharine Dexter McCormick, 68.572

35. *Autumn Foliage with Two Youths Fishing*,
about 1878
Watercolor over graphite
28.6 × 21.6 cm (11 ¼ × 8 ½ in.)
Bequest of Katharine Dexter McCormick, 68.571

36. *"Bo-Peep" (Girl with Shepherd's Crook Seated
by a Tree)*, 1878
Watercolor over graphite
17.8 × 21 cm (7 × 8 ¼ in.)
Bequest of John T. Spaulding, 48.724

37. *Boy and Fallen Tree*, 1879
Watercolor over graphite
20.7 × 28.3 cm (8 ⅛ × 11 ⅛ in.)
Bequest of Katharine Dexter McCormick, 68.570

38. *Boy and Girl on a Hillside*, 1878
Watercolor over graphite
22.7 × 28.7 cm (8 ¹⁵⁄₁₆ × 11 ⁵⁄₁₆ in.)
Bequest of Katharine Dexter McCormick, 68.568

39. *Driving Cows to Pasture*, 1879
Watercolor over graphite
21.7 × 34.5 cm (8 ⁹⁄₁₆ × 13 ⁹⁄₁₆ in.)
Bequest of Katharine Dexter McCormick, 68.569

40. *Girl on Swing*, 1879
Graphite and white watercolor
21 × 31.9 cm (8 ¼ × 12 ⁹⁄₁₆ in.)
Bequest of Katharine Dexter McCormick, 68.574

41. *Going Berrying*, 1879
Black crayon and white watercolor
21.2 × 33.7 cm (8 ⅜ × 13 ¼ in.)
Bequest of Katharine Dexter McCormick, 68.573

42. *Girl Seated*, 1880
Charcoal and white watercolor
46.7 × 37.7 cm (18 ⅜ × 14 ¹³⁄₁₆ in.)
Gift of Anonymous Donor in memory of Phyllis S.
Tuckerman, 1996.136

Cullercoats, England

43. *Fisherman's Family (The Lookout)*, 1881
Watercolor over graphite
34.2 × 49.2 cm (13 ½ × 19 ⅜ in.)
Bequest of John T. Spaulding, 48.726

44. *Coast Scene, with Boats on the Beach*, 1881
Watercolor and charcoal over graphite
23.2 × 35.6cm (9 ⅛ × 14 in.)
Bequest of John T. Spaulding, 48.725

45. *Girls on a Cliff*, 1881
Watercolor over graphite
32.2 × 48.5 cm (12 ¹¹⁄₁₆ × 19 ⅛ in.)
Bequest of David P. Kimball in memory of his wife,
Clara Bertram Kimball, 23.522

46. *A Fresh Breeze (Fishergirls, England)*, about 1881
Watercolor over charcoal
35.6 × 50.8 cm (14 × 20 in.)
Gift in memory of Ward and Louisa Hooper Thoron
from their son, 1998.581

47. *Fisherwomen*, 1881–82
Charcoal wash with white chalk over graphite
26 × 36.2 cm (10 ¼ × 14 ¼ in.)
Bequest of John T. Spaulding, 48.728

48. *Tynemouth Sands*, 1881–82
Watercolor with charcoal over graphite
37.2 × 54.6 cm (14 ⅝ × 21 ½ in.)
Bequest of Mrs. Arthur Croft—The Gardner Brewer
Collection, 01.6232

49. *Women on the Sands (Mussel Gatherers)*, 1881–82
Charcoal wash, white watercolor, and white chalk
21.9 × 33.0 cm (8 ⅝ × 13 in.)
Gift of the estate of Mrs. Sarah Wyman Whitman,
09.213

50. *Girl with Red Stockings (The Wreck)*, 1882
Watercolor and charcoal over graphite
34.2 × 49.5 cm (13 ⁷⁄₁₆ × 19 ½ in.)
Bequest of John T. Spaulding, 48.727

51. *An Afterglow*, 1883
Watercolor and charcoal over graphite
38 × 54.7 cm (15 × 21 ½ in.)
Bequest of William P. Blake in memory of his mother,
Mary M. J. Dehon Blake, 22.606

52. *Bridlington Quay*, 1883
Watercolor over graphite
33.9 × 45.3 cm (13 ⅜ × 17 ¹³⁄₁₆ in.)
Bequest of Ralph W. Gray in memory of his father,
Samuel S. Gray, 44.681

53. *Storm on the English Coast (W. H. Flamborough
Head)*, 1883
Watercolor and charcoal over graphite
59.7 × 76.5 cm (23 ½ × 30 ⅛ in.)
Gift of Theodore M. Kinch, 2018.357

Florida and the Caribbean

54. *Harbor Island, Bahamas*, 1885
Watercolor over graphite
31 × 41.7 cm (12 ³⁄₁₆ × 16 ⁷⁄₁₆ in.)
Gift of Mrs. Robert B. Osgood, 39.622

55. *Street Corner, Santiago de Cuba*, 1885
Watercolor over graphite
35.6 × 50.9 cm (14 × 20 ¹⁄₁₆ in.)
Anonymous gift in memory of Horace D. Chapin,
1978.300

56. *Fox Hill, Bahamas*, 1885
Watercolor over graphite
40 × 37 cm (15 ¾ × 14 ⁹⁄₁₆ in.)
Gift of Faith T. Knapp, 2003.352

57. *Thornhill Bar (Florida)*, 1886
Watercolor over graphite
35.56 × 50.8 cm (14 × 20 in.)
Gift of Mrs. Robert B. Osgood, 39.620

58. *Hunter in the Everglades*, about 1886
Watercolor over graphite
35.7 × 23.6 cm (14 ¹⁄₁₆ × 9 ⁵⁄₁₆ in.)
Gift of Mrs. Robert B. Osgood, 39.619

59. *The Sponge Diver*, 1898–99
Watercolor over graphite
38.1 × 54.3 cm (15 × 21 ⅜ in.)
Gift of Mrs. Robert B. Osgood, 39.621

60. *Rocky Shore, Bermuda*, 1900
Watercolor over graphite
35.7 × 53.5 cm (14 ¹⁄₁₆ × 21 ¹⁄₁₆ in.)
Bequest of Grenville H. Norcross, 37.487

61. *Palm Trees, Florida*, 1904
Watercolor over graphite
50.2 × 35.2 cm (19 ¾ × 13 ⅞ in.)
Bequest of John T. Spaulding, 48.731

The North Woods

62. *Adirondack Lake*, 1889
Watercolor and charcoal over graphite
35.6 × 50.8 cm (14 × 20 in.)
Warren Collection—William Wilkins Warren
Fund, 23.215

63. *The Guide and Woodsman (Adirondacks)*, 1889
Watercolor over graphite
35.6 × 50.8 cm (14 × 20 in.)
Bequest of John T. Spaulding, 48.730

64. *Rising to the Fly*, 1861
Watercolor and graphite
16.5 × 24.8 cm (6 ½ × 9 ¾ in.)
RISD Museum
Anonymous gift 78.156

65. *Trout Breaking*, 1889
Watercolor over graphite
35.2 × 50.4 cm (13 ⅞ × 19 ¹³⁄₁₆ in.)
Bequest of John T. Spaulding, 48.729

66. *Woodsman and Fallen Tree*, 1891
Watercolor over graphite
35.56 × 50.8 cm (14 × 20 in.)
William Sturgis Bigelow Collection, 26.778

67. *The Blue Boat*, 1892
Watercolor over graphite
38.6 × 54.6 cm (15 ³⁄₁₆ × 21 ½ in.)
William Sturgis Bigelow Collection, 26.764

68. *The Fallen Deer*, 1892
Watercolor over graphite
35.2 × 50.3 cm (13 ⅞ × 19 ¹³⁄₁₆ in.)
The Hayden Collection—Charles Henry Hayden
Fund, 23.443

69. *Hudson River*, 1892
Watercolor over graphite
35.6 × 50.8 cm (14 × 20 in.)
William Sturgis Bigelow Collection, 26.785

70. *Leaping Trout*, 1892
Watercolor over graphite
35.6 × 50.8 cm (14 × 20 in.)
Warren Collection—William Wilkins Warren
Fund, 99.24

71. *Old Settlers*, 1892
Watercolor over graphite
54.7 × 38.6 cm (21 9/16 × 15 3/16 in.)
Bequest of Nathaniel T. Kidder, 38.1412

72. *The Adirondack Guide*, 1894
Watercolor over graphite
38.5 × 54.6 cm (15 3/16 × 21 1/2 in.)
Bequest of Mrs. Alma H. Wadleigh, 47.268

73. *Hunting Dog among Dead Trees*, 1894
Watercolor over graphite
38.4 × 54.6 cm (15 1/8 × 21 1/2 in.)
William Sturgis Bigelow Collection, 21.1432

74. *Montagnais Indians, Pointe Bleue, Quebec*, 1895
Watercolor over graphite
35 × 51 cm (13 3/4 × 20 1/16 in.)
Warren Collection—William Wilkins Warren
Fund, 99.28

75. *Trout Fishing, Lake St. John, Quebec*, 1895
Watercolor over graphite
27.9 × 50.8 cm (11 × 20 in.)
Warren Collection—William Wilkins Warren
Fund, 99.29

76. Fragment of *Trout Fishing, Lake St. John*, 1895
Brush and black wash, gray wash and white
gouache over graphite
7.5 × 50.6 cm (3 × 19 7/8 in.)
Cooper Hewitt, Smithsonian Design Museum
Gift of Charles Savage Homer, Jr., 1912-12-199

77. *Ouananiche Fishing, Lake St. John, Province
of Quebec*, 1897
Watercolor and charcoal over graphite
35.56 × 53.34 cm (14 × 21 in.)
Warren Collection—William Wilkins Warren
Fund, 99.30

78. *Fishing for Ouananiche, Lake St. John, P.Q.
Canada, no. 2*, 1902
Watercolor over graphite
35.2 × 53.0 cm (13 7/8 × 20 7/8 in.)
From the Estate of Henry O. Underwood,
Bequest of Francis W. Davis, 1978.344

79. *Grand Discharge, Lake St. John, Province of Quebec*,
about 1902
Watercolor over graphite
35.6 × 53.4 cm (14 × 21 in.)
From the Estate of Henry O. Underwood,
Bequest of Francis W. Davis, 1978.345

Prouts Neck, Maine

80. *Haul of Herring*, 1884
Charcoal and white chalk
37.8 × 59.1 cm (14 7/8 × 23 1/4 in.)
Gift of George Nixon Black, by exchange, 37.374

81. *Breaking Wave (Prouts Neck)*, 1887
Watercolor with trace of graphite
38.7 × 54.6 cm (15 1/4 × 21 1/2 in.)
William Sturgis Bigelow Collection, 26.788

82. *Clamming*, 1887
Watercolor over graphite
39.1 × 54.6 cm (15 3/8 × 21 1/2 in.)
Gift of John S. Ames, 65.1713

83. *The Dory*, 1887
Watercolor over graphite
38.7 × 54.2 cm (15 1/4 × 21 5/16 in.)
The Hayden Collection—Charles Henry Hayden
Fund, 23.115

84. *The Dunes*, 1894
Watercolor over graphite
35.6 × 50.8 cm (14 × 20 in.)
Gift of Mr. and Mrs. Samuel Cabot, 67.1164

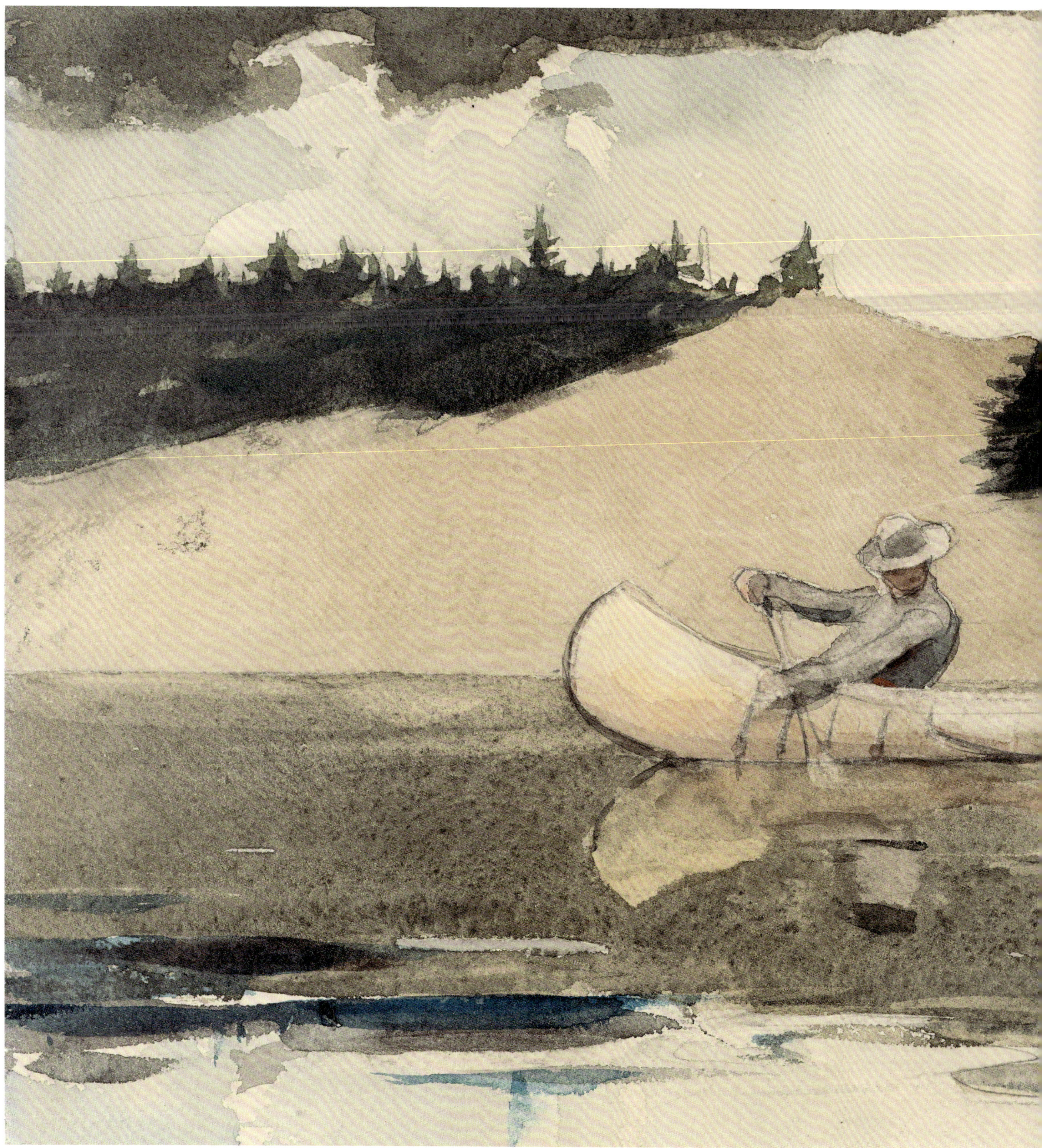

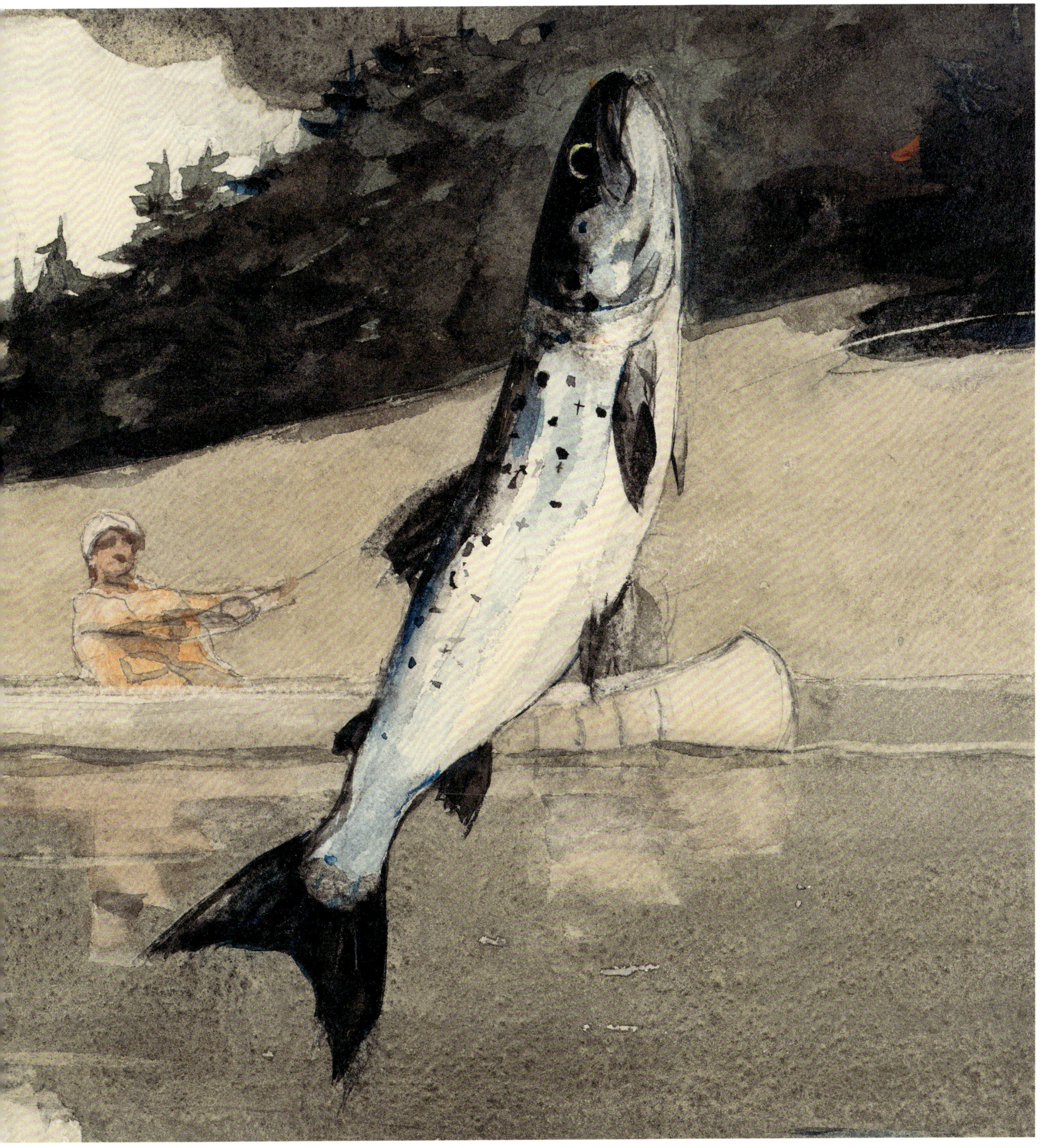

Acknowledgments

This publication and the exhibition *Of Light and Air: Winslow Homer in Watercolor* offered an exceptional opportunity to review and celebrate the Museum's collection of Winslow Homer works. We are deeply grateful to co-curator Ethan Lasser, John Moors Cabot Chair, Art of the Americas, for his thoughtfulness, enthusiasm, advocacy, and collaborative spirit.

This project would not have been possible without the visionary efforts of Edward Saywell; Pierre Terjanian, Ann and Graham Gund Director; and Matthew Teitelbaum, Ann and Graham Gund Director Emeritus, as well as the support of wonderful MFA colleagues, especially Michiko Adachi (Bettina Burr Associate Conservator, Asian Conservation), Layla Bermeo (Kristin and Roger Servison Curator of Paintings, Art of the Americas), John Carleton, Lauren Cosio, Kristen Gresh (Estrellita and Yousuf Karsh Senior Curator of Photographs), Karen Haas (Lane Senior Curator of Photographs), Anne Havinga (Estrellita and Yousuf Karsh Chair, Department of Photography), Erica Hirshler (Croll Senior Curator of American Paintings), Melissa Krok-Horton, Angela Lugo (Claire W. and Richard P. Morse Fellow for Advanced Training in Conservation of Works of Art on Paper), Alison Luxner, Rhona MacBeth (Rose-Marie and Eijk van Otterloo Director of Conservation and Scientific Research, and Head of Painting Conservation), Meghan Melvin (Ruth and Carl J. Shapiro Senior Curator of Prints and Drawings), Patrick Murphy (Lia and William Poorvu Associate Curator of Prints and Drawings), Katrina Newbury (Saundra B. Lane Conservator), Darcy-Tell Morales (Patti and Jonathan Kraft Chief of Learning and Community Engagement), Roy Perkinson, Stephanie Stepanek, Marina Tyquiengco (Ellyn McColgan Associate Curator of Native American Art, Art of the Americas), Ben Weiss (Leonard A. Lauder Senior Curator of Visual Culture, Department of Prints and Drawings), and Marcie Wiggins (Schorr Family Associate Research Scientist).

In addition to the colleagues listed above, Annette would especially like to acknowledge past MFA conservators Roy Perkinson and Elizabeth Lunning as well as former curators Cliff Ackley (Ruth and Carl J. Shapiro Curator of

Prints and Drawings Emeritus), Sue W. Reed, Stephanie Stepanek, and Barbara Stern Shapiro. Their passion for Homer and deep fascination with artists' materials and techniques formed the foundation of current work. Annette remains profoundly grateful to Mark Laning for his steadfast support.

It was a joy to work with Team Homer at the MFA: Ashley Bleimes, Kat Bossi, Sarah Cowen, Keith Crippen, Jordan Cromwell, Karen Frascona, Catherine Johnson-Roehr, Amelia Kantrovitz, Olga Khvan, Cordelia Leigh, Jared Medeiros, Angie Morrow, Cynthia O'Brien, Nick Pioggia, Michael Roper, George Scharoun, and especially Luisa Respondek. This book quite literally would not exist without Hope Stockton, whose patience, advice, and experience were a constant guide, and our colleagues from the Photo Studio including Maggie Loh and Saravuth Neou. We also thank Margaret Bauer for the book's elegant design.

We are also grateful for the insights and feedback from the following colleagues: Ross Barrett, Mary Broadway, Perry Choe, William Cross, Kristi Dahm, Sari Edelstein, Kathy Foster, Anne and Frank Goodyear, Joachim Homann, Justin Kedl, Conor Moynihan, Bruce McColl, Karen Papineau, Eli Portman, Juliet Sperling, Miriam Stewart, Kurt Sundstrom, Martha Tedeschi, Gordon Wilkins, and William Vareika. Christina would like to offer special thanks to Ramey Mize and her colleagues at the Portland Museum of Art, who, along with James Prosek and Judith Walsh, elevated this project to new heights, and she is thankful for the unwavering support of Mike Seiler.

The exhibition *Of Light and Air: Winslow Homer in Watercolor* is sponsored by the Abrams Foundation. Generous support provided by the Governor Carlton Skinner and Dr. Solange Skinner Fund for the Exhibition of Art of the Americas and by Kate Enroth and Dana Schmaltz. Additional support provided by the Jean S. and Frederic A. Sharf Exhibition Fund, the Dr. Lawrence H. and Roberta Cohn Exhibition Fund, and the Eugenie Prendergast Memorial Fund.

Generous support for this publication provided by the Andrew W. Mellon Publications Fund.

CHRISTINA MICHELON *Pamela and Peter Voss Curator of Prints and Drawings*
ANNETTE MANICK *Head of Paper Conservation*

MFABoston

MFA Publications
Museum of Fine Arts, Boston
465 Huntington Avenue
Boston, Massachusetts 02115
mfa.org/publications

Published in conjunction with the exhibition
Of Light and Air: Winslow Homer in Watercolor,
organized by the Museum of Fine Arts, Boston,
November 2, 2025–January 19, 2026.

ABRAMS

FOUNDATION

Sponsored by the Abrams Foundation.

Generous support provided by the Governor
Carlton Skinner and Dr. Solange Skinner Fund
for the Exhibition of Art of the Americas and
by Kate Enroth and Dana Schmaltz.

Additional support provided by the Jean S. and
Frederic A. Sharf Exhibition Fund, the Dr.
Lawrence H. and Roberta Cohn Exhibition Fund,
and the Eugenie Prendergast Memorial Fund.

Generous support for this publication provided
by the Andrew W. Mellon Publications Fund.

ISBN 978-0-87846-906-2
Library of Congress Control Number: 2025943352

COVER / front: *The Dunes* (detail, fig. 84);
back: *The Blue Boat* (detail, fig. 67)
ENDPAPERS / front: *A Fresh Breeze (Fishergirls,
England)* (detail, fig. 46); back: *Autumn Foliage
with Two Youths Fishing* (detail, fig. 35)

Details: pp. 2–3, fig. 38; pp. 4–5, fig. 75; pp. 8–9,
fig. 62; p. 10, fig. 70; pp. 34–35, fig. 31; pp. 44–45,
fig. 39; pp. 60–61, fig. 46; pp. 78–79, fig. 56;
pp. 94–95, fig. 67; pp. 124–125, fig. 84; pp. 132–133,
fig. 81; pp. 136–137, fig. 50; p. 93, fig. 61;
pp. 144–145, fig. 77.

The Museum of Fine Arts, Boston, is a nonprofit
institution devoted to the promotion and appreciation of the creative arts. The Museum endeavors
to respect the copyrights of all authors and creators
in a manner consistent with its nonprofit educa-
tional mission. If you feel any material has been
included in this publication improperly, please
contact the Department of Intellectual Property at
617 267 9300, or by mail at the above address.

The objects in this publication necessarily represent
only a small portion of the MFA's holdings. To
learn more about the MFA's collections, including
provenance, publication, and exhibition history,
kindly visit mfa.org/collections.

For a complete listing of MFA publications,
please contact the publisher at the above address,
or call 617 369 4233.

Illustrations in this book were photographed by
the Imaging Studios, Museum of Fine Arts, Boston,
except where otherwise noted.

Editing and production by Hope Stockton
Proofread by Kathryn Blatt
Principal photography by Saravuth Neou
Design by Margaret Bauer
Typeset in Adobe Garamond and Adobe Profile
Printed and bound at Graphicom, Verona, Italy

Distributed by
ARTBOOK | D.A.P.
75 Broad Street, Suite 630
New York, New York 10004
artbook.com

First Edition
Printed and bound in Italy
This book was printed on acid-free paper.

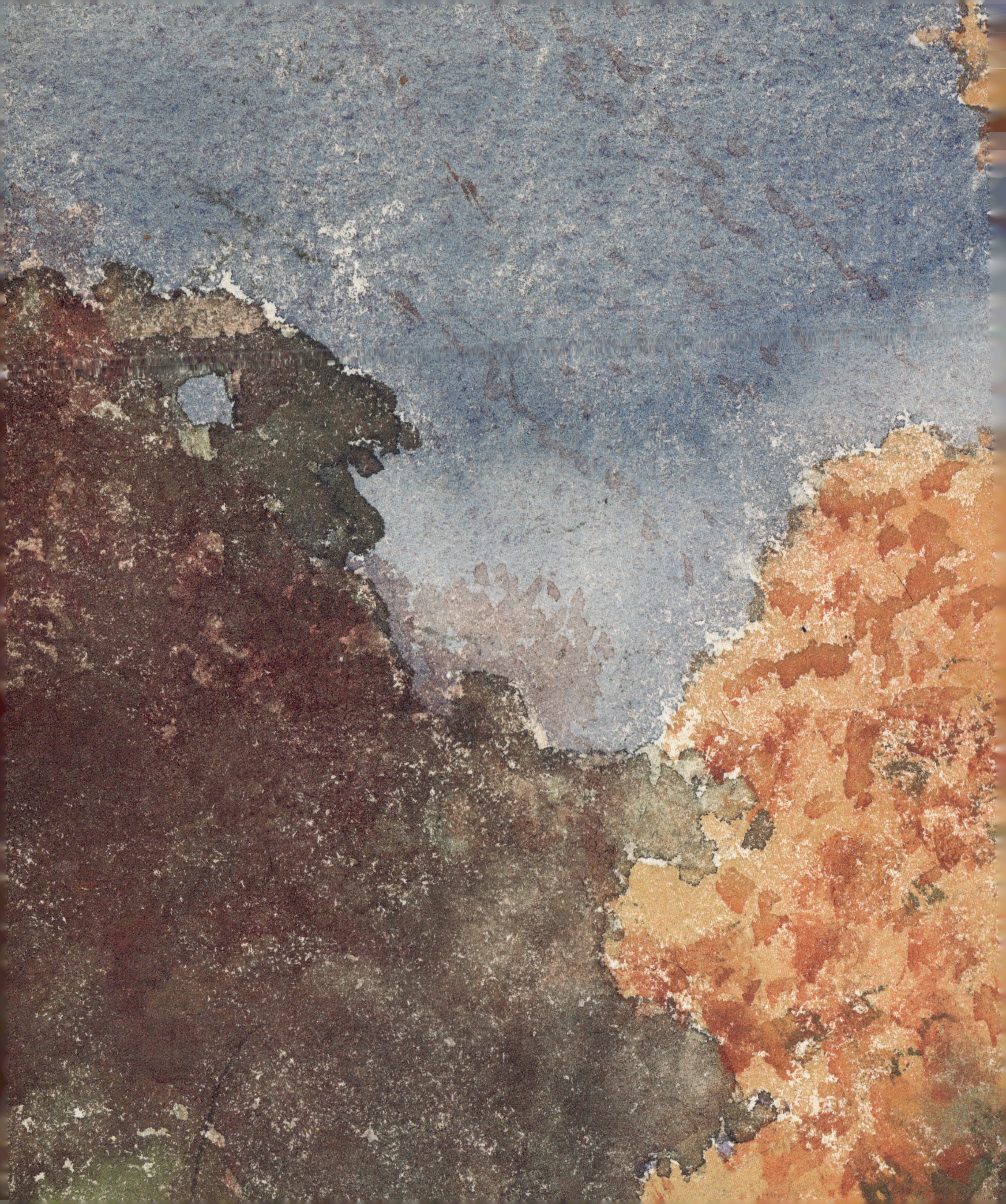